Visionaries In Our Midst

Ordinary People Who Are Changing Our World

Allison Silberberg

Oct. 6, 2013

To Sue —
Thank you for all you
do for our community.
Be a Visionary!

— Allison
Silberberg

University Press of America,® Inc.
Lanham · Boulder · New York · Toronto · Plymouth, UK

Copyright © 2009 by
University Press of America,® Inc.
4501 Forbes Boulevard
Suite 200
Lanham, Maryland 20706
UPA Acquisitions Department (301) 459-3366

Estover Road
Plymouth PL6 7PY
United Kingdom

Library of Congress Control Number: 2009929686
ISBN-13: 978-0-7618-4718-2 (clothbound : alk. paper)
ISBN-10: 0-7618-4718-9 (clothbound : alk. paper)
ISBN-13: 978-0-7618-4719-9 (paperback : alk. paper)
ISBN-10: 0-7618-4719-7 (paperback : alk. paper)
eISBN: 978-0-7618-4720-5
eISBN: 0-7618-4720-0

Front cover photography by © Allison Silberberg
Top left: Shakuntla Sapra with a toddler at Bright Beginnings.
Top right: Mary Brown of Life Pieces To Masterpieces.
Bottom left: Mobile Medical Care's Dr. George Cohen helps a patient while the
nonprofit's clinical director, Barbara Clark, looks on.
Bottom right: Maria Gomez with a patient at Mary's Center.
More photographs may be viewed at www.allisonsilberberg.com

Grateful acknowledgment is made to Maxwell Taylor Kennedy and the Estate of
Robert F. Kennedy for permission to reprint an excerpt from *Day of Affirmation* delivered
at the University of Cape Town in South Africa by Senator Robert F. Kennedy, copyright
© 1966 by Robert F. Kennedy.

Grateful acknowledgment is also made to Russell & Volkening as agents for Eudora
Welty for permission to reprint an excerpt from *One Time, One Place: Mississippi in the
Depresion/A Snapshot Album* by Eudora Welty, copyright © 1971 by Eudora Welty.

Praise for *Visionaries In Our Midst*

"This is a book of wonders—and hope. It tells us of extraordinary things 'ordinary' people can do."
 — Studs Terkel, oral historian/Pulitzer Prize-winning author

"This book will not just help save America; it will help save the world."
 — Pete Seeger, songwriter/song leader

"*Visionaries In Our Midst* by Allison Silberberg is a great book about very wonderful people who gave their heart and soul for others. It will inspire many others to do the same if they care. And who doesn't?"
 — Helen Thomas, Dean of The White House Press Corps

"In this age of cynicism, here is a book about good people doing good things. What a refreshing change! What a delightful and uplifting read!"
 — Marvin Kalb, the Edward R. Murrow
 Professor Emeritus at Harvard

"Strong stories of unsung heroes who ought to help give the rest of us courage to act."
 — Paul Loeb, author of *Soul of a Citizen*

For my parents, Al and Barbara Silberberg,
who sacrificed much,
gave me wings and values,
believed anything is possible and believed in me.
I only wish my father were still alive
to know my gratitude.

A PERSONAL NOTE

IT'S ALL ABOUT the dash. That's what my Uncle Erwin used to say. He
heard about the dash while attending a funeral on one of those stifling
summer days in my hometown of Dallas. A preacher in a colorful robe
stood beside the pulpit in an old black church in South Dallas, gazed upon
the casket, and honored the dead man within. Men wiped their brows with
wrinkled handkerchiefs and women fanned themselves as everyone praised
the Lord. The preacher led the gathering in prayer, and the choir sang out.
And there was my uncle, a Jewish man up in his years who always cherished gospel music, and on that day, Uncle Erwin was with real gospel and
surrounded by a strong black community mourning one of their own, an
employee my uncle had come to rely upon.

As anyone in town can attest, Uncle Erwin on most days had a joke to
tell, a bet on a game, a political story to relate, or all three. In many ways,
and not just physically, he was larger than life and reminded me of Jackie
Gleason's character in *The Honeymooners*, only far more polished and successful. When my uncle arrived at his office every morning, my cousins like
to recall that that was when the great debate began almost immediately—
the debate about where they would go to lunch. Uncle Erwin knew how to
enjoy life, sometimes to the hilt. He was not always perfect, mind you, but

he meant well and did his best, trying not to focus on mistakes or disappointments that eat most of our souls as we age. No doubt, as he might say, he had a great ride.

So there he was one afternoon in a church, attending a funeral for an employee, and the preacher gave what Uncle Erwin described as a eulogy for the ages. My uncle's exact words.

Each of us, the preacher called out, has on our tombstone a date of birth and a date of death. We celebrate our birthdays all our lives and never know when death will come—though death always comes. The preacher wanted those gathered not to focus on the date of birth or death, but rather on the dash between. The dash that represented a life—full of hope, achievement, joy, heartache, and recovery. It is all about the dash, he said, while everyone in the church called back an "Amen." What the preacher said stayed with my uncle long after the service. Sometimes, with family and close friends, my uncle discussed the dash and what we're all doing with it.

A few years later, at a packed funeral for Uncle Erwin, grown men fought back tears, to no avail. His dear friend Ben gave the eulogy, in which he spoke of the preacher and the dash. Ben said that no one made that dash more delightful, more memorable, than Erwin Schwartz. He said that Uncle Erwin would want us to remember that it's all about the dash, what we do while we are here, to make the most of our time.

For some, life is long, but they never reach out to others. For others, a giving soul's death touches so many in the community that it gives everyone pause. Almost sixteen when she died in a concentration camp at the end of World War II, Anne Frank continues to touch millions with her diary. Her dash, though short, is immense.

My father died a year after Uncle Erwin. Now and then, especially when something remarkable or horrible or humorous happens, which is basically every day, I find myself thinking about my dad and my uncle and other loved ones—our lives together and the dash. All of it is connected—those who influenced our lives, showed us the way with their courage, and instilled in each of us an ability to live with courage.

And so it is all about the dash.

PROLOGUE

Each time a man stands up for an ideal,
or acts to improve the lot of others,
or strikes out against injustice,
he sends forth a tiny ripple of hope,
and crossing each other from a million different
centers of energy and daring,
those ripples build a current which can sweep down
the mightiest walls of oppression and resistance.

— Robert F. Kennedy
University of Cape Town, South Africa, 1966

BEHIND AN INVISIBLE VEIL

IN OUR MIDST, an invisible veil of suffering exists. It is a side of America not often noticed. In the past, it took a Great Depression or a massive civil rights movement to spur action. Before there was even a hint of a global economic crisis, it first took a storm called Katrina to force a nation to pay attention to the most vulnerable and to care. One woman outside the Superdome in New Orleans, after days of deprivation and terror, put it best when she cried out in pain to America that she is a person, too.

Millions of Americans sat in front of their televisions, transfixed and angered. Though Hurricane Katrina might appear to be a story of the past, it was a harbinger. Now with the economic crisis, which began in late 2007 and reached historic proportions in 2008, the whole nation suddenly has a deeper and more personal understanding of that woman's sense of despair and vulnerability. The number of people receiving unemployment benefits is at an all-time high. Every week, corporations announce thousands of job cuts; millions of Americans have lost their jobs; millions more are cobbling together part-time work. Those with jobs sit with fear. Home foreclosure is epidemic. The stock market has fallen by over 50 percent. Savings and pensions have been severely hurt. It is a time when community is as important as ever.

When the hurricane hit in 2005, its aftermath seemed to pull back a sobering curtain and deliver to our living rooms what leaders in the nonprofit sector see every day all across the nation. But you don't have to go to New Orleans to see poverty. All you have to do is pull back the curtain and look in your own community, no matter where your home is. With the financial disaster hitting the nation, tens of thousands of middle-class American families, often for the first time in their lives, are flooding area food banks and health clinics. Families that went to a food bank or health clinic *before* the recession struck are no doubt having an extremely tough time now balancing food, medicine, and heating bills.

Why does it take a catastrophe for the voices of the poor to be heard and felt? Despite the financial downturn, ours is still in many respects a nation of plenty and even great prosperity for some, but what can be done to remind our nation that poverty exists all the time in New Orleans and in many parts of the nation? How can one person make a difference when there is much to be done and when many of us also feel strapped and nervous about our jobs, assuming we have one? The voices in this book say boldly that there is much that can be achieved. They are not famous; they're not members of Congress; they're not necessarily wealthy. Rather, they are people who took it upon themselves to right a wrong, people who had a morsel of courage and stepped forth on behalf of others, people who are like you and me.

Most of us, perhaps inadvertently, live in some kind of bubble, shielded from the stark reality of poverty around the corner. New Orleans exemplified this drastic divide until Katrina ripped the façade away. Most visitors to that remarkable city would not have spoken of grinding poverty but of memorable meals and mesmerizing jazz. But when the storm exposed desperation there, many Americans were shocked. Much like the hurricane, a perfect metaphor for our times, various factors in society are brewing out at sea and creating a growing underclass.

Despite government ineptitude after the hurricane hit, Americans did rally once they saw and heard the desperate pleas. Hence the phrase often heard at the time: This could not be in America. The tragic situation in New Orleans became a clarion call—that Americans expected better of their nation, of themselves, and of their government. It was as if America's moral compass had been reawakened.

Like a fog that creeps into our view until it envelops us, a new age of poverty has quietly entered our daily world, a disturbing era of class polarization, as the divide between the haves and have-nots continues to widen. Alongside that poverty is a rebirth of activism fighting each unmet social need. But today, the needs are intersecting and creating a daunting wave. Health insurance is out of reach for over forty-six million Americans. Even with coverage, the rising cost of health care is breaking budgets for families and companies. Hunger is on the rise. The savings rate in America, which had been *below* zero for years, has recently increased to 5 percent as families drastically curb their spending and struggle to pay down debt. The rising cost of a college education is too much for more and more families at a time when financial aid has been cut. Even with the new stimulus package and its college tax credit, college will continue to be an intimidating expenditure for most families struggling to keep up with basic bills.

Of all the statistics about suffering, children cast the longest shadow within our country's invisible veil. As Douglas W. Nelson, president of the Annie E. Casey Foundation, noted in 2005, "In all, more than fourteen million, or 21 percent of all kids under eighteen, still live in poverty—a higher proportion than in 1975."

For the first time in our nation's history, the next generation may not do as well financially as the previous generation. How can that be? The American dream is that common thread that binds us all to an abiding hope for a better tomorrow for the next generation. If the American dream continues to be out of reach for a growing segment, then that realization will ultimately threaten the foundation and ideals on which this great nation was forged over two hundred years ago. The Founders' principle that all are created equal—that all have an equal chance—is not a given anymore. It's as if our nation stands on a precipice and doesn't see it.

A nation's greatness is judged not only by its GDP and most successful, but also by its compassion for its most vulnerable. There was a time when the government tried to shoulder responsibility for the downtrodden. In an era long since Franklin Roosevelt's New Deal, John Kennedy's New Frontier, and Lyndon Johnson's Great Society and War on Poverty, public initiatives have mainly been dropped in the laps of what I call the do-gooders. In turn, the nonprofit sector has developed dynamic remedies and produced a number of true public leaders.

One key difference is that in the 1930s and 1960s, government was willing and able to step up and do something. Until the stimulus package passed in early 2009, the power of the state had turned elsewhere.

The fact that private individuals, nonprofits, and philanthropists have stepped up to tackle social ills does not mean the government can walk away. These nonprofit leaders are the heroes of our times, and in order for them to survive and flourish, they will need consistent support from public and private dollars to replicate their innovative solutions for social problems. This is a central theme of this book—that it is incumbent upon the state and the private sector to do more to help fund these heroes and their proven programs. In his inaugural address on January 20, 2009, President Barack Obama implored all Americans to be of service and to care for the less fortunate—especially in these turbulent times. The Edward M. Kennedy Serve America Act of 2009, which was co-sponsored by Senators Edward M. Kennedy and Orrin Hatch, is a bold step in the right direction. It expands national and community service opportunities for all Americans, and increases the number of service corps entities, jobs in the nonprofit sector, and volunteerism. It also provides incentives for students to engage in service as well as much-needed funds for nonprofit capacity building to assist small and midsize organizations.

The invisible veil of suffering is not only in small pockets; it reaches all across the nation, from New York to Los Angeles. Ironically, the invisible veil is no more clearly evident than in the shadow of the nation's capital. Washington, D.C., and its surrounding neighborhoods represent a cross-section of the nation. Focused on visionaries in the Washington region who are tackling problems with successful approaches, the stories are case studies in courage. The visionaries, problems, and solutions in this community exemplify problems and potential solutions throughout the country. Even if there are different unmet needs in your community, they are all part of the fabric of America today. By addressing national poverty issues on a gripping human level, these stories reveal the can-do spirit of a nation and demonstrate how each of us can take part.

This book captures a moment in time. The stories were researched and written beginning in 2004 and through 2008, providing a sense of how the individuals and their programs have evolved as well as depicting the growing depth of unmet social needs *before* the economic downturn.

While the programs in this book can be duplicated—in fact two are now in the process of replication—one of my goals is to make the process of getting involved as easy as possible, no matter where someone lives in the nation. With help from numerous contacts and community leaders throughout the country, I developed a national list of effective, innovative programs. Several are listed after each chapter. The conclusion of the book provides information about online resources.

In addition to the programs, it's the people behind the programs who are compelling: who they are, why they do this work, and what the work has meant to them and their staff and volunteers, not to mention those they serve. This book profiles the courage and innovative solutions with which ordinary Americans are forging ahead, often against tremendous odds.

Authors of other generations have reminded our nation of grinding poverty. In some small way, I have endeavored to document America's confrontation with poverty, much like James Agee and Walker Evans did in the 1930s with their classic, *Let Us Now Praise Famous Men*, or as Michael Harrington's *The Other America* spurred action in the 1960s. Now in the first decade of a new century and new millenium, America stands at the height of its power coupled with a crippled economy and unrealized goals of a better society for all.

Breaking through the invisible veil every day and making a noble effort to remove it forever are countless hands. This is a book about those who inspire hope, about those who struggle, and about what it means to care and do something about it. This is a book that tells a different kind of profiles in courage, focusing on catalysts—visionaries who innovate and work for change for the greater good. This is a book that asks about our priorities and our values as a nation. And this is a book to discover what is possible when people stand up for one another. But first, before the stories of the visionaries, here is a snapshot of our nation's growing needs.

THE CASCADING EFFECT FOR AMERICA'S MOST VULNERABLE

WHILE THE UNITED States remains the wealthiest nation in the world, the United States is also a nation of about thirty-eight million people in poverty, according to the U.S. Census Bureau in 2005. Included in those thirty-eight million is nearly one child in six. Those statistics reflected realities on the ground before the economic disaster hit, before the unemployment rate skyrocketed, and before foreclosures became commonplace.

In addition to the thirty-eight million in poverty, millions of other Americans of all ages are on the verge of poverty. Deemed the working poor or the "near poor," these Americans live on the margins—stressed about bills, working without health insurance, and living a paycheck or two away from financial disaster. It wouldn't take much to tilt such a family into ruin. There have been price increases in food, education, shelter, and health care. Basic needs often merge with one another until there is a disturbing critical mass effect, and things snowball. Cutting back on food is one of the first considerations.

This is not only about the lower class. The middle class, which historically has been the backbone of the American economy, is faltering. Millions of Americans, whether employed or not, are strapped with bills while drowning in debt. The growing division between the haves and have-nots is not only a concern for the nation's sociologists and economists; it is a threat to the fabric of our democracy, the ideal that everyone has a voice and a chance to realize their potential.

The situation for children is clear. When parents struggle to meet basic needs for survival, children suffer. Lacking consistent nourishment affects a child's ability to learn and grow. These children often go to school without school supplies, and have parents who either cannot read to them or who are too tired to do so. Special needs, such as early diagnosis and treatment of reading and learning disabilities, inevitably take a back seat. These children are behind before the whistle blows. And so the cycle begins.

Without a change in direction, our nation will soon be at a crossroads—economically, socially, and spiritually.

While the statistics reflect urban poverty in major cities, those same statistics also reflect a growing, stealth-like *suburban* poverty in our midst. Though rural poverty goes beyond the scope of this book, it is also crushing, and in rural America, there are fewer services within easy access. The essays here go on a journey from urban to suburban poverty in the heart of wealthy suburbs and back again. Much like our nation, the Washington, D.C., region is a tale of two cities with great wealth and a growing underclass. A microcosm for the rest of the country, the Washington region became my laboratory. The stories may appear to be about one region, but this is a tale about America.

In our nation of plenty, hunger is a growing reality, according to the U.S. Census in 2000. The census reported that 56,000 children in Washington were hungry or at risk of hunger. ("At risk of hunger" refers to households that are food insecure, meaning that they could not afford to buy adequate food on a regular basis.) According to D.C. Public Schools, half of the children enrolled live below 185 percent of poverty, which means they qualify for free or reduced-price lunch and breakfast.

As of December 2008, just over 100,000 D.C. residents (about half of whom were children) participated in the Food Stamp Program. That figure was up 12 percent since a year earlier. And what does the Food Stamp Program buy you? Not much. The program, which is now known as the Supplemental Nutrition Assistance Program (or SNAP), provides less than $115 per person per month, which translates into about $1.28 per person per meal. According to the Congressional Budget Office, once the stimulus benefits go into effect in the coming weeks, the average amount per person per meal will be about $1.50.

While hunger is not new, hunger in D.C. has increased significantly since 2001 and even more since 2008. According to the Capital Area Food Bank, a D.C. nonprofit, between 2001 and 2006, the need for food supplies increased 39 percent. Of the 380,000 people served at the Food Bank in 2005, 50 percent of the households reported they had at least one working adult. In early 2009, the network of agencies that the Food Bank serves reported an increase of need between 30 and 80 percent over the previous year. The Food Bank's "hunger lifeline" helps people who are in crisis and need food the day they call. In late October 2008, a spokesman for the Food Bank stated in the *Washington Post* that "calls from needy residents to the food bank's hunger lifeline have jumped 248 percent in the past six months." In short, there was significant need before the recession hit in late 2007. Now, the need is overwhelming.

Hunger is not only a D.C. issue, though D.C.'s hunger rate is staggering. Hunger is a national issue and a bellwether of other crisis points. According to Census Bureau data in 2007, over thirty-six million Americans lived in food-insecure homes, including twenty-five million children. As of early 2009, approximately thirty-two million Americans were receiving help from the Food Stamp Program, an all-time high and almost double the number of people receiving benefits in 2000, according to the U.S. Department of Agriculture. Like the canary in the coal mine, the Food Stamp Program is one of the first indicators of increased hardship.

The nation's largest charitable, domestic hunger-relief organization is Feeding America, which serves twenty-five million Americans a year throughout the nation. In early 2009, Maura Daly, vice president of government relations for the nonprofit, explained, "More than thirty-five million Americans, including twelve million children, are living on the brink of hunger each year. Nearly 40 percent of the people we serve have at least one adult working in the household."

Hunger is only one growing need, but it has tragic ripple effects, especially for children, because hunger is directly tied to a child's ability to learn in school and succeed in life. First, a child who goes to bed hungry has incalculable disadvantages at school in the morning. Dr. Deborah Frank, an expert on the connection between food insecurity and children's health, testified before the U.S. House Budget Committee in 2007 that "infants and toddlers from food insecure families are 90 percent more likely to be in fair or poor health." Dr. Frank also reported that "in older children food insecurity is associated with poorer physical health, decreased school achievement in reading and math, and more behavior and emotional problems, including risk of suicidal thoughts in adolescent girls." Without consistent nutrition, a hungry child's growing mind and body cannot be nourished properly. A hungry child has a hard time falling asleep or will sleep too much. That child doesn't know if there will be three nutritious meals a day; that child doesn't know why he or she doesn't have a great attention span. That child only knows fatigue and restlessness all at once. How can that child be expected to learn when his or her brain is literally hungry and yet striving to grow?

Then, there are the children of the homeless—the children whose parents are on a waiting list for a shelter, or whose families are staying in emergency shelters, transitional housing, or permanent supportive housing. Nationally, one out of every fifty American children, or approximately 1.5 million, is homeless, according to a 2009 report from the National Center on Family Homelessness, which analyzed data from 2006. Times are far more difficult now: Millions have lost their jobs, and many families are facing foreclosure and risk homelessness.

In 2008, on any given day in D.C. alone, there were 1,149 children (age seventeen and younger) whose families were in emergency shelter or transitional housing, according to the Community Partnership for the Prevention of Homelessness. Approximately half of the 1,149 children were age five or younger.

The numbers are far higher for the region. The Fannie Mae Foundation reported in 2004, "On any given day, 14,000 people in the greater Washington metropolitan area are homeless. A third are employed. Half are families, and a quarter of them are children." Though the Fannie Mae Foundation has ceased day-to-day operations, other organizations have had similar findings. And that was prior to the recession.

Another issue is health care, a top priority of the Obama administration. According to the *Washington Post* in 2005, "In the District [of Columbia], an estimated 15 percent of the population has no health insurance and one in three residents receives health benefits from a patchwork of government programs."

Nationally, as of early 2009, the number of Americans without health insurance was at an historic level of forty-six million. That statistic does not include the tens of thousands of Americans who have recently lost their jobs and are therefore on the verge of losing their health coverage.

Yet, employment is not a guarantee of health coverage. In early 2009, a Robert Wood Johnson Foundation report noted that more than 80 percent of America's uninsured are working but cannot afford insurance. A 2005 foundation report stated that 35.5 percent of working Hispanics in the United States are uninsured, compared to 11.8 percent of working whites, and 18.5 percent of working African Americans. And these are the people we can document. We know there are about twelve million undocumented people in the country, and they are not counted in those statistics.

Whether documented or undocumented, they're immigrants who came here for the American Dream and who are working and raising families. Many are living paycheck to paycheck at best. They clean our offices, homes, and restaurants; work two or three jobs a day; share an apartment with two or three families and have little or no benefits and little or no savings. They and their children are part of the invisible veil of suffering.

But it is not only immigrants who make up those behind the veil. It is white America, black America, and every kind of America. Go to a soup kitchen, a free clinic, or a shelter, and you will see that poverty touches all kinds of Americans.

These are our nation's "working poor"—the millions of Americans who work hard and who can barely keep up, much less save. They have to pay for their own health insurance or go without coverage. Many cannot afford major medical insurance, so if possible, they make do with what one friend, a single mother, calls her "disaster health insurance" plan. Thus, she is under-insured. She pays out-of-pocket for minor things and lives in dread of her son's broken arm from a fall on the playground. She also dreads the day that her measly "disaster health insurance" will raise her rates or decide to cancel her policy and leave them in worse shape.

ON THE COLDEST OF NIGHTS

LAST WINTER, ON the coldest of nights, I remember leaving a party in Washington and chuckling at how freezing it was as I rushed to my car and waited for the seat warmer to send warmth through my body. On the way home at one in the morning, I got stuck at an eternally long stoplight in full view of the White House grounds and the Washington Monument.

Even though I was wearing my heaviest winter coat and had the car's heat blasting, I was still shivering. To my right, there was a steady flow of hot steam billowing into the sky from the grates on the ground. I knew who would also be there. Glancing over and watching the steam float up and away, I knew I would see the homeless people huddled under their worn, gray blankets, trying to harness warmth from the grates. I had seen them there many times before. Somehow I hoped they wouldn't be there on this coldest of nights. But there they were—all within a stone's throw of the White House grounds—shrouded under a dark gray blanket, which made them blend in with the landscape and appear invisible.

Nearby, their few belongings sat in a pile in a shopping basket. I imagined how painful, physically and spiritually, it must be to stay outside in the freezing cold for hours on end. How do they choose what they keep in that basket and how will they ever survive such a bitter night? On these freezing nights, homeless people are encouraged to seek shelter, but some refuse. By a certain time, the shelters fill up. No doubt they had filled up by that point.

I thought about those huddled on the grates as I drove the empty streets of Washington, past the White House and the glorious monuments honoring Abraham Lincoln and Thomas Jefferson. What would Lincoln and Jefferson say or do about homelessness? I thought about when Lincoln and Jefferson lived in hardship. Lincoln as a boy was dirt poor, and Jefferson, after his presidency, fell on hard times and worried about expenditures. Lincoln educated his way out of poverty. Jefferson managed the best he could. Any one of us can fall on hard times. There but for the grace of God go I.

Whether urban or suburban, the stealth-like poverty in our midst demands investment—both private and public dollars—if all of our nation will be able to flourish. A sliver of the massive stimulus package might offer that opportunity. If dollars were invested in replicating innovative, well-managed nonprofit programs, then the programs would pay for themselves by saving our society from dealing with the unmet needs later. Imagine if government and business forged public-private partnerships to support and replicate successful nonprofit "business" models, and if more citizens donated even an hour per week to a nonprofit that is making a similar difference. Every volunteer would be enriched. And imagine the impact on those in need, on the community, and on our nation. Imagine the tiny ripples of change throughout the land. Living a life of active engagement and citizenship is critical to the life of a nation, according to the American scholar Benjamin Barber.

There are many ways to be actively engaged. But why get involved with the public good when there are so many other things to do?

I know an elderly couple, Peggy and Alvin Brown, who answer that question with a simple phrase they call "psychic pay." In their late eighties and early nineties now, they have been married for nearly seventy years. I met them in the late 1990s when they commissioned me to write their memoir. They were seventy-eight and eighty-three, and still very active. But unbeknownst to us then, Alvin was on the verge of aging fast. Though he is alive, his brilliance and wit have faded. To know Alvin was to know someone who savored life and wanted to share that with others. Working with them on the memoir, I witnessed the magic between them and absorbed their wise counsel about creating and living a meaningful life.

Peggy and Alvin came out of the ruins of the Great Depression, did well in business after World War II, and then became philanthropic, making a difference in the region and the nation. Much of the book I wrote about them focused not only on how they made their wealth, but also on what they did with it, enriching their lives all the more.

As they said consistently, so much can be gained by giving to those you will never know. It was more than giving back; it was about being part of a grander, positive force, a measure of character, of not forgetting what it was like to be cold in the winter, not having enough to eat, not being able to go to camp or college. They never forgot any of that and were always grateful for their good fortune, for their ability to give. Through the decades, they have supported numerous nonprofits that help children, the elderly, the ill, and the unemployed. The main thrust of their giving is focused on education, for they believe education creates the greatest opportunity for achievement and change.

Peggy believes that "psychic pay" is a perfect phrase, for it captures the essence of what you get paid for your involvement, which is nothing and yet you get paid everything. It's not something you can hold onto in your wallet but rather in your heart, in your soul. While most of their giving has been financial, there are countless ways to give.

THE EIGHTEEN VISIONARIES

Choosing to focus on eighteen visionaries carries special meaning. In Judaism, the word *chai* means the number eighteen. *Chai* has another meaning, and that is life. Many have heard the phrase, *l'chaim*, which means "to life." Any multiple of eighteen works in giving. (Such is my religion's logic, and there may be a pop quiz on this part later for those of you who are skimming this introduction.)

Therefore, I chose to focus on eighteen, because of the meaning behind the number eighteen and how it related to the mission of the individuals in the book, expressing their commitment to helping a life and giving someone another chance with life. Their commitment to another is an example of *tikkun olam*, which is a Hebrew phrase meaning world repair and refers to making the world a better place. All part of doing a *mitzvah*, or a good deed and any act of human kindness. All of it is part of a commitment to *tzedakah*, which literally means justice, or as it is commonly interpreted, charitable giving.

As a priest once said, being present is critical. The stories of this book remind us all what it is to be present, to be human. Those mentioned in this book choose to be present, to be for others. How bountiful their lives have become. Hearing their words with all their impact only requires a listening heart.

"May your life be a blessing," a Jewish prayer implores. It is a far higher calling than to pray for blessings. Saint Francis of Assisi knew what that meant, for he chose to have his life be a blessing for others. It is a choice.

As Eudora Welty wrote about photographing poverty during the Great Depression, "…my wish, indeed my continuing passion, would be not to point the finger in judgment but to part a curtain, that invisible shadow that falls between people, the veil of indifference to each other's presence, each other's wonder, each other's human plight."

To part a curtain and ultimately remove that invisible veil of suffering in our land—that is this book's aim.

If we create something for others, something bigger than ourselves, something that will live through the ages, only then are we truly living and only then can we have a small understanding of what the stars must know: what it is to live forever. But people do not live forever. They live on through the memories of those who loved them and through the good they leave behind for those they never knew.

Allison Silberberg
April 2009

Please note: The contact information for the organizations mentioned in this book was up-to-date at the time of publication.

I can see the beauty and happiness in life, which many people take for granted. I think you gain a keener perception of life if you have faced adversity...This is what I [would] like to convey to people. That it is the greatest blessing, not to take for granted what you have...I think that the thought of God is the thought of love. If you can engage in doing something good, then you are a part of that. And that is very fulfilling.

— Gerda Weissmann Klein
Author & Holocaust Survivor
Excerpt from an interview on
ABC News' *Nightline*, 2000

THE EIGHTEEN

THE FISHING SCHOOL

STANDING IN A packed banquet room at a fancy Washington restaurant near Capitol Hill, the crowd cheered loudly for a frail Tom Lewis as he slowly made his way to the podium. The mayor of Washington, D.C., various congressmen and senators of both political parties, the British ambassador, and countless supporters—many with tears in their eyes—applauded for this former police officer and his beloved Fishing School, which was celebrating its fifteenth anniversary. An after-school program, The Fishing School has a sterling reputation as a miracle worker for children in a neglected part of the city; the fact that Tom was standing and about to give a few remarks was a miracle, too. As Tom leaned on the podium for strength, the crowd cheered even louder and emotion came to his eyes.

If a stranger wandered into the room, he might ask, "Who is this fellow? Why all the tears?" Tom Lewis. Utter the name around Washington and you will hear a story that will force you to pause. If I hadn't witnessed some of the story myself, I'm not sure I would have believed it. It all began with a selfless decision on Tom's part to create something for children in need. Then, many years later, Tom's life was saved not once but twice because of his work for the children. Not that that was why he created The Fishing School. It just worked out that way.

To no avail, Tom tried to quiet the people at that reception, but the crowd would have none of it. It felt too good, too right to cheer. And there was Tom, humble about the whole thing and heartened by the outpouring. The good he instilled in a small nonprofit is carrying on. This is a story about an individual whose faith in children led him to make a difference in a neighborhood no one would touch.

When I first met Tom and his wife, Lucille, a few years earlier, there was no hint of illness. They were dressed to the nines in formal wear. He reminded me of Sidney Poitier, and, like Poitier, his voice was calm, soft, and deliberate. We were all at a charity event in the fall of 2002, and Tom's Fishing School had been honored. At the end of the event, I sought him out and waited my turn to shake his hand. He was unbelievably gracious and distinguished. In that moment of chatting with him, I felt a kinship. His enthusiasm was compelling and contagious, and he had a sweetness that was genuine. I knew instantly I was in the presence of quiet greatness. I remember the glow of pride and humility in the faces of Tom and Lucille Lewis. At once, I felt emboldened and grateful for having met them, and I felt tears as well. The story of Tom and the children of his Fishing School made me cry.

A retired District of Columbia police officer after twenty years in the line of duty, Tom decided he wanted to do something for children in need. So in 1990, he started The Fishing School. His mission was to bring hope, skills, and belief in oneself to economically disadvantaged children and youth in Northeast Washington, D.C.

Tom's community involvement had evolved, beginning during his years in the police force and even before that. At one point, he was a PTA president at his children's elementary school. He also helped out with his church on Sundays and assisted the pastor by working on plays with the children during the holidays.

Only a couple of years on the police force, Tom was assigned to be on the streets right after the assassination of the Reverend Dr. Martin Luther King, Jr., in 1968. The news of the tragedy stunned and saddened millions of Americans. For Tom, as an African American as well as a witness to the riots and destruction around D.C.'s U Street corridor, those days remain a poignant and painful time.

Soon, the police department realized it had an eloquent officer in its ranks—an officer whose words touched people, especially children. After years of assigning Officer Lewis to a beat, the D.C. police assigned him to work in the Community Relations Division, where he and four other officers became known as "Officer Friendly." This meant they went to all the schools and other community forums to speak with students about "being good junior citizens." As an "Officer Friendly," Officer Lewis saw so many children living in desperation and destitution that he felt compelled to act. The Fishing School was born from his belief that the promise of America can only be realized if all of our children get the love and care that will enable them to mature into responsible adults and leaders of tomorrow. Tom wanted to give these kids a fighting chance to realize their potential, so he devoted his life to them.

"The Fishing School is an after-school family and child support center that provides a safe haven, intervention, and education for vulnerable children and youth," Tom wrote for the entity's mission. "The Fishing School is inspired by the adage, 'If you give a man a fish, you will feed him for a day. Teach him how to fish, and he will feed himself for a lifetime.' Through a variety of programs and services, we help children develop into independent, productive, and contributing members of society."

Blessed with the fine ability to tell a story, Tom enjoys sharing the Biblical story about Lazarus, a story I did not know. I've heard him tell it twice, and I could hear him tell it again and again. There is something about Tom that is unassuming and yet confident. With a gentle voice, he reminded me of Fred Rogers.

But by 2004, his voice was not the same due to serious illness. Though convalescing, he was still short of breath. Tom wanted me to know the correct story of Lazarus for the sake of the book, and he said in a weak, gravelly voice, "Lazarus was very sick, and his family had sent for Jesus. But Jesus was in another town, and Lazarus died three days before Jesus could arrive. Lazarus was buried in a tomb, and a big stone blocked the entrance of the tomb. When Jesus came, in order for Lazarus to be set free, Jesus demanded that they roll the stone away. And when they rolled the stone, Jesus called Lazarus by name and told him to come forth. Lazarus walked out of the tomb, and he was brought back to life."

Tom linked the miraculous story of Lazarus to The Fishing School's mission. He explained, "The correlation is that over there where The Fishing School is, the area is full of people, families, and children who are the walking dead because of their economic and living conditions, drug-infested neighborhoods, etc. The people in the neighborhood can't go anywhere. They're living, breathing, and walking, but they're not living.

"Stones are in their way—stones of illiteracy, stones of poverty, stones of prejudice, stones of drug abuse and alcoholism. What The Fishing School is trying to do, what I'm trying to do with The Fishing School is to roll those stones away. What we need is stone throwers to help roll those stones away."

Since 1990, The Fishing School and Tom Lewis have helped push rocks out of the way for over 2,500 youngsters—giving the children a sense of community, a deep well of love and understanding, and a strong foundation for setting and achieving goals.

One day, three of the kids Tom had helped were able to be there for him. Tom was on his way to work one morning and felt pain in his chest as he drove. He recalled, "When I got to work, I called my doctor, and he told me to get someone to drive me to the hospital right away. And when I got in the door of the hospital, I saw a young man. There were three EMTs there and they started to help me, and one of the EMTs stopped and shouted, 'Mr. Lewis?!' All three of the EMTs had gone to The Fishing School."

Tom had helped all three of them as youngsters. Now he was on a gurney, and they were helping him.

He shrugged, "Everywhere I go around the city, I run into people who used to go to The Fishing School. Some of them are doing quite well, and some of them are just doing. It's enlightening to hear them call my name," he said with a touch of glee.

"It must give you a great feeling," I said.

"Oh yeah," he replied with his softness.

Married since 1970, Tom and Lucille Lewis have three children of their own, two sons and a daughter, all doing well. And he said proudly, "And three grand-boys! Got a big picture on the wall. I was just looking at it."

"They call you Grandpa?"

"Yeah, Grand-daddy. I LOVE to hear that! Grand-daddy!"

"So with The Fishing School, you just enlarged your family."

"Yes, you could say that. That was my life. It wasn't just some nice thing that I did. It was my life."

Recalling how it all began, Tom said, "In the late 1980s, I was in church one Sunday, and I had a vision. I guess people call it a vision. So I knew I was supposed to be doing something, and I didn't know what it was. And I realized I had [a place,] that old, ragged house in Northeast [D.C.], and I saw how bad that area was. And I decided to open the program there."

He also remembered that it didn't happen overnight and said, "There was a long time before I got the community to help me. They thought I was running an office to trick them or something. But I had made up my mind that I was going to stay there and do the work whether I got any help or not."

And work he did. His property was a dilapidated row house in a rough neighborhood by anyone's standards, but today there are parts in the midst of some gentrification. Back in 1990, it was a rougher area, and Tom transformed that old row house into a clean spot of heaven. He had the outside painted a pale shade of yellow, and put a small sign above the front door. Tom made the various rooms into classrooms for after-school programs that include homework assistance, tutoring, and classes in reading, math, and computer technology. One room is full of computers so that the children can learn computer skills.

The school's commitment is clear: "Our year-round focus is to provide safe havens for children during critical out-of-school hours, intervention through academic help and personal nurturing, and positive social activities. Several special initiatives allow us to accomplish our objectives: the Female Youth Enrichment Program, the Male Youth Enrichment Program, the Homework Assistance/Tutoring Program, the Computer Program, the Spanish Program, the Fishing School Gospel Choir, and the Parent/Community Resource Center."

Speaking of how critical it is to include parents in the nonprofit's mission, he explained, "We meet with parents and invite them to The Fishing School and have different kinds of programs. I think that helps the children to see their parents involved."

Among the many awards, Tom received a prestigious national award called The Jefferson Award for Public Service in 1997, and was chosen as a Washingtonian of the Year by *Washingtonian* magazine.

In the fall of 2002, within weeks of meeting Tom and Lucille, I visited The Fishing School around 7 P.M. About thirty children, ages six to fifteen, had already worked on homework and were eating dinner. Tom's office was upstairs in a tiny, crowded room. How he accomplished so much from that desk is amazing. There he was, a tall man working at a regular-sized desk, which was covered with piles of papers, grant proposals, files, clippings, and letters. It was a lot of hard work, but a labor of love. All of a sudden, while standing behind his desk, Tom had a bothersome cough and shrugged, saying it was a nuisance lately.

Within a month or so, Tom had an incessant cough that was even deeper. Finally, he was diagnosed with advanced cancer, lymphoma to be specific. By the time it was caught, he was getting weaker by the day. Five years earlier, Tom had been treated for lymphoma and had recovered. Having a recurrence was terrifying. Lucille recalled looking him in the eye: "I told him, 'We're in this together. And we're gonna fight it and get through this together.' And we did. And he cheered up after that."

Tom was sent to an oncologist at Kaiser Permanente. When the doctor asked Tom about his work, Tom told him about The Fishing School and the children. The oncologist was so moved by Tom's work with the children that he paused and then said half-jokingly, "Well then, we gotta keep you alive."

Remarkably, the doctors did just that.

By sheer coincidence, his oncologist had trained at Johns Hopkins and was familiar with a special program there that might save Tom. He made some calls on Tom's behalf, because Hopkins would need to accept Tom into what was then an experimental and risky stem cell transplant program. At age sixty-three in early 2003, Tom had the surgery.

Recovery was slow, and it was a turbulent couple of years for Tom and Lucille. The stem cell transplant at Hopkins was successful and gave him another chance at life, but recovery had its own daily challenges. Less muscular and energetic, Tom was in the midst of a slow but stunning comeback for many months. Getting shingles, a painful nerve disorder, after two bouts of lymphoma didn't help matters. As stressful as it was for Tom, it was at least that stressful for Lucille.

He feels blessed and said, "She had a tailor shop for twenty-eight years, and she closed that down so she could take care of me."

Due to his illness, Tom slowly handed the reins of The Fishing School to his niece, Jackie Walls. At first, Jackie was the acting executive director, and about a year later, she became the executive director. Tom could no longer be the president of the board of directors either. The board found a replacement and made Tom president emeritus.

Always focused on the well-being of the children of The Fishing School, Tom reflected on the good he has done. "Quite a few of them are in college now. I got very ill. I'm still sick," he said in a hoarse voice while lying on the couch on a hot summer day in 2005, resting before a brief visit to The Fishing School. Each sentence took his breath away and forced him to pause. "The board of directors hired a replacement for me. I'm not complaining that I'm still sick."

On another steamy and humid July afternoon that summer, Tom was determined to go to The Fishing School for an hour to see the garden that the nonprofit was working on. Though short of breath, he was determined see all the volunteers who were going to be weeding and planting the garden across the street from The Fishing School. He wanted to be there.

On the heels of turning sixty-six in August, Tom visited The Fishing School as often as he could and helped out when he felt up to it. During those months of endless recovery, he visited the children one afternoon and was thrilled that the children had made him a collage. He was also there for Jackie and the staff if they needed a guiding hand. It was a tough transition for someone so connected to and touched by the work at The Fishing School. And a tough transition for the nonprofit that loves him.

The kids (or the alumni) of The Fishing School continued to come by looking to say hello to *their* Mr. Lewis, but Tom was at home recuperating. Tom said, "One of the kids who came by was Natalie, now an adult. She came by The Fishing School to see me, and they said I wasn't there. Jackie asked her what she was doing now, and Natalie told her that she was a pharmacist technician. Jackie also asked how The Fishing School influenced her life. Natalie said, 'If it wasn't for The Fishing School, I would not have finished high school.' She said that her mother did not care if she went to school or not, but that I taught her how important it was for her to get her education. Natalie said that my daughter, Tisha, who is now pursuing a doctorate, was a real inspiration to her. Natalie asked for my home number, and she called me here at home the other day. That made me feel good."

There is a reason for Tom's ability to understand the struggles endured by the children of The Fishing School. He was once like those children. And like Lazarus, someone came to push a stone away for a young Tom Lewis. Someone gave him a chance. It was about fifty years ago, and Tom was seventeen and barely able to live. That's when things began to change, because Tom met a man named Gilbert Paisner and his family.

Tom was born and reared in a small, rural town in North Carolina, and it was rough in the segregated South. As Tom put it, "I had dropped out of school in tenth grade. I was one of sixteen children. My mother and father didn't have any education. My mother was trying to keep meat on the table, but we didn't always eat. I went hungry a lot of days. There were a lot of mouths to feed."

At age sixteen, Tom left home and went to work on a migrant farm. "There was a bus and a bunch of people would go from state to state and work the land," he remembered. "So we'd go from Virginia to New Jersey to upstate New York, back down to West Virginia and back to Florida. I was picking tomatoes, potatoes, peas and beans, apples and oranges, doing seasonal work."

Around age seventeen or eighteen, Tom made his way to New York City. He remembered, "I had no place to stay. Some North Carolina friends let me stay with them and sleep on the floor. For about six months, I had no job and borrowed forty cents a day from a friend so I could eat. Then I saw this sign at 708 Broadway that said they were looking for a floor boy in the factory. This Jewish family named Paisner owned the factory, and the father and son managed things together. The son, Gilbert, gave me a job and got me a place to stay. I became a floor boy in his family's factory. They were making different things—materials and fabrics like nylon, wool, cotton. They made braids. I'd get on the bus and deliver samples. There were eight ladies working on various machines, and I would take their samples to the garment district. This fellow, Gilbert, was so good to me. Being a country boy, I sometimes went out to their house on Long Island to do some gardening and helped around the yard. They were very nice to me, and they helped a lot of people. Everyone who worked for them at the factory—it was like a big family. When I left and went to the military, I was overseas. Once, I needed some money. I sent word, and Gilbert sent me some money. Years later, when I started The Fishing School, Gilbert chipped in and was very supportive.

"No question. If he wasn't there to help me, I wouldn't have been able to help others. I'd be in jail myself, or I don't know where I'd be. And of course, the Lord helped me."

Eventually, Tom would be the first in his family to go to college. While working full-time in the D.C. police department, he earned a college degree from American University. It took him eight years to graduate because of work and family commitments, but he did it. With Tom's strong work ethic and Gilbert's help, the endless cycle of poverty in Tom's life had finally ended.

Poverty in Tom's family began long ago, for Tom's father struggled for years. There was no Gilbert Paisner to help Tom's father find stability in life. It wasn't until Tom was a grown man with a family that he learned more about his father's youth and what had shaped his father's life.

The story came to light because some relatives in North Carolina asked Tom to organize a family reunion, and he said quietly with a shaky voice, "I found out something about my Daddy I never knew. We thought he was very mean, but—"

Gathering his thoughts, he continued, "He was three years old when his father killed his mother. So his dad went to jail, and for fifteen years, three months and a day, that little boy [Tom's father] barely scraped by. For all that time, no one in the family wanted him. Someone would keep him for a while and then send him around to someone else. My great-grandfather was a white man. So that had something to do with it."

Eventually, Tom's father got emphysema; he lived to be seventy-four. Tom added, "My mother was eighty-one when she passed. She had sixteen children. Her twin sister had fourteen children and lived to ninety-two."

Tom got a little choked up speaking about Gilbert Paisner and the Paisner family. There are no words for how grateful he feels, for Gilbert and his family didn't have to help him change the course of his life, but they did. And that, in turn, enabled and inspired Tom to be there for hundreds of youngsters. Today in 2009, Gilbert Paisner is 84.

There is almost always a story behind the story. Success stories like The Fishing School do not happen in a vacuum. Someone inspires another to take action. Each of us can be that person—the one who inspires others to go farther, achieve more, do more. A Tom Lewis does not merely arrive. Taking a chance on someone and believing in them when they are not even sure about themselves can be the difference between a broken spirit and a determined, giving soul. This story behind the genesis of The Fishing School exemplifies Robert Kennedy's ripple upon the water, for who can tell where all the youngsters of The Fishing School will land and how many others they will help?

The Fishing School continues to provide rewarding moments for the children as well as the staff and volunteers, including Jackie Walls. She confessed, "I spent almost thirty years in corporate America, but I didn't start living a life that was purpose-driven until I began working at The Fishing School. I tell people that all the time. When I came to The Fishing School, even though I had worked for years with the girls on the Saturday enrichment program, it wasn't until I was brought on full-time that I felt the full breadth of service that The Fishing School brings forth to the children. It's life-changing. I see why we call this heart work and not hard work."

Prior to running The Fishing School, Jackie had been its director of operations and finance. She is devoted to the nonprofit and observed in 2005, "The children are interested in learning everything."

Jackie is doing her level best to fill Tom's shoes and continue the entity's successful record. Fair Chance, a D.C. nonprofit that helps local nonprofits strengthen their programs for at-risk youth and their families, selected The Fishing School to help it grow and provide more services. It is a tremendous honor to be selected.

Since its fledgling start, The Fishing School has come a long way. By 2005, with an annual budget of almost $660,000, The Fishing School was helping 150 children per year, providing a safe place for learning, personal growth, and friendship. Not bad for a retired police officer who had a vision and knew the children needed and deserved more attention and guidance.

In 1996, Jackie put together a book about the Lewis family. Her father is Tom's older brother. Born in Chadbourn, North Carolina, Tom grew up nearby in Elizabethtown, North Carolina. In 1998, Tom replicated his program and started a Fishing School in Chadbourn. One of his cousins runs the program. In her family book, Jackie included the following Ettiene De Grellet quote to describe her feelings about Tom's life of service:

> I expect to pass through this world but once; any good thing therefore that I can do, or any kindness that I can show to any fellow creature, let me do it now; let me not defer or neglect it, for I shall not pass this way again.

The Fishing School's year-round, academic-focused, after-school and summer programs provide what any child needs: attention, structure, learning, encouragement, and love. During the school year, its programs include academic instruction, tutoring, homework assistance, and cultural enrichment, as well as music and dance lessons. The Fishing School also provides the children with life skills training and field trips, not to mention a parent support component.

Jackie explained, "Our summer program includes academic enrichment in the mornings. Classes are in reading, math, music appreciation, and computer technology. This summer, we have three new programs: martial arts, rites of passage for male youth, and a financial literacy television program called *Money Savvy Kids*, which is an award-winning PBS program out of Chicago.

"The *Money Savvy Kids* program was introduced by one of our board members, Julie Anderson. Julie produced the PBS program in Chicago where she is based and brought the program to The Fishing School's attention. In addition, she arranged for the creators of the program, Susan and Michael Beacham, to train The Fishing School's teachers. They have provided all the materials for us to do this program. Julie is amazing. She flies in from Chicago for every board meeting."

The children's afternoons are filled with recreational activities such as bowling, skating, swimming, and intramural sports. Intramural sports programs include basketball, baseball, and volleyball. The Fishing School serves children from two sites, and they form teams and play against each other, which teaches teamwork and sportsmanship. Sometimes, they go to a recreation center, which partners with The Fishing School.

"Thursdays are museum trips for our cultural awareness," Jackie specified. "Fridays are all-day field trips, such as to the Maryland Science Center, an interactive museum where there are different ways to feel and experience science. We have field trips to King's Dominion and other water parks, so they get a chance to experience plain fun. For the last two years, we have also taken the children to tour the White House.

"Every year, we partner with U.S. Fisheries and Wildlife and they sponsor a fishing trip. Not only do the children learn how to fish, but they learn character traits such as patience, perseverance, focus—a blend of fun and learning.

"Today, the children had a trip to the World Bank, and that was sponsored by Siemens Corporation. We took thirty children down there, and the Bank gave them handouts and a briefing about what the World Bank does. Our activities coordinator asked what our children would need to do in order to work there.

"The Bank's representative told about her background. First, she was part of the Peace Corps; she knew four languages and had a college degree, maybe more. Well, the children saw that education was important," Jackie concluded and then had to get everything ready for the group to redo the garden.

It's almost as if Tom does not need to be present at The Fishing School every single day, for he is present even while at home. His imprint has not and will not fade. The children will continue to come to The Fishing School and find a sanctuary from the troubled streets and empty homes. Tom created a haven out of nothing. It's not fancy at The Fishing School. Not everything is perfect, but it's a special place. You know it when you walk in. It's a place of encouragement and hugs and belief. It's a place that looks after the children, guards them from the wrong path, and guides them through their studies and hopefully to a full life. The Fishing School shows them a way, pushing stones out of the way for so many. It calls out to each of them to come forth—and, like Lazarus, miraculously live.

A CELEBRATION FOR THE CHILDREN OF THE FISHING SCHOOL

IN LATE AUGUST 2005, The Fishing School held its "Gifted & Talented Celebration," an end-of-summer talent show with refreshments. Tom was supposed to be there, but it was a rainy day and he had a doctor's appointment that cut too close to the time of the event. I went to the celebration to photograph the children. What I found was a memorable day of anxious joy, endless smiles, and true pride.

The celebration was the culmination of The Fishing School's Summer

Enrichment Program, and the children had prepared different presentations individually and as small groups. In front of a large gathering in a banquet hall on the lower level of a nearby old church, the children overcame any nervousness and stood on a narrow stage and sang, read, and performed—all for their families and supporters of The Fishing School. It was a proud moment for the children and their families, not to mention the beaming teachers and volunteer helpers. Jackie and the teachers stood near the stage to shepherd the children and guide them through the program. Some children recited short speeches and poems while others performed musical numbers, skits, and songs about what they had learned in the summer program's classes.

One of the brightest moments was when the children sang "This Land is Your Land." Dawn Reynolds, the music teacher, took "God Bless America" and merged it into "God Bless The Fishing School." She also added some words to "This Land is Your Land" that brought tears to my eyes as the children sang it in their high-pitched voices; the verse that did me in follows:

> I live in D.C. This town is my town.
> From up in Northwest, to Anacostia.
> You'll find the White House—lots of famous places;
> This town belongs to you and me.

With tremendous gusto, the children then sang The Fishing School's official song, which is called, "The Mighty, Mighty Fishing School."

I was so taken by the celebration on stage and in the audience that I stayed for most of the program and kept photographing the children. Then something happened when I was about to take two last photos before leaving. I had a perfect shot lined up of a little girl who was captivated by the other children onstage. I bent down and just as I took the shot, the little boy sitting next to her leaned forward and jumped in the shot on purpose.

I was stunned and said, "Hey! Why did you do that?" He looked down, and I suddenly realized of course that maybe he wanted to be in the shot as well. I felt bad about that. The girl's expression was now gone, and he had ruined the shot, or so I thought. Of course, it was *only* a photo, not the end of the world. He said softly that he was sorry and looked down and began rubbing his eyes.

"Oh no, I'm sorry. I didn't mean to make you cry," I said softly to the little boy, putting my hand on his shoulder and bending down to his eye level.

"No, that's OK. I'm not crying," he said with tears going down his face.

"My eyes water whenever I see a camera flash."

"Well, I'm sorry, honey." He nodded and said he understood. I offered, "Here, can I take your picture? Would that be OK?" The little boy brightened and smiled. After I took the shot, his eyes really started to water. So he was telling the truth! He wasn't crying!

He said with a big smile, "Thanks so much! My eyes just do this. I have this condition."

"Kinda like cutting onions." He looked up at me and shrugged. I realized he was too young to know about cutting onions and tearing eyes. "My name is Allison. What's your name?"

"Christian." And we shook hands. He was really quite adorable. If he hadn't jumped in front of the camera, I probably wouldn't have noticed him. I told him I was sorry one more time, and I told him how terrific he is. Then he thanked me for taking his picture. And then I knew that's all he wanted. A simple photo. To have someone focus on him.

It was a day of achievement, a day to seal the relationship of The Fishing School with the youngsters. The children will go forward and know that they are special and loved, and they will have had a memorable summer of lessons and friendships made.

Identifying strongly with the story of "The Dash" at the beginning of this book, Jackie reflected about her role with the children, "When you become a mother or a leader, you cease being the picture and you become the frame. It's not about us. It's about what we contribute to other people's lives." She paused and added, "We all should be aspiring to participate in or have a purpose for being involved with something that's bigger than ourselves. And that's what The Fishing School has done for me."

When I read that last passage to Tom, there was silence on the other end of the phone. Then, all he could utter while choking back tears was, "For me, too."

Update about The Fishing School

In January 2007, Tom Lewis, at age sixty-seven, had an excellent medical report. His appetite had returned, and he looked dapper again.

Under Jackie's leadership, The Fishing School added more tutoring and activities for the children. During the summer of 2007, due to family priorities, Jackie left The Fishing School and began working as a counselor. Tom served as the interim executive director until the board selected Leo Givs to be the new executive director. Under Leo's leadership, The Fishing School continues to be primarily academic focused. With a new board chair named Sally Sullivan, he has recruited new board members, expanded programs, and enjoyed success in the area of fund development. After a year on the job, Leo said, "Mr. Lewis' story of personal sacrifice for the benefit of others—namely the children we serve—is an awe-inspiring and inspirational story that continues to serve as my motivation every single day to help actualize his vision."

Now that Tom is feeling stronger, he has the energy to be more involved again. Everyone associated with The Fishing School is already anticipating the nonprofit's twentieth anniversary and celebration in 2010.

Christian, the little boy in the essay, continues to do very well.

Tom and Lucille's daughter, Tisha, moved back to D.C. in 2006 to finish her doctoral dissertation, and for over a year, she worked as a reading specialist with the children at The Fishing School. By the fall of 2008, Tisha was writing the final chapters of her dissertation.

In August 2008, Tom and Lucille celebrated their thirty-eighth wedding anniversary. By November, Tom needed a follow-up appointment with his oncologist at Johns Hopkins. Back in 2003 when Tom had his stem cell transplant, it was experimental and risky. He has not forgotten that other patients around him didn't make it through. It took a long time for Tom to become stable, and he was told they would check him each year for five years. The year 2008 was that fifth year.

Barely a week after that appointment with his oncologist, Tom said, his voice brimming with joy and relief, "My doctor tells me I'm his miracle patient. He said, 'Let me hug you. Your five years are up. You're wonderful and good to go!'"

"You've shown real courage throughout," I said to Tom.

He replied, "My wife is my courage. My earth angel."

Contact information for The Fishing School:

Leo Givs
Executive Director
The Fishing School
1240 Wylie Street, NE
Washington, D.C. 20002
Phone: 202-399-3618
Web site: www.fishingschool.org

If you like The Fishing School, you might be interested in these organizations:

1) The Child & Family Network Centers
   Alexandria, Virginia
   Web site: www.cfnc-online.org
   Phone: 703-836-0214

2) Griffin Center
   East St. Louis, Illinois
   Web site: www.griffincenter-esl.org
   Phone: 618-874-2500

3) Lopez Island Family Resource Center
   Lopez Island, Washington
   Web site: www.lifrc.org
   Phone: 360-468-4117

4) YouthFriends
   Kansas City, Missouri
   Web site: www.youthfriends.org
   Phone: 816-842-7082

MARY'S CENTER

THE FIRST TIME I spoke with Lyda Vanegas, I didn't know that we would become friends or that I would eventually feel strongly about the entity that helped her get back on her feet. I didn't even know the name of the executive director. All I knew was that I kept hearing nonprofit executives suggest Mary's Center for Maternal and Child Care (or Mary's Center) for the monthly charitable event that I used to organize.

With a focus on families who work in jobs where health insurance is not available, the mission of Mary's Center is "to build better futures through health care, education and social services." The center is committed to providing an individual with "the highest quality of care, regardless of their ability to pay." I learned that and more reading their Web site. But I needed to do more due diligence.

As was my habit, I called one day and asked for the executive director or the director of development, but those people were in meetings. As someone in the development office of Mary's Center, Lyda happened to pick up the phone.

Even though I had read about Mary's Center online, I asked Lyda a slew of questions. The founder was still on board; she was Mary's Center's president and CEO, Maria Gomez.

Lyda asked gently about my charity events and became enthusiastic about the idea. She told me all kinds of information and didn't flinch when I peppered her with questions. I had found that if the nonprofit is not focused on your phone call when all you want to do is give them money, then they aren't worth the donation. Lyda was totally focused on our conversation, and if she didn't know something, she said she would ask and get back to me. I could tell she was taking notes on things she needed to find out.

She urged me to choose Mary's Center, and their work was impressive, but I still had one last question. I asked about the annual budget, and she said it was $8 million. That sank it like a torpedo. I praised all the hard work and worthiness of the place, but I said that unfortunately that budget was way out of my range. I was helping small, well-managed nonprofits, usually well under $1 million. Some had budgets of $200,000 or less. My paltry donation from my monthly charitable event would not make a difference.

Lyda had a calming voice, which kept me from saying goodbye, yet I was pretty much clear that they weren't right for my purposes. How could $500 or $1,000 be critical to them? I needed to make a difference with these monies. But Lyda asked if I could give her a couple of more minutes so she could explain some things about the center.

"We help so many people every day," she said with her perfect English. I could still detect some Spanish background, and I could detect a genuine quality about her that was refreshing.

"With all due respect, y'all sound great, but...well, this is your job. To raise money."

"Oh, no. Mary's Center is much more than that to me."

Lyda told me how she first came to Mary's Center—as a patient. She was pregnant with her first child in a new country. I would soon see that she was expecting her second. When she and her husband, Gerardo, came to the United States from Colombia, she was pregnant and without health insurance. She went to Mary's Center to get prenatal care and then volunteered for something. Soon, they had an opening and she was hired as an administrative assistant for the pediatrics department and then moved over to women's health. And now she is in the development office. The story put a lump in my throat. I was sold.

It's not that Mary's Center is a job bank. Hardly the case. It's that Lyda came with nothing but her heart in the right place. And she found the most caring people.

Lyda urged me to come for a site visit any time, something I didn't usually do. But then one day, I changed my mind.

It was an emotional afternoon at George Washington Hospital, where I had a follow-up mammogram—something all women can say is a little stressful, especially when the radiologists think they see something suspicious. The numerous women in the waiting room were all ages, a few with children in tow. We all knew that statistically one of us would have breast cancer, and many of us gave each other reassuring looks as we took turns with endless calls of our names. Everything turned out to be OK for me. I was so relieved and grateful that when I got back to my car, I called Lyda and asked if it would be all right to come by for a quick visit. She was delighted.

Mary's Center is located in Adams Morgan, a D.C. neighborhood known for its Greenwich Village-like atmosphere and hip restaurants. It is also known at times for its crime spikes; in fact, at times, police have listed Adams Morgan as a crime hot spot in the city. I had passed Mary's Center dozens of times and yet had never noticed it. The sign was small at that time, and it's tucked away a couple of blocks behind the main row of restaurants, in an area that some might call transitional. Many of the old apartment buildings were filled with two or three families in each apartment. That was the only way they could afford it. Prices have shot up dramatically as development has quickened. Thus, some parts of the neighborhood remain low-income while other areas have been bulldozed for pricey lofts and condos. The Latino population, which has inhabited this area for a long time, is slowly being forced to move elsewhere. It's classic gentrification, good for urban professionals who own condos there, but detrimental to a family that is barely making rent every month in that neighborhood.

Walking into Mary's Center, the first thing I noticed was how professional, clean, and bright it was. Children were huddled around a computer terminal while their mothers, or both parents, sat nearby. Numerous mothers, some pregnant and some with babies, were waiting and chatting quietly. One woman sat with four children, while another held a newborn closely. The front desk had three or four women who greeted everyone and helped with paperwork and charts. It was like any other doctor's office I had seen, not as I had imagined it. There was even art on the walls. Later, I found out that the art was donated to Mary's Center, part of an ongoing fundraiser. There was a lot of energy at this place. The staff had a calm and friendly demeanor; and yet, there was a hustle in the air.

Lyda showed me around the Women, Infants and Children (or WIC) area, where low-income women, infants and children up to age five can get federal-supported health care.

Between patients, while a mother left with a child and another parent came in with two other youngsters, one of the pediatricians told me that she loved what she was doing at Mary's Center. She knew that she was making a difference. I got the impression that her days flew by and that she thrived on it. I asked her about any special needs that a small donation could handle, and she encouraged me to donate funds for a booklet they had to help children who have asthma. The booklet is about Leo the lion and his asthma and how he copes. The young doctor said each booklet costs them about $4 to produce and really helps the children learn to cope with their asthma.

Next, we were standing in the expectant mothers' area, and Lyda and I chatted with a Spanish-speaking woman who was due any day. Lyda translated for me. The expectant woman's mother was sitting nearby, full of anticipation. A midwife joined us and explained that they work with various hospitals in the area, and that the mothers go to different hospitals for delivery.

I asked the midwife about her practice's needs, and she said that above all else, they needed dopplers to check the fetus in utero. She explained that they have two or three. But two are always broken or on the mend. They are always waiting for each other to share the working doppler. I decided that was critical and that the funds from my charity night would purchase two new dopplers and any extra funds would buy the booklets about Leo the lion's asthma.

Mary's Center exemplifies the growing inequality in our nation so poignantly. Without Mary's Center, where would these people go without health insurance? They're certainly not counted as part of the forty-six million Americans who are uninsured and the millions who are the underinsured. These are people who have lived in the United States for perhaps fifteen years, but who have not received full citizenship yet. It is expensive to go through the citizenship process, and even done correctly, it can take up to eight years or more. One immigration lawyer I know charges each client $7,000 *up front* to handle their green card, and that can take a year or two. That is not even citizenship. So I know this is a whole part of society that is not officially counted but is definitely part of our nation's fabric.

I got back to my car and tears came to my eyes as I thought about how blessed I was to have health insurance and some of the best care at George Washington Hospital. If a child has undiagnosed or badly treated asthma or diabetes, isn't it counter-productive for that child with regard to school and their long-term well-being? Isn't that putting that child at unnecessary risk not to mention at a huge disadvantage? Just knowing of a place like Mary's Center gave me a sudden sensation of pride. Its social services embrace this culturally diverse community with a focus on families who work in jobs where health insurance is not available. Every $350 raised provides a year of medical visits for a newborn baby.

As Mary Center's president and CEO, Maria Gomez knows how to work with people, and she is incredibly gracious and always grateful for any and all help. One afternoon in 2005, Maria, Lyda, and I sat in a corner of their expansive waiting room and discussed Mary's Center. Mothers and a few fathers chatted while rocking their babies. A half dozen children shared the computer terminal nearby while other children played board games with each other, waiting for their turn to be called to see a doctor. Once in a while, a mother would emerge with a crying child, who had just gotten a vaccination or an injection. The scene reminded me of sitting in a waiting room with my mother when I was a toddler, but I always flinched and started to get nervous upon seeing or hearing another child cry in a doctor's office. The numerous children at Mary's Center didn't flinch. They appeared happy to be there.

Accustomed to the fun chaos, Maria and Lyda described the origins and mission of Mary's Center.

With a genuine, thoughtful spirit and her trademark dynamic personality, Maria explained, "In 1988, a group of us started Mary's Center because of the influx of Salvadoran immigrants who were fleeing the civil war that was going on. A lot of the women had been raped by the *coyote*, the guide who was bringing them up from El Salvador. The women were coming here to make money to send home and their husbands were fighting the war, many of them getting killed."

Like many, I was a little familiar with some of the horrors of El Salvador's twelve-year civil war. But I had an outsider's perspective. I had studied international relations in college and recalled protests on campus in the early and mid-1980s about the Reagan administration and its position on Central America. In 1983, I had also interned in Senator Edward M. Kennedy's Capitol Hill office, where in addition to standard mail-room duties, I was assigned to the Senator's foreign policy advisor and given minor tasks dealing with Central American issues. Therefore, while I knew something about the war from a foreign policy standpoint, speaking with someone firsthand about the atrocities or aftermath was totally different.

Maria patiently explained how these women came with nothing but the shirts on their backs and traveled a treacherous journey after paying the *coyote* dearly to lead the journey. Throughout the strenuous journey, the *coyote* raped the women and threatened them with worse. Now these women found themselves in a strange land, not knowing the language, traumatized by the journey and rape, pregnant by a man not their husband, and scared to death without any means of getting any health care.

A nurse with a master's in public health who worked at the D.C. Department of Health at the time, Maria felt that the health department was not meeting the needs of these immigrants. Others agreed wholeheartedly. As Maria put it, "There were barriers, including fear and difference in language, and other needs weren't being met. These women needed prenatal care and understanding and counseling. They were having a child, the product of a rape. There was no documentation, fear of being found out, fear of going to the government, having to walk into a government office… after seeing what they saw in their homeland with their government. The Department of Health wasn't set up to do that. There was this movement [of people] because of the war, and the city wasn't prepared to deal with it. They weren't welcomed here." Moved by the women's plight, Maria saw a need and founded Mary's Center. That was in 1988.

Over 80 percent of those who go to Mary's Center are Latino. Maria explained that the Latino immigrants in the late '80s were different from other immigrants who had come to the United States, saying, "If they were coming from Vietnam, after the war, they were considered refugees and given support and help to start over."

Initially, Mary's Center was created to provide a place that was safe for women and their children. The mission has evolved as the need has evolved. In 2003, Mary's Center opened a clinic for men on Tuesdays, and follow-up care was handled on any other days with an appointment. By 2005, the center was providing health care to men all the time. As Maria explained, "There are so many families intact. The women kept saying to us that they wanted us to take their husbands. So today, you often see a whole family at the clinic."

As the services at Mary's Center have grown, so has the nonprofit's budget. In 2005, Mary's Center provided over two hundred physician visits per day. By 2007, Mary's Center was seeing about 11,000 patients annually at two sites in D.C., and it has since added a new service site in Silver Spring, Maryland. In 2008, over 14,000 patients were seen.

Celebrating its twentieth anniversary in 2008, Mary's Center, which began with an initial budget of $250,000, had an annual budget of $14 million. Here is a sampling of what that expenditure achieved. Of infants born to Mary's Center patients, 97 percent arrived at a healthy birth weight. In addition to health care, Mary's Center has a program to help teens build self-esteem and set life goals. One goal of the Teen Program is to prevent teen pregnancy, and 75 percent of the girls between the ages of thirteen and eighteen who have participated in the Teen Program have not become pregnant.

Originally from Cali, Colombia, Maria Gomez arrived in the United States with her family when she was thirteen. They lived in Adams Morgan, and every day, Maria took two buses to junior high and high school across town to the heart of wealthy Georgetown. It was the early 1970s, a tumultuous time in Washington and the nation. And Maria soaked it all in.

By her late forties, she could see the remarkable trajectory of her life, and admitted, "It's one of those things about being young. You don't paralyze yourself with analysis. But I've gotten older now."

She hesitated and said about her inspiration, "One is my mom—her example. Just do what's in your heart, she used to say. If there's something that pains your heart—that you really believe in—it will all work out well for everyone. We often don't do things because we analyze it too much. But it's all possible. That's the beauty of being young and not being bogged down with bad experiences. Do what's in your heart. You don't have to figure it all out. You do that with simple things. If you have a homework assignment, don't think about it too much. Get your things or tools, and things will come together. She always simplified things. She lived that kind of life to get things done.

"As I was working in the Health Department, I was frustrated, seeing all the barriers that prevented me from serving the community that came to me in need. All this was happening at the same time that we got the opportunity to create an organization that would answer specifically those needs. And we would be able to do it without the Health Department's bureaucracy, which was how fast you had to see patients, whether the patients had the proper paperwork, and being open certain hours. The fact that it was a government institution itself was a barrier [for immigrants who had been traumatized by government officials]. All the things came together with the money and opportunity to create Mary's Center. My mother motivates me subconsciously. It's part of my fabric now."

As Maria spoke of her mother, I thought about how Maria and her husband have a school-age daughter, who has a wide-open look in her eye that I imagine Maria had as a youngster. Enthusiastic about Mary's Center, their daughter is bright and curious about the world. Above all else, she is close to her parents, just as Maria was with her mother.

The other inspiration for Maria was a schoolteacher. Maria recalled, "I'm really lucky. I had a great civics teacher at Western High School, which is now the Duke Ellington School for the Arts [in Georgetown]. Taking the bus to school, I had to transfer buses, and I remember Dupont Circle being under siege by tanks around the circle and the protests inside the circle.

Dupont Circle was the place to gather, still is. Jim Nathanson was my civics teacher when I went to school in the early '70s. Later, he was on the D.C. City Council for several years. I had so many interests in the social issues of the day and the war in Vietnam. The most crucial years of shaping me as an adult revolved around the War on Poverty. I got involved in everything that was happening—a lot of civic participation. That your vote counts, that one by one becomes millions, that it's a powerful process in this century of change. Jim Nathanson made what was happening with social uprisings, with Martin Luther King and the effects of the marches, and he made all that real in class in the sense of responsibility, that you as an individual have a responsibility in humanity as a whole. In my heart, that's what makes me tick." She interjected quietly, "I think about civics class."

"I remember I got in some trouble in what I was doing in the '70s," she admitted. "And I remember him sitting me down and saying, 'What a waste. You're so talented.' Oh my God! The light went off. If I don't graduate from school, I'm not educated. All those things came together. It was a way of calming down all this chaos that was happening around us, and trying to figure myself out."

For all those teachers and parents who are reading this story, one person can and does make a difference. Maria's mother and Jim Nathanson helped guide Maria Gomez to make better choices. Today, Maria helps thousands.

"There was a time in the '80s and '90s that was comfortable for so many Americans, except for those who were hidden," she philosophized. "A whole generation was raised in comfort. I hope that nobody has to walk barefoot to know loss. To be able to serve, whether you volunteer or make it your living, that's what I want to say. Every time I think why continue to serve? There's a sense of responsibility. I have to demonstrate so others can take on and do it in their own way. Just do it. That's what my mom used to say, long before it was a Nike ad.

"Those are the kinds of things that seem to influence you to create a just society. It was the era. It's the moment in time. It's about following your heart. You're doing good but you're doing well for society. That's what civics class taught me, and my mom showed me with her life," she concluded. And then she added softly, "I was very lucky."

Contact information for Mary's Center:

Maria S. Gomez, R.N., M.P.H.
President and CEO
Mary's Center for Maternal and Child Care, Inc.
2333 Ontario Road, NW
Washington, D.C. 20009-2627
Phone: 202-483-8196
Web site: www.maryscenter.org

If you like Mary's Center, you might be interested in
these organizations:

1) alley's house
   Dallas, Texas
   Web site: www.alleyshouse.org
   Phone: 214-915-9945

2) La Clinica del Pueblo
   Washington, D.C.
   Web site: www.lcdp.org
   Phone: 202-462-4788

3) Hopelink
   Redmond, Washington
   Web site: www.hope-link.org
   Phone: 425-869-6000

4) The N.A.T.I.V.E. Project
   Spokane, Washington
   Web site: www.nativeproject.org
   Phone: 509-325-5502

5) Wesley Community Center
   Phoenix, Arizona
   Web site: www.wesleycenterphx.org
   Phone: 602-252-5609

TAHIRIH JUSTICE CENTER

SOME GO TO law school to save the world and defend those in need. Then, for one reason or another, those idealistic dreams are put away in a drawer and forgotten—replaced by life, work, and money. This is a story about someone who kept her dream alive and created a stellar team to save thousands of people. With steady determination and a vision for justice, Layli Miller-Muro lives her dream each day and encourages others to join her. This is a story that demonstrates what boundless courage can achieve—the courage of Layli and the clients of a nonprofit called the Tahirih Justice Center. When you save one life, you save the world. This core belief fuels the Tahirih Justice Center.

Farida Azizi stands only about five and a half feet tall but is a fearless giant in her work on behalf of women and girls in her homeland of Afghanistan. Not that long ago, she walked for days between Pakistan and Afghanistan, trying to help women and girls. That was in the mid-1990s, and the Taliban would have loved to stop her—permanently. After the Americans toppled the Taliban and installed a new Afghan government, the warlords controlled (and still control) the Afghan countryside and wanted to make Farida go away. Soon, it became too dangerous for her and her small children. With the help of the Tahirih Justice Center, Farida and her family found asylum and a new life in the United States.

Today, speaking beautiful English, Farida wears American jeans, lives in Northern Virginia with her growing family, and is a program officer for

Vital Voices, a nonprofit that works with women all over the world and trains them in political activism. Farida could sit back and enjoy her life. But that would not be Farida Azizi. When she speaks to you, you know she is speaking from the heart, and she is but one person of *thousands* saved by Tahirih, which got its start because of a gutsy law student named Layli Miller-Muro.

In 1997, right out of law school, Layli founded the Tahirih Justice Center, a nonprofit committed to helping immigrant women and girls who are seeking justice in the United States from gender-based cruelty such as forced female genital mutilation, torture, rape, trafficking, honor crimes, gender apartheid, forced marriage, and domestic violence. In addition to legal representation, the Tahirih Justice Center has a holistic approach and puts its clients in touch with other services that help heal the physical and emotional pain and trauma of their journey.

With Tahirih, there is hope, for they are committed to "promoting justice for women and girls worldwide." Based in the Washington area, Tahirih (pronounced "*Tah-heh-ray*") has thus far assisted more than 9,000 women and girls by providing direct legal services and referrals. Combining those efforts with public policy advocacy, the nonprofit is having a significant impact in the States and worldwide.

I first learned about Tahirih during a photo shoot for the *Washington Post* in 2003. Tahirih was having its annual dinner in a Washington hotel, and I was supposed to run in and get a couple of shots of the executive director with the honoree and maybe a shot of some of the people at the event. An easy shoot, the editor said.

When I arrived, I was told that a tall, polished woman in the back corner of the room was a well-known reporter from Afghanistan. Tahirih had saved her from the Taliban. I didn't know the whole story but I went to her table and took some shots of her with the others at the table. I turned to the next table and photographed little children eating some ice cream and drinking Cokes and laughing a lot. They climbed onto a parent's lap and gave hugs to grandparents. I kept writing down names in case we used the shots in the *Post*. Soon enough, I noticed that everyone's last name was the same.

One of the older women at the table leaned over to me and said proudly, "We're all related."

"You mean at this table?" I asked.

A member of the Tahirih staff explained that the three tables in this part of the room were full of people who were all related and that they had all fled Afghanistan.

"That's quite an exodus. Why?"

Pointing to the reporter from Afghanistan, the staff member said, "Because the Taliban had issued a *fatwa* on that woman's life because of things she had been reporting that were critical of the Taliban's treatment of women. The *fatwa* extended to her whole family, not just to her. Tahirih intervened and made it possible for them all to come to the States."

"So the Taliban would have killed this whole family—all these people?" I asked quietly.

The staff member nodded. I looked over at the Afghan reporter standing about twenty feet away and then at all three tables of her extended family, all of whom were enjoying their time together, all of whom I had just photographed. I simply stared in amazement and knew that all the faces on the roll of film I shot existed by the thinnest of threads. They would have all been dead. Men, women, children from age one to eighty.

It's one thing to understand the Taliban intellectually; it's a whole other thing to see, photograph, and chat with an extended family that would not have survived. I suddenly felt the air was sucked out of the room and I was no longer aware of the noise in the banquet hall.

Something was tugging at my jacket, forcing me to snap out of my daze and look down. It was one of the children, a little boy with huge brown eyes, tugging away, wanting me to take his picture with his cousins. I gladly took a few pictures, making the children giggle. I smiled with the children but suddenly felt like crying.

After the dinner, a woman from Nigeria stood at the podium and spoke about her life, about how her American husband beat her nearly to death and threatened their toddler if she left. The husband, who had never done anything for the child, also threatened to turn her into authorities and have her shipped back to Nigeria, knowing she would never see their child again.

Instead, this Nigerian woman took her child and fled to another location in the States. Somehow, she heard about Tahirih, which helped her find a job and shelter and provided the encouragement to help her get her feet back on the ground. Tahirih also handled her case and won. Today, this woman is in graduate school and looking at a bright future.

Hearing the Nigerian woman's story, the large collection of people sat silenced by her words and her emotions. The only noise in the room was that of tissue and handkerchiefs, men quietly blowing their noses. I was not the only one in the room with tears. It was a story of courage, and Tahirih made it possible. Tahirih gave her life back to her.

For Layli, the journey began when she went to Africa and later when she was in law school at American University.

"Right before I went to college," Layli remembered, "I was in The Gambia, West Africa. I was there with my religious community, the Bahá'í faith, participating in a social and economic development project. It was there that I was first exposed to female genital mutilation. I was hanging out in the marketplace, and women were talking a lot about planning the circumcision celebration, what to wear, what needed to be done.

"When I came back home to the States, and went to college, it was the topic I was interested in and I tried to write papers about it. Then when I went to law school, I had a Refugee Law class. And I decided to write a paper on whether or not you could receive asylum because of female genital mutilation, because it was being hotly debated at the time."

Then, the young law student received an opportunity to put her ideas to work. It was a case about a young woman named Fauziya Kassindja, a case that would change more than one life.

Layli recalled, "I was working for an immigration lawyer. I was his law clerk and he assigned the [Kassindja] case to me. It was while I was working for him that I argued the case before the immigration judge. On appeal, I brought the case to American University's Human Rights Law Clinic and continued to work on it as a student."

Layli had only four days to put together her case for Ms. Kassindja. Against all odds, Layli proved her case and won a landmark decision that to this day is helping countless individuals.

As Tahirih's written materials explain, "The case was that of Fauziya Kassindja, a seventeen-year-old woman who fled Togo in fear of a forced polygamous marriage and a tribal practice known as female genital mutilation (or FGM). After arriving in the United States and spending more than seventeen months in detention, Ms. Kassindja was granted asylum on appeal. Her case established national precedent and revolutionized asylum law in the United States, opening the door to those seeking protection from gender-based persecution."

"Ms. Kassindja was mistreated in prison here," Layli elaborated. "Her nightmare included rancid food, losing forty pounds, bleeding ulcers, being given two left sandals, not being allowed to change clothes or shower for weeks, being given men's underwear to wear—horrible conditions overall."

After this triumph, Layli saw a need and knew she wanted to help others. She wanted to serve the needs of women facing international human rights abuses, especially with regard to immigrant and refugee women. Thus was born the Tahirih Justice Center with its mission, which is "based on the belief that the recognition of the equality of women and men is a moral imperative and a practical necessity for the advancement of society. To this end, Tahirih provides legal protection for women facing human rights abuses and assists in the provision of certain social programs…[and] revolves around a core of projects aimed at serving women's legal, health care, and social needs…addressing the full range of women's issues."

The center is named for Tahirih, a nineteenth-century Persian woman, poet, and scholar who rejected Persia's traditional subordination of women and publicly removed her veil in 1848. A member of the Bahá'í faith, Tahirih was killed for her beliefs and actions in 1852 at age thirty-five.

Typical of the other visionaries in this book, Layli is not self-promoting. Her preference is that the focus be on the work of Tahirih. But the fact is that Tahirih began because of her vision for a more just world. This core value—her sense of justice—was forged long ago in her childhood during a tumultuous time for our nation.

Though reluctant to discuss what influenced her, Layli spoke of growing up in Atlanta. Mainly, she spoke about one of her heroes, the Reverend Dr. Martin Luther King, Jr.

Born in 1972, Layli grew up in the aftermath of a chaotic time when everything seemed to be on the line. Back in 1963, even four little black girls at a church were not spared but rather killed by a bomb in Birmingham. The church had been a meeting place for the civil rights movement at that time. Throughout those years, the Ku Klux Klan was a dominant force; lynchings and marches filled the nation's television screens. Those working for civil rights were threatened, arrested, beaten, jailed, and sometimes killed. Atlanta was at the center of much of the debate and not only because of its geographical location. The King family lived in Atlanta, and Dr. King's life was under constant threat. Layli remembers the stories about the bombing of Dr. King's family home.

Those who hated Dr. King and his words about freedom and economic opportunity for all did not weep when he was killed in 1968. They hoped that his death would be the end of civil rights. But Dr. King's dream of a better America did not die with his death; rather, it launched a thousand ships. In the intervening years, many have carried on the work.

Just as Gandhi influenced Dr. King, Dr. King influenced countless Americans, one of whom was a young girl named Layli, who knew she did not want to stand by.

Layli has a distinct point of view. As she put it, "Even though I was white and growing up with all the privileges of a comfortable life, I witnessed loved ones endure the tinge of discrimination." Her compass was set.

And like Dr. King, Layli has an ability to see an unjust situation and speak movingly about it.

She explained, "Growing up in Atlanta, many of my closest friends lived in the inner city. I began hearing their stories of how they were being pulled over by the police and other issues of injustice. It became apparent to me at an early age that there was a disparity, largely through my friendships. It helped me have an understanding about the social inequities, which I am not sure most white people had.

"One time, a father from the inner city called my father at three in the morning to help his son. His son had been put in jail because of a misidentification. My father helped him," she recalled. "My father is a person of privilege and he wears a suit and is very convincing. He's a management consultant, a businessman who is committed to social justice issues. Because of my father's income, my mom had the luxury of working on social justice issues full-time. She was a commissioner for the Martin Luther King Federal Holiday Commission. She was a very close friend with Mrs. King. They met on an airplane. Literally.

"Another example was a very good friend who was in tenth grade in high school, and though he wasn't a junior yet, he took the SAT and got a perfect score. Incredibly smart. He ended up getting a full scholarship to Georgia Tech. But the scholarship wasn't enough money for books and everything, so he had to get a job while he was in school. He couldn't keep up his grades on top of his job, and he had to keep up his grades to maintain the scholarship. So he had to drop out.

"Today, he is a security guard in a bank. Has been for many years." She was silent for a moment and then said with disbelief, "He's way smarter than I am, and he should have had other opportunities. But his family didn't have the money—growing up in the projects of Atlanta and as an African American.

"What that says to me is that it's unfair. And it makes me realize that I had this gift of growing up in the Bahá'í community so that I got to know a wide range of people who had many experiences in society that made me passionate about social justice issues.

"The Bahá'í faith is very committed to issues of justice and the equality of women and men. As I grew up, the importance of structuring one's life to be of service and promote those principles always echoed in my head. I always envisioned my life in large part about the promotion of justice. I couldn't contemplate my life not being about the promotion of justice."

After college, Layli worked for four years as a nonviolent student coordinator at the Martin Luther King, Jr. Center for Nonviolent Social

Change in Atlanta. Then she went to law school.

Layli's work on behalf of others is another example of the ripple effect that Robert Kennedy envisioned. A child of a time that cemented her path, she learned early on that a more equitable world is worth fighting for. In her way, she is carrying on Dr. King's dream from all those years ago. Layli remarked, "I knew I wanted to be of service, to work on social justice issues."

The genesis of Tahirih was a gradual process. Without a grand plan, one thing led to another. As Layli put it, "I created Tahirih right out of law school, but I didn't know how to be a lawyer, much less be a manager. I needed more growth as a lawyer and a manager. I was advised to join a firm and get experience. So while I served on the board of Tahirih and helped it, I worked as a litigator for four years at a large D.C. firm called Arnold & Porter. During that time, program staff was hired, and the executive committee of the board served as management. Then after four years, Tahirih grew and needed a full-time, on-site executive director. Concerned that I was not skilled enough for the job, I took a year leave of absence from my law firm. The idea was to go to Tahirih temporarily, help raise money, and 'get the house in order,' and then Tahirih would hire someone who knew what they were doing, and I would return to the firm. Eight years later, I am still here. I still don't think I know what I am doing, but I keep trying."

Arnold & Porter is still involved with Tahirih. One of their partners served as president of the board for a time. Today, lawyers from Arnold & Porter and many other top law firms in the Washington area give of their time to Tahirih's clients. In fact, Tahirih assigns 75 percent of their new cases to pro bono lawyers from the region's law firms, and Tahirih has a 99 percent success rate.

Tahirih started small but by 2007 had grown to a staff of twenty-seven and a budget of $1.2 million, plus nearly $5 million in donated professional services. For every $5,000, Tahirih can provide free legal services to a client. Layli and Tahirih have won numerous awards and national media attention for their triumphs and humanitarian work.

In recent years, Tahirih has taken a high profile, national leadership role in fighting the abuse of international marriage brokers who pair American men with so-called "mail-order brides." Layli explained, "Marketing women as 'submissive' and 'subservient,' the international marriage broker industry brings in an estimated up to 14,000 foreign women annually to the United States to marry American men looking for traditional wives. The result is often violent and can be deadly, as predatory abusers use the agencies to find their next victims."

As a recognized public policy advocate, Tahirih has successfully pushed Congress to bring more pressure and resources to the frontlines of this issue. On January 5, 2006, President Bush signed into law The International Marriage Broker Regulation Act of 2005, which was attached to the bill to reauthorize the Violence Against Women Act.

As Tahirih continues to grow, the need for their services also continues to grow. One example is the highly contested issue of forced marriage as grounds for asylum. As recently as 2007, the Justice Department filed a *writ of certiorari* to ask the Supreme Court to reverse a federal court's grant of asylum to a young woman from China who was sold into a forced marriage. Tahirih advocated at the time that "this decision to contest the asylum grant could roll back historic progress made over the last decade in gender-based asylum law and could deny future clients...the ability to seek protection in the United States from forced marriages."

In addition to celebrating its tenth anniversary in 2007, Tahirih won the prestigious 2007 *Washington Post* Award for Excellence in Nonprofit Management, and the staff began planning national growth and replication of their program. In 2008, after much discussion and research, Layli announced their plan to establish a Tahirih Justice Center in Houston.

It was a little over a decade ago that law school gave Layli her legal knowledge as well as an opportunity to expand her critical thinking skills. With a measure of moxie, Layli took that knowledge and made the laws work for those without any voice or power. While Layli's work with Tahirih has assisted thousands, her work has also given her own life something she cannot measure. Yes, she is compensated, but her work is not about the money. It is that psychic pay, or the knowledge that she has helped another, that her life has made all the difference. It is immeasurable. All those who work or volunteer with Tahirih know that feeling, too.

To think it all began with a trip to Africa and learning about women and girls who had little or no choices in life. But none of those images or experiences would have meant very much if Layli had not known in her gut what was right. She is not a person who will ever have to question why she gets up in the morning, and she has made countless, deep friendships based upon this shared mission.

And the mission is clear when worldwide, according to a 1999 report from The Johns Hopkins Bloomberg School of Public Health, one out of every three women is a survivor of gender-based violence. Without people like Layli and nonprofits like the Tahirih Justice Center, the unthinkable cruelties and horrors of the world would continue to go unchecked. The fate of thousands of women and their families would have been sealed.

With untold courage and the help of Tahirih, thousands of women and girls have stepped out of the shadows of terror and have begun a new life. Farida Azizi and her children, the reporter from Afghanistan and her extended family, the Nigerian woman and her child, and Fauziya Kassindja all know how hard it is to live in fear every second of every day, and now they live in peace. Justice has been done. Originally, they had to fight to save themselves, but now they speak out for justice, for those who are silenced forever and for those who are shackled today. Tahirih provides a measure of hope and action to stem the tide of inconceivable acts.

Contact information for the Tahirih Justice Center:

Layli Miller-Muro, J.D., M.A.
Founder/Executive Director
Tahirih Justice Center
6402 Arlington Blvd, Suite 300
Falls Church, Virginia 22042
Phone: 571-282-6161
Web site: www.tahirih.org

If you like the Tahirih Justice Center, you might be interested in these organizations:

1) Abused Women's Aid in Crisis
   Anchorage, Alaska
   Web site: www.awaic.org
   Phone: 907-279-9581

2) Aid to Artisans
   West Hartford, Connecticut
   Web site: www.aidtoartisans.org
   Phone: 860-756-5550

3) Peter C. Alderman Foundation
   Bedford, New York
   Web site: www.petercaldermanfoundation.org
   Phone: 888-764-1804

4) Save Darfur Coalition
   Washington, D.C.
   Web site: www.savedarfur.org
   Phone: 800-917-2034

5) Solar Cooker Project
   (A Relief Campaign of Jewish World Watch)
   Encino, California
   Web site: www.jewishworldwatch.org
   Phone: 818-501-1836

6) Southern Poverty Law Center
   Montgomery, Alabama
   Web site: www.splcenter.org
   Phone: 334-956-8200

BRIGHT BEGINNINGS

W E ALL KNOW about the plight of the homeless, the souls who fill our nation's shelters or somehow sleep on a cold street. What we don't usually see or hear about are the children of the homeless. But rest assured, children of the homeless exist.

Living a life of constant upheaval and noisy environs, the children of the homeless go where they can with their parent or parents as well as a few, treasured belongings. These children might recall a more stable life before the upheaval began, or they might not know anything else, but they do know they are constantly on the move and often see their mother or father under stress. The children of the homeless are among the most vulnerable in our midst.

As mentioned in the introduction, in the Washington region, it is estimated that there are over 14,000 persons who are homeless at any given time—a quarter of that number being children. About half of all women and children who are homeless are fleeing domestic violence, according to the National Coalition Against Domestic Violence.

Only a few blocks from the U.S. Capitol, where the Congress debates our nation's priorities, there is a determined nonprofit that is focused on the children of the homeless. Since 1991, Bright Beginnings has been committed to serving homeless families with children in Washington, D.C. The organization provides "comprehensive developmentally appropriate child care and family support services to improve the quality of life of children and families who are homeless and residing in poverty or other vulnerable conditions."

There is no one person who envisioned Bright Beginnings. Rather, it was a group of people who helped make it possible. Today, some hard-working souls are resolute about keeping it going. In their own way, each of them is a visionary. Bright Beginnings creates a nurturing world for the most defenseless: the children of the homeless. This story is for those children and the hopes of everyone associated with Bright Beginnings.

Driving to Bright Beginnings on a bitterly cold day in 2005, I easily found the historic, red, square building standing proudly. The old brick building with its bold letters that say The Perry School exists right in the heart of a troubled neighborhood and yet within the vicinity of the U.S. Capitol. The school sits directly next to a major thoroughfare with steady traffic zooming by at all hours. Within that crime-ridden area, the Perry School has a fence but is surrounded by numerous beige, low-rise apartment buildings. If apartment buildings could look tired, these run-down structures did. People have been shot at night in front of the school. The afternoon I was there, the streets were strewn with trash; ice covered the sidewalk.

After looking for a spot, I parked my car as close as possible, but that was about two blocks away on a side street. As I got out of my car, I noticed some folks hanging out. One leaned against a fence, another near a stoop. They didn't seem to have anywhere to be. One fellow walked closer to me and my car. Though polite, he and another person on the street asked me for some money so they could eat at the nearby Hardee's. As difficult as it was, I shrugged and said, "Sorry. Don't have anything on me today." I trudged up the street with my camera gear in each hand and one camera bag thrown over my right shoulder.

As I entered the Perry School and checked in with the guard, I noticed that other nonprofits are based there and serve those in need. Bright Beginnings fills the first floor, but could serve many more children if it had the room.

Bright Beginnings has three top priorities. First, it provides a safe, nurturing environment. Second, it prepares children for kindergarten so that they are ready to learn. Third, it helps parents stabilize their home life and achieve self-sufficiency. Three main points make up the whole program: an intense educational program, therapeutic services, and a family service team that works with the parents to help them progress toward a better situation.

When I visited Bright Beginnings, the ratio of caring teachers to children was impressive. I was told that there was one adult for every three babies, one adult for every four or five toddlers, and one adult for every six or eight pre-schoolers, depending upon the size of the room. (D.C. requires the ratio in preschool to be no more than eight children for every adult.) There are seven early childhood classrooms, and each room was clean, bright, and organized with books and games for learning. In one classroom, three or four children were sitting in those itty-bitty chairs that only a two year old can sit in. One child (not quite two) was eating a nutritious meal, and he was using a spoon as if he had been eating with utensils for many years. The children hugged their teachers and each other and laughed and played. These were the faces of children under the age of five, all of whom were homeless.

As I photographed them, I wondered where would they be if they were not able to go to Bright Beginnings? On the street most likely, or on the go with their mother or father, who needs to work or look for work. Without Bright Beginnings and programs like it, there is no place for these children to be cared for, nurtured, fed, kept from the elements.

Dr. Betty Jo Gaines is the executive director who has been at the helm of Bright Beginnings since 2001. With a doctorate in education and over thirty years of experience working with children and youth in D.C., Dr. Gaines has brought a business savvy and nonprofit compassion while growing the program.

Lindsey Waldrop, the director of development, has also been with Bright Beginnings since 2001. As Lindsey said about the increasing number of at-risk children in the District, "Bright Beginnings is doing all it can and would love to do more."

Both Dr. Gaines and Lindsey and the whole staff work with a remarkable amount of positive energy. And they're very successful at their jobs because they see their work as a cause worth fighting for.

In early 2005, Lindsey explained the need in D.C. this way, "A January 2002 study by the Community Partnership for the Prevention of Homelessness showed that 487 homeless children under the age of five had nowhere to go during the day. And that's the number we know about. There might be other children. It does seem to get worse every year. In 2003, we did our own preliminary research to determine the need of services. What was the need for these kids? What was the percentage of these families in D.C.? We found there were over 700 children under the age of five who had nowhere to go during the day. It's case by case. We have families waiting to get into shelters that are living in cars. Some families are doubled and tripled up in an apartment with relatives or friends. They are homeless because they don't have permanent residences. Bright Beginnings takes children from every shelter or from families waiting to get into a shelter. D.C. does not require shelter for the homeless except for hypothermia season."

With a $2 million annual budget, Bright Beginnings makes every dollar stretch. It has thirty-four teaching staff, two social workers, a family service/health coordinator, an executive director, a development director, a development associate, an administrative assistant, and an information technology manager. When I've discussed the nonprofit sector with other executive directors in Washington, Bright Beginnings is often mentioned. The nonprofit makes a difference in concert with other organizations.

One brilliant aspect of the program is its location. Though the neighborhood is known for its poverty and crime, the old, red school building stands as a beacon of hope. Inside the Perry School Community Center, Bright Beginnings offers a safe, pleasant place for children to spend their day. The building itself, once the first African American high school in the District, was rescued and restored through neighborhood efforts. With ten other nonprofit organizations in the center that provide much-needed services to the residents, Bright Beginnings families have access to a health clinic, job training, after-school tutoring, and enrichment opportunities, among other services, in the same location as their childcare.

Summarizing the shelter system for the homeless, Lindsey chose her words carefully and said, "There are some excellent shelter programs in D.C., and then there are some that are just solely trying to get people off the streets. They don't have any additional income to provide support services. In the evening, some families might be at a shelter in a room for families, but they might not have specific programs for the children. And if the families are doubled or tripled up in a small apartment, that's not a nurturing environment for the children either."

One key point is that *before* the age of five, children are not required to be in school. Providing some background, Lindsey explained, "The most critical need in childcare is infant and toddler care. There are Head Start Programs for these children, and those are mainly for the three and four year olds, the year *before* kindergarten, but officially it's for children who are from two and a half to five years old. Early Head Start is for the six-week-old babies to age two and a half, but all these programs have significant waiting lists. It's unreal. You're reimbursed per child, and the reimbursement is so low. It's not even profitable. Head Start and Early Head Start are for low-income families. Bright Beginnings is for homeless families who are obviously low-income. What differentiates us is that we are primarily serving homeless families, and the needs of homeless families are tremendous. We're not only giving parents peace of mind. We're also helping them to achieve self-sufficiency."

Bright Beginnings does receive some Head Start reimbursement, but it accounts for less than 10 percent of the annual budget. The nonprofit's fundraising efforts have to make up the difference.

Among its programs, Bright Beginnings provides on-site therapeutic services to even the playing field for each child. As the Web site points out, "Poor nutrition, exposure to violence, and the chronic stress of poverty contribute to delays in development of language, motor, and social skills among many of the children at Bright Beginnings. In response, Bright Beginnings screens each child in its care individually for developmental delays. When deemed necessary, on-site therapeutic services are provided by a speech/language therapist, an occupational therapist, and/or a psychologist. About one-third of the Bright Beginnings children need these services. These professionals evaluate the child, design a plan to remedy his or her problem, and implement the plan with parent and teacher assistance. Our goal is to prepare the children at Bright Beginnings to enter kindergarten ready to learn."

"Ready to Learn" is a fundamental base for each child's future. This is Bright Beginnings' overarching mission.

Lindsey recalled with heartfelt enthusiasm, "When our kids graduate to kindergarten, part of the graduation ceremony is that we give each child a batch of new school supplies to start off their next year at an equal level as the other kids. That would include a new notebook, paper, pencils, pens, a glue stick, child scissors, a ruler, and it's all in a new backpack! It's so cute. They do a pomp and circumstance. Usually, the kids will transition to an older class even if they are not going just yet to kindergarten. They go through the ceremony, too. That's in mid-August. Then we have an intense staff development week. We bring in specialists from all over the District, and make sure our teachers are up-to-date in the best practices of early childhood development. We put a big push toward making sure our staff is well-prepared, as ready as they can be…so that they are as ready to be the best they can be—so that our kids get a chance to succeed.

"All of our lead teachers have a four-year degree in early childhood education or some related educational field with some experience. D.C.'s standards require only a child development certificate, a nine-class program that takes under a year. And it's not nearly as comprehensive.

"We also have a Parent-Aide Program. If a parent would like to go into a career in early childhood development, then they meet with their social worker and get approval and go through training with our education coordinator, who is like the principal of the program. Then we put them in the classroom, and they shadow the other teachers. The position is a part-time position, so they can take classes. It's not a full job, but it's a way to get them work experience, build their resume, gain skills they need.

"They're all homeless parents. After they're finished, they can get hired somewhere. Or maybe they realize this is not something they want to do, but they can get a reference from Bright Beginnings. It's a great program, and then the parents have a sense of ownership of the program, because they know the day-to-day activities and how hard the staff works to make it a nurturing, educational atmosphere.

"Another great reason for our success is the involvement of the parents and the commitment that our organization has to the parents. And we have a Parent Policy Committee, and it meets monthly. They review program matters. They serve as advocates for the other parents if there is an issue to discuss. Each year, the Parent Policy Committee signs off on the annual budget. There is nothing that we are doing that they do not know about. And they see how much it costs to run a program like this. We want them to have commitment and ownership. We're here for the children, but we're not serving children unless we're helping the parents as well.

"At Bright Beginnings, we believe a parent is a child's first teacher. We're here to help parents learn how to support their child's early childhood development," Lindsey emphasized.

Originally, Bright Beginnings began in 1988 as a Junior League of Washington (or JLW) project when the JLW secured a grant from the Department of Health and Human Services to start a child development program for homeless preschoolers in Washington. The JLW had conducted an extensive community needs assessment, and they concluded that the greatest need in D.C. was childcare for homeless families living in shelters and transitional housing. During 1989 and 1990, Junior League volunteers established a nonprofit structure, secured day care center licensing, and hired staff. In 1991, with its own board of directors, Bright Beginnings officially opened its doors at the YWCA in the Shaw neighborhood of D.C. with a capacity to help twenty-two children.

Throughout the organization's history, Bright Beginnings has assessed the needs of the homeless community and has tailored its growth accordingly. In 1998, Bright Beginnings recognized a serious need to expand in order to serve more children, so they moved to The Perry School Community Services Center. This move enabled Bright Beginnings to increase capacity from forty-two to eighty-four childcare slots, including fifteen children from the local community whose families are desperately poor and in need of Bright Beginnings' services. The expansion also supported the nonprofit's infant and toddler childcare program.

Lindsey recalled, "Historically, we went from twenty-two children in 1991 to eighty-four children in 1998, and this year we are looking to expand and serve more children. It ends up being around 150 children per year because most children are here around ten months. We need to grow so we can serve more children."

Bright Beginnings works with the children until they are five years old. And then the children move onto other programs and/or school. The follow-up is hard to maintain with such a mobile population, but Bright Beginnings does what it can.

Before families move forward after Bright Beginnings, the social work staff helps the families develop a realistic plan of action. They keep track of their progress as long as possible. They also help parents locate the resources they need, such as clothing, food, furniture, job training and placement, and assistance for financial or legal problems.

Lindsey said, "Bright Beginnings is not sure where the children go after Bright Beginnings. If the kids get into kindergarten, Bright Beginnings can know about that. If the parents secure permanent housing while they are in the Bright Beginnings program, then they're allowed to stay with Bright Beginnings for the remainder of the school year. About 120 families a year go through Bright Beginnings, and we're trying to set up a tracking system that respects their privacy. It's the nature of the homeless population. They might pick up and move where they grew up or have family. That's especially hard on the social workers and teachers who don't know if the children and families will be back tomorrow. It's not that we have a huge turnover."

Lindsey has seen many families and children come through the doors of Bright Beginnings, each family with its own story.

"My point here is that it takes a lot to become homeless, but it can take just a little, too," Lindsey summed up. "It can be a lost paycheck or a lost job or a medical disaster. But there is a significant number of homeless families with mental health issues. And that is why we have the family service team. We have two social workers and a family service/health coordinator, who supports our families.

"One thing that is so great about Bright Beginnings is that if a family is in a shelter, they have a caseworker. But more often than not, they are overwhelmed. At Bright Beginnings, we're the secondary social workers. That's a big deal. We can really help our parents. We serve between sixty-five and seventy-five families at any time. Two social workers at Bright Beginnings are serving about thirty families at any time. Our social workers can go to doctor appointments and custody trials.

"The Therapeutic Service Team helps the parents understand their child's learning disability and what needs to happen in order to help the child. They don't just hand out a list of where to get this and that. They're there holding their hand through the process.

"Some of the women have left abusive situations and need help getting through the system. The vast majority of our families are single mothers. About two or three single fathers come in per year, and other fathers come in through the year. But most are single women with their children," she pointed out.

The fact that most of their clients are single women with children is a dramatic aspect of the feminization of poverty, which affects children directly. For example, if young girls have babies in high school, they hurt their own graduation rates and vocational and/or college options. Women who are in abusive relationships often find it difficult to leave a dangerous situation with their children. They might not know where or how to go and start over. Women often make less money than their male counterparts, and yet they are the primary caregivers for children and aging parents in this country. Women are also far more likely to outlive men and have fewer resources to support themselves as they age.

"In the end, we're a child development center, but we're so much more than that because of our comprehensive approach and our commitment to serving these families. And that's how we've grown," Lindsey concluded.

When its leaders see a need, Bright Beginnings strives to fill it. In late 2005, Bright Beginnings opened an evening care program for the children under the age of five. That way, the children are safe while a parent is working a night shift or attending a class at night.

Without Bright Beginnings in the community, where would these families go? How would these children start kindergarten with a fighting chance? And if that child had any kind of learning disability, that child would be at an incalculable disadvantage without Bright Beginnings. The nonprofit does what it can with what it has.

Lindsey recalled one little girl: "The mother came to the program, and her child wasn't crawling but should have been. The teachers recognized right away that there was a delay. So they brought in the occupational therapist and the mother. And what they found was that the shelter the mom was staying in was so filthy and so infested with cockroaches that she wouldn't let her daughter crawl on the floor. She kept her daughter in a carrier to protect her, but then she never was able to crawl around and develop those skills of rolling over, inching forward, crawling, standing up, and then eventually walking. It's a process. So with the help of the occupational therapist, they developed a treatment plan that the teachers and the mother could work on. Eventually, the child was meeting appropriate milestones. Kids are so resilient; it didn't take us long. If you can catch a delay early on, you can make a substantial impact. Can you imagine if she had not been in a program like Bright Beginnings?" Sometimes, the visionary in our midst is a program like Bright Beginnings and the people who make it possible.

Making a difference with Bright Beginnings is easy. Lindsey said one elderly gentleman showed up one day with a big box of diapers. A retired doctor, he only said that he had heard about Bright Beginnings from a friend. He comes by every month with a box of diapers. Lindsey said that they used to be on the verge of running out all the time. Not anymore.

With tears welling up, Lindsey said that a woman called one day on behalf of her family that was in mourning. The woman wanted to inquire about choosing Bright Beginnings as a designated charity in her mother's memory.

In addition to diapers, contributions come in all shapes and sizes, including clothes (new or almost new) for children five or under, Metro cards for the families, and even umbrellas. They need it all, and we'll distribute everything carefully to the needy families who are striving to change their lives.

Lindsey and I walked into one room of about six or eight toddlers. Some were taking an afternoon nap on one side of the room. Three or four were quietly eating a snack. One child had a plate with chicken and broccoli and rice and seemed to be enjoying the whole eating experience. And he was using a fork at his young age! There were three teachers in the room. Two of the teachers were in their mid-twenties. One of them was sitting at the table helping the children who were eating. Both of those teachers were hopeful that by the following year, in addition to working at Bright Beginnings, they would be in graduate school for their master's in social work.

The third teacher in the room, Shakuntla Sapra, was the lead teacher, a woman in her fifties. Originally from India, she was soft-spoken and thoughtful. She had a way with the children that I sensed was special and even spiritual. Working with Shakuntla for a season would be akin to getting a master's degree. By example, her teaching skills and patience demonstrated ways of reaching the children.

I shot a roll of film and asked the teachers about what they needed. One teacher said, "Bubbles."

"The kids love to blow bubbles," Shakuntla said with exuberance. We all chuckled. I thought about how all kids love to blow bubbles regardless of the situation they're born into.

Then Shakuntla said quietly, "There is something. A new playground. The playground is all muddy and run down. The children need a playground, a place to run and play and not get all muddy. It would make a difference."

I had one last shot on my roll of film. Shakuntla was holding one of the youngsters, and I didn't even really set up the shot. I just bent down and aimed, and she and the little one looked right into my lens. The shot is hauntingly beautiful. In an instant, it captured the abiding care the teachers and staff at Bright Beginnings feel for the children.

I packed up my camera gear and waved goodbye to the children and the teachers, thanking them all. One little boy, about age two, didn't say a word as he slowly walked over to me and looked up at me with his big brown eyes. Then his arms extended out. He wanted to give me a hug goodbye. I bent down and extended my arms. Though I intended to give him a big hug, it was this little boy with his rumpled clothes and bits of cracker on his cheeks who gave me a big hug goodbye, and it was that moment that has stayed with me more than anything.

UPDATE ABOUT BRIGHT BEGINNINGS

LINDSEY WALDROP LEFT Bright Beginnings to work for another nonprofit and pursue a graduate degree. She is now the associate director of the M.B.A. evening program at Georgetown University.

Under Dr. Gaines' leadership, Bright Beginnings continues to grow and garner many accolades for its hard work. In 2006, Dr. Gaines received the prestigious Exponent Award for Nonprofit Excellence from the Eugene and Agnes E. Meyer Foundation. The award, which recognizes strong and effective nonprofit leaders, provided $100,000 for leadership development and management training.

In 2007-2008, the Catalogue for Philanthropy selected Bright Beginnings as one of the best small charities in the Washington, D.C., region.

During the school year of 2007-2008, Bright Beginnings helped 188 children from 138 families. In 2008, in D.C., the families of over 1,800 children under the age of five registered for shelters and services available to the homeless.

Contact information for Bright Beginnings:

Betty Jo Gaines, Ed.D.
Executive Director
Bright Beginnings, Inc.
128 M Street, NW
Washington, D.C. 20001
Phone: 202-842-9090
Web site: www.brightbeginningsinc.org

If you like Bright Beginnings, you might be interested in these organizations:

1) ALIVE! and ALIVE! House Shelter
   Alexandria, Virginia
   Web site: www.alive-inc.org
   Phone: 703-837-9300
   (ALIVE! House Shelter's direct line: 703-684-1430)

2) Carpenter's Shelter
   Alexandria, Virginia
   Web site: www.carpentersshelter.org
   Phone: 703-548-7500

3) Children's House
   Fayetteville, Arkansas
   Web site: www.childrenshousenwa.org
   Phone: 479-443-5239

4) Educational First Steps
   Dallas, Texas
   Web site: www.educationalfirststeps.org
   Phone: 214-824-7940

5) Hopkins House
   Alexandria, Virginia
   Web site: www.hopkinshouse.org
   Phone: 703-549-4232

6) Vogel Alcove Childcare Center for the Homeless
   Dallas, Texas
   Web site: www.vogelalcove.org
   Phone: 214-368-8686

7) Wonderland Developmental Center
   Shoreline, Washington (in the Seattle metro area)
   Web site: www.wdcbirthtothree.org
   Phone: 206-364-3777

GEORGETOWN SENIOR CENTER

VIRGINIA LUCE ALLEN is a Georgetown version of one part Auntie Mame mixed with a good helping of Miss Marple. If you don't know the book and film references, I can only say that Auntie Mame was a Rosalind Russell character who loved life to the hilt and saw every day as a wonderful adventure. Virginia Allen loves life to the hilt, and people love her for that *joie de vivre*. The other day, she said she was thinking about trading in her old Honda for a Mini-Cooper sports car so she can zip around town more easily! (That is so Auntie Mame.) Miss Marple was an elderly British sleuth, who seemed soft and sweet but she also always figured out who the murderer was. Similarly, Virginia has grace and softness and yet stays focused on the task at hand and gets things done.

Virginia has more energy than most. Usually wearing a pretty floral-printed dress, she is understated with her spectacles and her slightly Southern speech pattern. Virginia Allen is all that. And much, much more. Like Auntie Mame and Miss Marple, Virginia has guts and gusto in an unassuming way. As she puts it, her calling is to ease "the plague of loneliness for seniors in Georgetown."

When Virginia Allen started the Georgetown Senior Center in 1981, she was not a senior herself. Now that she is a senior, she appreciates the center all the more.

In all candor, when I first contacted Virginia in late 2000, I was in no mood to call her. After numerous delays, I virtually forced myself to make the call. My father had died a month earlier, and I was calling Virginia from my hometown of Dallas to discuss her nonprofit and decide if her nonprofit met my criteria. Then, if I chose it, I knew I would need to make some arrangements since someone would handle my monthly charity event in my absence.

Virginia answered the phone sweetly but with very low energy. That caught my attention and forced me to slow down. I explained why I was calling, and we discussed her nonprofit at length. Though I knew quite a bit before making the call, I still preferred to speak with the person in charge. We discussed all kinds of programmatic and budgetary issues for the center. She answered all my questions with patience and grace. (I have found if the person representing the nonprofit has no patience, is clearly not focused on your conversation, does not invite you for a site visit, or cannot discuss the basics with you on the phone, then those are major red flags.)

From our conversation, I knew I would select the center. I wasn't sure how much money would be raised at my event and warned Virginia that it was not usually a huge sum by any means, but I told her that I would be happy to designate the Georgetown Senior Center as the nonprofit of the month. That meant that all proceeds from the door would go directly to the senior center. She was quiet for a second and said, "Well, Allison, that is the best news I have had in a long time, and your call couldn't have come at a better time. Here I was…sitting here and feeling so low I guess…and that's not like me. And your call came out of the blue. You see, my sister died recently, and I've just been…well, finding it hard to get my energy back up. But this call and your generosity make me feel so much better. I really want to thank you."

Her words nearly did me in. Only a few minutes earlier, I figured I would plow through the phone call. Something about her made me pause. This connection was what life was also about. I could understand quite a bit about how she felt. It was December and close to the holidays. We had both lost a loved one. In her case, losing her sister was all the more troubling, because as I later learned, Virginia was now the last of her immediate family to survive. And it was nearly Christmas, when most folks are with their families and loved ones, something many of us tend to take for granted.

When I returned to Washington, I visited Virginia Allen and her Georgetown Senior Center and saw all the good things the center does for the seniors. Since that time, we have become friends. The following story about how she started the center epitomizes how one person can start something and make a significant difference—all on a shoestring budget. And it all started because of an article in the paper.

Virginia had always been a part-time volunteer while working in the federal government. In 1978, while in her late fifties, she resigned her position and for a time enjoyed "retirement" and seeing friends for lunch, etc. But then one day, an article changed that.

"Having always done volunteer work, I felt the need to serve again," Virginia recalled in 2005. "I saw this article written by Bob Woodward in the *Washington Post* on the closing of a senior center in Georgetown that was run by the D.C. government. And they closed it down due to funding. He wrote of the need and the loneliness of the elderly, and all they wanted was a place to gather. I said to myself, 'Golly, I could do that!' So I decided to try it."

She explained, "Bob Woodward covered the story as a reporter, but the story came to his attention because a neighbor/friend of his was a member of the senior center that was closing. And Woodward wanted to bring attention to its closing and the needs of seniors. And I was moved by that."

Virginia called the Dumbarton Church where the senior center was located, and the minister told Virginia that the senior center had closed.

"Then one day," she continued, "the minister ran into a woman named Mary, the spokesperson for the displaced seniors, and told her that a woman called and seemed like she was very interested in starting a center. He did remember my name, and Mary looked me up in the telephone book and called and asked if she could come see me.

"So Mary came to see me and *begged* me to try and do something. I explained that I was not a cook, but she said that sandwiches and cookies would be great! The center was a real purpose in their lives—to know that three times a week, they could meet their friends and have it to look forward to. The seniors were very upset, and they wanted so little, really," Virginia felt. "So I began my search for a meeting place, which became a very difficult thing. But I did find one, and I sent out three hundred letters for funding...to people I knew. And received *nothing*. But I just decided I would go ahead and do it myself.

"And so we began in October of 1981 without anything, but we used to sit and talk about my dream of what the center would be one day, because I saw right away the amazing loneliness of seniors. So I had my dream and I worked to what it is today. I had high standards and I just persevered. It shows you what you can do. It's just been a very happy experience for me. I've loved it. I've loved seeing the changes that take place in a lonely person's life. And today, we're recognized as an outstanding senior center, because I have received many prominent national and local awards. And today the center is firmly established."

"So are you glad you quit your job?" I asked, half-joking.

Without hesitation, she said with a big smile, "Absolutely!"

But there were some rough patches. Virginia recalled, "The first two years, I had to pay for everything. I have given up much, but there is satisfaction that comes with the sacrifices. If you try to do the right thing, help comes in many forms."

And help did and does come in many forms, and Virginia made special efforts for the seniors, especially for Mary, the senior who begged her to start the center in the first place. Virginia said, "Mary had so little money and was so independent and was not well. I offered to pick her up and take her to her doctors and she finally agreed. She would always be on the outside waiting for me to pick her up. One day, I ran into a friend of mine at the center, and I told her that Mary wasn't outside waiting for me, and she didn't answer her phone. So we walked down to her house a block away, and I just had a gut feeling about it—the only way I can explain it. My friend said, 'Let's crawl in one of her windows.' So she was in the process of crawling in one of the windows when a policeman came by on a motorcycle and said, 'Ladies, what are you doing?' He said that could be housebreaking. And said, 'Let me go in.'

"Well, he did and he came to the door and told us that she was on the floor unconscious. He had already called for an ambulance. They worked on her and had to take her to the hospital, but she came to as they were putting her in the ambulance and said to me, 'I knew you would come and help me, Virginia.' And she died at the hospital within a day."

Some people, myself included, can sometimes make assumptions about Georgetown and assume that the wealth of that famous community extends to *all* of its residents. But that is simply not true.

Virginia explained, "Mary lived in a house in Georgetown badly in need of work. She had no real means but she told me she had a small pension from a leading department store that is now out of business. Her monthly pension was $1 for every year she had worked, and she worked for fifty years for that store. So that was $50 per month. Can you believe that?"

Mary's pension situation is hardly rare. Today, millions of Americans don't even have a pension, and thousands of those, who were promised a pension, are being told the pension was "under-funded." The need for senior centers around the country will only grow with time as the number of seniors mushrooms and as many of those seniors have fewer options in terms of their pensions.

The Georgetown Senior Center represents an ominous tale. Aging in

America is about to "boom" as the baby boomers continue to retire in the coming years—*eighty million* of them. It is not a question of whether we will be older someday. It will be us, each of us. Unless an early death hits us, those of us in our "working middle years" will be part of this aging trend in America. Any one of us could be like Mary.

Just because we go to college, enjoy being the belle of the ball, work hard, and have a family—none of that guarantees that poverty will not touch us directly or indirectly. And it does not guarantee that loneliness will not touch us. Some of us will be blessed by good health, good medical care, good luck, and live out our lives. But all of us will age, albeit differently, some far better than others. All those who survive into old age, most of whom will be women, are susceptible to this plague of loneliness that Virginia Allen describes. Assuming basic needs are met, and that is assuming a great deal, an elderly person's life could be lonely for many days on end with no circle of friends left alive, no conversation, no contact. Local government was providing places similar to the Georgetown Senior Center until funding was cut. Is that what we as a community want for our nation's elderly?

"In my experience," Virginia summarized, "at the center, in the beginning I had the very poor ones. But today, I have the very, very lonely housebound ones. None of them are wealthy but they are all lonely. By far, the majority, their husbands have died, and the women get the Social Security checks or pensions from their late husbands. Because none of them worked. But it's this plague of loneliness. The thing that inspires me is to see how they change once they become members.

"Today, there are twenty-five seniors in full attendance. I don't want it to get too big, because I'm really interested in quality, not quantity. Individual attention is a big part of what we do. If someone misses, they are called to see if everything is OK."

To join, a senior simply meets with Virginia at the center. The seniors do not pay to join, and they don't sign anything. It's more of an understanding.

Regarding the process of joining, Virginia said, "We discuss what the center consists of. And then it gives me an opportunity to talk with someone on a one-to-one basis. My specialty is lonely seniors. And I just want it to be a very pleasant place for the seniors. So my meeting them and interviewing them, I can see if the center would be the right place for them. Of course, we have seniors of all backgrounds regardless of race or religion."

There is a van that provides transportation for the members. Three-fourths of the seniors ride the van. The center asks the members to contribute

$1 each way to ride the van, but if they don't have the dollar, the service is still provided.

The Georgetown Senior Center has use of an expansive room in St. John's Episcopal Church – Georgetown Parish, a beautiful, cherished place of worship that sits on a tree-lined street in historic Georgetown. In fact, that tree-lined street is one of the few streets in Georgetown that still has the original cobble-stoned road. Shiny, buckled rails that the trolleys used in the 1800s and the first part of the 1900s run down the middle of the picturesque street. It's one of a handful of streets in Georgetown with the stones and rails still in place. Established in 1796, St. John's was founded by Georgetown business and social leaders, including Francis Scott Key and Thomas Jefferson. Dr. William Thornton, the architect of the U.S. Capitol, designed the building. The church donates its large hall and kitchen facilities to the center so that the seniors can meet three days a week on Mondays, Wednesdays, and Fridays. The other days, the center is not open. Their space is huge and feels larger because it is filled with light from the large windows that surround the room.

Virginia described, "A typical day at the center runs as follows. First, there is yoga with a professional instructor, followed by lunch, which is freshly prepared. After lunch is a program. One will be a representative from the National Park Service. Another one features Indonesian dancers. Another one will have an author who wrote *American Traveler*. Then once a month, we celebrate birthdays of that month. Also once a month, we take a field trip, which could be to a museum, theater, Annapolis, Normandy Farms in Potomac for lunch, or a movie. The last time we went to a movie, a contributor donated the tickets! Next week, the seniors are going to have lunch at a friend's home in Georgetown, and that has all been donated. It's a tremendous place we have."

During the holidays, Virginia ensures that each senior receives a wrapped gift. For some, that gift might be their only present.

The center's budget is only $50,000 per year, and they have many volunteers helping with the lunches, the field trips, and other needs. Without volunteers, the Georgetown Senior Center would not be able to run on such a small budget.

Virginia said, "The volunteers love helping the center and can see first-hand the good that they do as a volunteer." With pride, she added, "Our lunches are always well-planned and nutritious meals."

"Friends have put on benefits for the senior center and have been wonderful," she said with gratitude. "I so believe in the need of the center and the good that it does for the seniors *and* the volunteers. The volunteers just love it. One volunteer, Susan Smith, has been helping out on Wednesdays for the past three years. It's very easy for me to meet anyone and speak with them about the need of the center."

Virginia is the perfect spokesperson for the center. It's her integrity. But the most compelling spokespersons are the seniors, and the seniors have frequently and openly said how the center has changed their lives.

During one of their Wednesday gatherings in May of 2005, I arrived with my camera gear. Two of the volunteers, Grace Charbonnet and Cathy Applin, were busy in the kitchen with Virginia getting all the plates of food ready for the seniors. The seniors were in the main hall doing yoga with their instructor, Ophelie Chevalier. Virginia usually has a few volunteers who make a special lunch, but she was short-staffed that day. So Virginia shrugged and said, "We are making do with pizza and salad."

Grace and Cathy had already set the tablecloths and place settings. Everything looked nice. Soon enough, the seniors took their seats and began to enjoy lunch and conversation. Many of the seniors ate second helpings. Last week, they had a special outing to a nice restaurant and field trip to Potomac, Maryland.

Without the volunteers, the Georgetown Senior Center wouldn't have the same feel. Grace has been volunteering for the center for about two years. She said, "It keeps my brain going, and the people are interesting. And I go to this church, too." And with that, she was off trying to help with all the food and coffee and cookies for dessert.

I sat at a table with an open seat. Everyone at the table had a fun spirit to them, and each had a story that gave me a glimpse into their lives.

The woman sitting across from me was Ruth Hyde, who said she was relatively new to the senior center, maybe about half a year. She emphasized that she loved coming to the gatherings and was grateful to Virginia Allen for making the center possible. She said, "I think this [center] is considered the best one in the area. For example, it gives you the exercise program, the lunch, and the afternoon program. We're very fortunate."

Ruth joked with the lady next to her, Joan McDaniel. They had met at the senior center. Ruth was a Vassar graduate, class of 1946, and her new friend, Joan, said, "Aw, you're a young one. I went to Smith, class of '38." Joan said she didn't know about the senior center until late last year, but was glad to be a part of it now.

At one point, Ruth worked at The World Bank.

"But that was a long time ago," Ruth shrugged. "I learned about the senior center while I was at a doctor's office in Georgetown Hospital. I've had cancer a couple of times." Though a lady in her late seventies, her blue eyes and white hair made her look younger, and she seemed to be in good shape and wanted to talk about the state of the nonprofit sector, not about her health.

The only gentleman at the church that day was a fellow named Fred Kelly, a former mechanical engineer. Wearing khakis and a button-down shirt with a tie, Fred leaned over to me and asked me to take his picture, because he is looking for a wife. Being the only fellow there among all the seniors that day, he seemed to be enjoying himself. Some of the women still have their husbands, but not many. To give you a sense of his age, Fred remarked, "I think I'm the last person alive to shake the hand of Orville Wright!"

Joan McDaniel had her long, gray hair beautifully braided and wrapped around a bun on her head. Her cream-colored, silk blouse was elegant, as was she. She said, "This group means a great deal to me, because my children are all elsewhere, and so many of my friends have frankly died. And I've made new friends."

In fact, one of those new friends was Ruth Hyde. Joan said after she graduated from Smith in 1938, she spent a year in France and studied and traveled around Europe but did not go to Germany. But she said she did go to Austria, and it was a fascinating time to see Europe right before World War II broke out. She said that she had raised three children, one of whom became a doctor, and as soon as the children were grown, she became director of a United Way day care center.

One lady eating at our table, Eleanor Depenbrock, in her mid-eighties, told me, "I'm one of the originals, been coming for fifteen years I guess. I'm a volunteer. Through the years, I've been in a variety of roles, including entertainment! I'm still a volunteer. I take care of the Bingo games. I've enjoyed it. I'm still enjoying it."

Also at our table was Phyllis Bonanno, who has been coming to the Georgetown Senior Center for two or three years. Wearing a soft purple outfit, she had the sweetest face. She said she didn't work because her husband didn't want her to. "That's how it was done in those days," she shrugged. "So I did a lot of volunteer work." She mentioned that she was originally from outside of Boston, and I asked her if she was a Red Sox fan, and her eyes went wide as she exclaimed, "Sure!" Regarding the senior center, Phyllis said, "I didn't know that they had such a nice group of people. It's wonderful. They made me feel very comfortable just to be there. And a lot of it is due to Virginia Allen. She's been marvelous. She puts her heart into it."

One woman at the next table sat in a wheelchair and had a caregiver. She didn't seem as engaged in conversation as all the others. One of the women at my table told me that that lady used to own a well-known dress shop in Georgetown and that one of the shop's customers was Jackie Kennedy.

After lunch, it was time for the day's program to begin, which would last until two o'clock. The special guest speaker was Joe Fitzgerald, an artist who was chosen by the U.S. Mint to redo the nickel! He handed out nickels to everyone and explained our nation's intriguing history of coinage and the importance of currency. As he talked about how the original coinage was made from Martha Washington's own silver, he also talked about Thomas Jefferson's role and the artistry behind the design of our coinage. The seniors were all focused on him.

I went to say goodbye to Virginia and she handed me a letter. All she said was, "I just got this before lunch."

It was a hand-written note from Joan McDaniel, one of the ladies from my lunch table. Her letter, dated May 31, 2005, read:

> Dear Virginia,
>
> Summer is upon us, and I am grateful that the center will be open through June. It means a great deal to me, and I do want to express to you and to all your faithful volunteers, my *deep appreciation* for all the careful planning and hard work involved in providing the Senior Center programs throughout the year. Bless you, volunteers! Thank you!! We appreciate you so much!
>
> And of course, dear Virginia, the guiding light and the energy which animates the whole program—to you, *gratitude* for your creativity, energy and concern. Thank you. Thank you.
>
> Most sincerely, Joan McDaniel

Virginia didn't have to say anything. I could tell she was moved by Joan's note. She said she planned to include it in the next newsletter for the center.

The second of five children, Virginia Allen grew up in Georgetown and is the fourth generation of her family in that historic neighborhood. Virginia's father was a doctor who specialized in tuberculosis. Growing up at her family's dinner table was a virtual lesson in issues of the day and problems in the community. Virginia attended Immaculata. After that, she took special courses all over, studying business and then later design.

"I was my father's daughter, always doing things with him. He was a great community leader, and I guess I learned by example to be involved in doing for others. He loved serving and so do I. I loved him very much.

"Mother had five children and we were all very close. I'm the only one left…my mother, my father, my two sisters, my two brothers…all gone now," Virginia said softly. "I miss them very much. And here I am for some great purpose, doing God's work.

"But you see I'm blessed knowing so many people and having so many friends. I'm really blessed in that way. And I'm particularly happy that I have so many young friends. I love them. It's a great compliment to me."

What she doesn't realize is that young people like to be with people who are older and can guide them or just be their friend, too. That multi-generational connection is meaningful.

"Absolutely," she said with her signature gusto.

"Your father would have been proud of you and all you've done," I said.

She paused and said quietly, "I think so."

UPDATE ABOUT THE GEORGETOWN SENIOR CENTER

AFTER FALLING AND breaking her leg at home, Phyllis Bonanno died in October of 2005.

Joan McDaniel moved into a retirement community and is hoping to return full-time to the center.

Ruth Hyde tripped and hit her head, but she recovered and continues to enjoy the center.

Eleanor Depenbrock broke her ankle in two places and though that healed, she suffers now from arthritis and can hardly walk. She moved into a retirement center, and she will be part of the Georgetown Senior Center again if she can arrange a ride.

In November of 2006, Virginia Allen broke her ankle in two places. While getting a cast put on her lower leg at the hospital, her blood pressure skyrocketed, and results from her blood work were worrisome. Fearing she was on the verge of going into a coma, the doctors hospitalized Virginia to stabilize her. She was in the hospital for eleven days. Though a painful recovery process for over eight months, Virginia finally began to move better and recapture her energy. One thing this episode demonstrated is that her beloved nonprofit can sustain and flourish in her absence. Virginia was relieved to see how the community and her team of part-time staff and volunteers rallied to keep the Georgetown Senior Center fully operational, especially during the holiday season and through the winter and spring of

2007. The community also rallied to be of help to Virginia in her time of need. Amazingly, that was the first time in her life that Virginia needed help. By late summer of 2007, Virginia was able to use a walker. By the spring of 2008, she was only using a walker on occasion and was more apt to use a cane. She admits reluctantly that her ankle has never regained full strength and that her back is painful, but she doesn't let any of that stop her. Except for not driving, she is basically back to living a full and busy life.

During Virginia's long recuperation, the members of the center took it upon themselves to vote in a nominal charge of $6 per senior for each day they attend. They said that they wanted to help Virginia pay for the van and its driver and other costs. If a senior cannot afford the fee, then it is a personal matter with Virginia and she handles it in a discretionary way.

By the fall of 2008, the Georgetown Senior Center had thirty-one members, eight of whom were now men, and Virginia continues to receive more and more requests for membership. "That's the success of the center. They know they're loved," Virginia figured. "One lady, who had a deep depression, was going every day to see a psychiatrist. When she met with me, she made it a point of telling me that she wasn't hospitalized but was an outpatient there. Through her social worker, she started coming to the Georgetown Senior Center and she hasn't missed a day since. Not long ago, her social worker called me and said, 'Virginia, you perform miracles.' And if you were to see this woman today, she's laughing and talking. Just wonderful! It's more like a private club. You would never know that any of them have problems. When they first come, they're reluctant to eat and open up. But after a while, they're totally engaged."

One glorious day in the spring of 2008, a pianist donated his talent to the center and played music from the 1920s and 1930s for the seniors after they had had their lunch. According to Virginia, "The seniors loved it. Fred Kelly, who is ninety-six, just got up and started dancing the Charleston! Almost all the seniors were dancing. They danced up a storm. They didn't want it to end."

Contact information for the Georgetown Senior Center:

Virginia Luce Allen
Founder/Director
Georgetown Senior Center
3127 P Street, NW
Washington, D.C. 20007
Phone: 202-338-2219
No Web site

If you like the Georgetown Senior Center, you might be interested in these organizations:

1) The Campagna Center
   (In addition to the elderly, this nonprofit serves children and families.)
   Alexandria, Virginia
   Web site: www.campagnacenter.org
   Phone: 703-549-0111

2) Experience Corps
   (A national program)
   Washington, D.C.
   Web site: www.experiencecorps.org
   Phone: 202-478-6190

3) The 92nd Street Y
   (In addition to numerous programs for seniors, it has programs for all ages, and some programs are intergenerational. Scholarships are available where applicable.)
   New York, New York
   Web site: www.92y.org
   Phone: 212-415-5500

KIDS R FIRST

SOME TEACHERS MAKE an indelible mark and inspire their students for a lifetime. With boundless enthusiasm, those teachers make learning a joy. Their contagious energy envelops the students, making each one want to work harder. Until retirement, Susan Ungerer was that kind of teacher. Now retired, she still loves students but she has created a different way to give.

I first learned about Susan's nonprofit, Kids R First, when I read about it in the *Washington Post* in 2003. But before selecting her nonprofit for one of my charity events, I had to ask why she was focused on giving school supplies to kids in the Fairfax County school system when I knew that Fairfax County was one of the wealthiest counties in the country. (Located just south of D.C. in the heart of Northern Virginia, Fairfax County was named the wealthiest county in the country in 2005.) It seemed odd to focus on Fairfax. Susan explained that there is an untold story going on in Fairfax County, and the story is a bellwether for what is going on in counties across the nation.

Susan quoted a 2002 statistic that was reported by the Fairfax County Department of Family Services. That statistic stated that 33,000 out of 155,000 students received free or reduced-price meals. A surprising statistic, because I knew that families had to qualify for that national food program in the public schools. This also meant that these students most likely did not have three meals a day. In fact, the majority of these students also received breakfast at school. Often, these two meals were the only ones they would receive in a twenty-four-hour period. The fact that one in five students in Fairfax County needed this food program was shocking, and I knew I wanted to support Susan's endeavors.

In 2005, Susan elaborated, "The need has only grown. That is, the number of students qualifying for this school lunch program has increased. Most of these children are without health care as well. But that's another topic."

In short, in 1998, Susan saw a need and decided to do something about it. It has been a whirlwind ever since.

Today, Kids R First is a nonprofit, all-volunteer organization that is dedicated to education. It has two special programs. The main program is to provide school supplies to children from families in need in grades K through twelve. The second one is a college- and career-bound program that provides funds for those with financial need. Kids R First donates funds annually to high schools in Northern Virginia, and those dollars are then monitored by school counselors and given to students based on need and an interest to attend college or to seek a career. Every year for the past five years, Kids R First has given more money to more schools. By spring 2005, Kids R First had given a total of 2,500 mini-scholarships. The need continues to grow.

Susan has the energy of a dozen people, and the only way to describe her is to say that she has an understanding soul and a belief in another's potential. Because of all that, people are drawn to her. She is the kind of person that people want to be around. She also knows firsthand about students, because she was an elementary schoolteacher for twenty-three years at Fairfax County schools in Northern Virginia and then retired. Fairfax County is often cited as having one of the best school districts in the nation. While teaching for all those years, Susan got to know her students and their families and saw how some students did not have enough funds to get new school supplies.

"It just seemed so unfair for these students. What a disadvantage," she felt. "Some students were understandably embarrassed, and their self-esteem was compromised. I followed a pattern of many teachers who quietly gave supplies to students to get them on an even keel with the others. I was no different from a lot of the teachers. But there are students who sometimes would be in a classroom where these supplies were not quietly offered. Maybe a schoolteacher in another classroom couldn't afford it. Therefore, some students suffered academically and emotionally by virtue of the classes in which they were placed. Pure luck. The older the students, the more problems seemed to exist due to a lack of supplies. This was especially hard on boys. Sometimes, this created a situation where the boys would act out with negative behavior, which then affected their academic achievement. Cause and effect.

"When I first left teaching, I volunteered with another organization called F.I.S.H., which met emergency needs for families. F.I.S.H. stands for Friendly Instant Sympathetic Help. I served on their board as the family assistance coordinator. Through the emergency phone calls that came into the hotline in August, September, and October, it was very clear to me that the need for children's school supplies infringed on the family's necessary budget. Therefore, I asked the board of F.I.S.H. for funds to purchase school supplies for these needy families. This, in turn, allowed the families to use their own income to pay their own rent, utilities, and/or food. I then went to local retailers and persuaded them to donate school supplies at a greatly reduced rate." Through F.I.S.H., Susan named the program, the Good Start Stay Ahead Program.

Susan laughed and explained, "That first year, in 1995, the school supplies were stored in and distributed from my garage. The program was received with such success, I was asked to continue and double the effort the following year. School administrators, teachers, and parents were thrilled with the program. In 1996 and 1997, the program tripled. Here are the numbers. In 1995, 450 children were assisted at four schools through this program. The second year, 1,250 students at eight schools were given supplies. The third year, 2,000 students at twelve schools were helped.

"After the third year, I realized there was a special mission and therefore resigned my volunteer position from F.I.S.H. and founded Kids R First in 1998. The first year of Kids R First, the numbers continued growing from 3,000 students at twenty schools in 1998 to 13,000 students at seventy schools in 2005."

Susan is thrilled about a new development for Kids R First. A local middle school in Northern Virginia donated its cafeteria for two weeks in August so that Susan's garage is not overflowing anymore. In essence, that local middle school became the distribution center for two weeks.

Kids R First gives $1,500 annually to each of the nine schools in the Dulles corridor, which is located in Northern Virginia right outside Washington. The communities it serves include Reston, Herndon, Sterling, Ashburn, portions of Leesburg, Centreville, and Chantilly. Within that $1,500, there are mini-scholarships that are given to help pay for numerous costs for these students. Through school counselors, these special funds, ranging from $25 to $150, are given to students. Some of these funds help defray the costs of SAT tutorial courses, college application fees, leadership training opportunities, and TOEFL exams, which are for English-as-a-second-language students.

Kids R First hopes that these monies will help students go from one level to the next. These students do not have the luxury of asking their parents for these funds. Every dollar their families make covers the basic costs of existence, such as rent, food, clothing, utilities, and transportation.

But the main focus of Kids R First is distributing school supplies.

Susan stated in 2005, "This past year, we purchased over 100,000 units of school supplies. For example, one unit could be one notebook, one packet of pencils, one box of crayons, or one three-ring binder.

"The difference between our program and others that just collect and donate supplies to schools is that we have a selected custom-ordered list that we provide each of the schools. In May, the schools give us their order for the students who are on free or reduced-price lunch, and we then purchase all of our supplies based on an exact list. We custom order the student supplies so that they have the exact same supplies that their classmates have. And every dollar donated to Kids R First purchases three to four dollars of school supplies. This is made possible by the retailers giving us huge cuts on the supplies that we custom order. The two retailers are Office Depot and Wal-Mart."

This is also possible because of the outstanding, all-volunteer team that Susan has put together for Kids R First, and they have a ball in the process.

"The board of directors has up to this point consisted of mostly retired educators who volunteer their time," she said. "But now it is extending to other community and business leaders. We also have another group of volunteers called Friends of Kids R First. These are non-board members who help with events such as the annual golf tournament, holiday gift wrap, and the distribution of the school supplies."

Susan and her Kids R First team have monthly board meetings, and they do year-round fundraising. "At the present time, 86 percent of our monies raised comes from small donations from individuals and other non-profit organizations; 14 percent comes from corporate support," she said, planning to focus on increasing corporate support in the coming months.

Describing their budget, she detailed, "Eighty-six percent of our budget goes to school supplies, and 12 percent goes to the college- and career-bound programs; 2 percent is for administrative costs."

Susan has many stories about how meaningful her work with the children has been. But one story, a story about a boy named Tommy, stays with her every day.

Susan spoke of Tommy softly, "I would like to share a story that happened back in 1995, the first year I started helping children with school supplies through F.I.S.H. I stopped by Terraset Elementary School in Reston, where I had formerly taught. It was one of the four schools originally selected. I stopped to visit one of my former colleagues named Merri Wiggins in her fourth grade classroom, and I asked if she had received supplies from F.I.S.H. for any of her students in need. Merri said that she had not. The amount of school supplies given that first year was minimal, and she had not been able to get them."

Susan continued, "Merri had four little boys that had come into the class without even a sheet of paper or a pencil. She had been quietly giving them the supplies on a daily basis thinking they might bring their supplies in from home like other kids, but they hadn't. So I asked Merri for her grade-level school supply list, and went out to my car to get some remaining supplies that I happened to have with me. I took them in, and we put them on each of the four boys' desks.

"The next morning, one of the four boys, Tommy, said to Mrs. Wiggins, 'I cannot find my desk.'

"'Tommy, it is where it has always been,' she replied.

"And Tommy said, 'No, Mrs. Wiggins. It's not there.'

"'Yes, it's in the same place it has always been.'

"So she walked over to his desk, which was covered with a neat stack of new school supplies. Tommy then picked up the one box of crayons from the desk, and said, 'Mrs. Wiggins, I have never had my own box of crayons before. Why are they here? Where did they come from?'

"And Mrs. Wiggins explained, 'Tommy, there were people in the community that cared enough about you that wanted you to have these supplies so that you can learn as well as the other children.'"

Susan was quiet for a second and then said, "After hearing that story from Merri, I knew there were so many Tommys out in the community that needed help, and I knew that a mission had been established."

As Susan pointed out, Kids R First might have started in Northern Virginia, but it is everyone's hope to expand to school districts throughout the state and then nationally.

"My hope is that we are going to encourage other volunteers, teachers, and communities to develop their own Kids R First programs. The legal process to form additional boards in other communities is very doable. The groundwork has been laid. A new chapter formed in Bowie, Maryland. All we need are volunteers to make the commitment to help kids in their own communities," she concluded.

SUSAN UNGERER AND KIDS R FIRST GO THE EXTRA MILE

IN EARLY SUMMER of 2004, I called Susan to see if by chance she would be able to provide school supplies for two fifth graders I had tutored a year earlier in Alexandria's public schools. The two girls, Inez and Lillian, were now preparing for the sixth grade, and I wanted to make sure they had every advantage for the new school year. Susan said that she would have to wait and see if she had any extra school supplies left over from what they had committed to the 11,000 students in Fairfax County and its vicinity.

Susan called me in August and said she had enough supplies left over and to bring the supply list that the girls received from the school. So I picked up the official supply list and drove to Susan's home and saw the piles of supplies that had been donated or almost totally donated.

We created a pile of supplies for Inez and a pile for Lillian. Something about Susan made the process of creating the piles a riot. I would say a set of blue pens, and Susan would throw in two sets. I had told Susan about my experience as a volunteer tutor for Inez and Lillian, whose families had emigrated from El Salvador. Of course, Inez and Lillian were as American as the kids who were born here, but they were first-generation American. One set of parents spoke some English. The other set of parents did not speak any English, and they were not literate in Spanish. They were from the countryside of their native land and came here for a better life. But having a parent who cannot speak English with ease or a parent who is not able to read in their native language puts a child at a huge disadvantage, especially when the child has homework.

Susan and I put the supplies in my car, but there were some items that were not at her home. Susan insisted that we drive to Office Depot; she said she had to go by there anyway to get supplies for some students in Reston. At Office Depot, we got everything that remained on their list and more. The store's manager could not have been more helpful. Everything had been pre-arranged.

In the next couple of days, I took the supplies to the apartments where Inez and Lillian's families live. I had met their siblings as well as their parents on occasion, and everyone seemed to be expecting me. The girls and their siblings helped me carry the supplies up the flights of stairs to one of the apartments. As we sat on the floor and divided up the bags of supplies, Inez and Lillian were very excited and grateful. The siblings sat with us and helped find which supply went in each batch. It was like Christmas. Except for one thing. I quickly realized that I didn't have "gifts" for all the siblings, just for Inez and Lillian. The siblings did not say a word or even hint at jealousy, but I felt bad about it just the same. Lillian has one little sister, and Inez has two sisters. Each set of supplies would normally cost about $100. How could their families afford this?

The next day, I called Susan to thank her again. She was enthusiastic as ever and asked how it all went. I told her that Inez and Lillian were overwhelmed with gratitude and would be writing her a thank-you note. I mentioned the siblings sitting there and how I hadn't taken into account how they would feel about it.

Immediately, Susan said, "Oh well, we have to take care of that."

Next thing I knew, Susan drove to Alexandria, and we arranged to meet the girls at their apartment complex. Susan's car was full of supplies based on the siblings' supply lists, which Susan had me fax to her. Now the siblings had their supplies and were thrilled. The mothers came outside to meet Susan and thank her. Unbeknownst to me, Susan spoke Spanish, and she chatted with the mothers.

The various siblings had places to be, so Susan and I took Inez and Lillian around the corner for some ice cream at Baskin-Robbins. Sitting at a tiny table with all our different scoops of ice cream, Susan asked the girls about their experiences at school and their goals for the future. With her former teacher's abilities, she listened carefully, encouraging each one's interests. They told Susan that they both would like to go to college. Lillian was not sure what she wanted to be when she grows up, but she definitely planned to go to college. Inez said she wanted to go to college and become a teacher. As a former teacher and a grandmother herself, Susan beamed. Inez and Lillian were both on their way to a positive future. Susan's efforts with Kids R First helped make their dreams a little more attainable.

Please note: Inez and Lillian are not the real names of the children. Their names were changed to protect their privacy.

UPDATE ABOUT KIDS R FIRST

In 2008, Kids R First celebrated its tenth anniversary, and in August of that year, the volunteers gave new school supplies to 14,000 students from families in need at eighty-five schools in Northern Virginia. Since its founding, Kids R First has given new school supplies to more than 101,000 children. In those ten years, Kids R First has custom ordered and donated more than one million units of school supplies. The nonprofit has also expanded its

College and Career Bound Program Fund, which in 2009 plans to give seven hundred mini-scholarships to students at nineteen high schools.

Need continues to be significant and will likely increase throughout the nation, even if that need is in one of the nation's wealthiest counties, such as Fairfax County. As of January 2009, there were 170,000 students in the Fairfax County Public Schools. Of the 170,000 students, just over 37,000 (or about 22 percent of the students) were receiving the free or reduced-price meals. In early 2009, according to the Virginia Department of Education, the poverty rate at schools in Fairfax County varied widely, from zero to 78 percent, demonstrating the wide income disparity as well as the need for programs like Kids R First. It is too soon to know exactly how Fairfax County's students will be affected by the economic collapse. The total fallout from the crisis has yet to be fully realized. If reports from food banks around the nation are any indication, there will be a sizable increase in the number of students whose families qualify for the free or reduced-price meals. The fact that the number of calls to the "hunger lifeline" at the Capital Area Food Bank more than tripled in the second half of 2008 is a strong indication of growing needs. As Susan Ungerer can attest, if a child is hungry, then it is unlikely that that child's family will be able to afford the necessary school supplies. And so the cycle of poverty begins or carries on. Ironically, education is critical to breaking that cycle of poverty.

Contact information for Kids R First:

Susan Ungerer
Founder/President
Kids R First
P.O. Box 3242
Reston, Virginia 20195
Phone: 703-850-2255
Web site: www.kidsrfirst.org

If you like Kids R First, you might be interested in these organizations:

1) Hungry For Music
    Washington, D.C.
    Web site: www.hungryformusic.org
    Phone: 202-674-3000

2) Kids Against Hunger
    New Hope, Minnesota
    Web site: www.kidsagainsthunger.org
    Phone: 866-654-0202 (toll free)

3) World Care
    Tucson, Arizona
    Web site: www.worldcare.org
    Phone: 520-514-1588

4) Youth Guidance
    Chicago, Illinois
    Web site: www.youth-guidance.org
    Phone: 312-253-4900

FOOD & FRIENDS

Do justice, love kindness and walk humbly
with your God.

— Micah 6:8

THOSE ARE THE words engraved on a small plaque as you enter the
spiffy, new headquarters of a nonprofit called Food & Friends. If
you were in a hurry, you might miss the plaque; yet it captures
the essence of this exceptional nonprofit, one of the most organized and
enthusiastic in the Washington area. Talk about high impact. As the name
of the nonprofit states, it is about food but it is *all* about the friends—the
people of Food & Friends—those who are being helped and those who are
helping.

Food & Friends' mission is direct and slightly witty: "For people living
with HIV/AIDS and other life-challenging illnesses, the battle is far from
over. We just make sure no one has to do it on an empty stomach."

Walking in the door, there is an immediate sense of zeal, camaraderie
and passion for life. Though serious about the task at hand, the people of
Food & Friends have a lot of smiles and a strong sense of humor permeating
all that they do. Maybe it's because they know they are making thousands
of lives better each year.

Providing specially prepared meals to those who have a debilitating illness may sound like a simple goal, but it takes a highly organized team
and plan of action to be so effective. According to their Web site, "Food &
Friends is the only nonprofit organization in the Washington, D.C., area
providing meals and nutritional services to men, women and children living with HIV/AIDS and other forms of life-challenging illness. Founded
in 1988 in the basement of the Westminster Presbyterian Church, Food &
Friends has rapidly grown from a dedicated band of twenty volunteers and
sixty clients, to more than fifty full-time staff, over 1,200 volunteers and

more than 1,500 clients today." In 2005 alone, they prepared and delivered over a million meals.

To understand Food & Friends today, you have to think back to how things were in the late 1980s. Originally, Food & Friends started because many with HIV/AIDS were shunned and seen as outcasts. The AIDS patients in the region needed attention, food, and support. Even though the mission of Food & Friends today includes serving those with all kinds of life-challenging illnesses, Food & Friends' efforts began because of the massive tragedy of HIV/AIDS.

Despite massive outreach and public education over the past twenty-five years, the increasing rate of HIV/AIDS continues to astonish epidemiologists. According to a 2009 report funded by the Centers for Disease Control and Prevention, at least 3 percent of D.C. residents have HIV or AIDS, a rate that is considered a "severe epidemic." That rate translates into just over 15,000 residents, or nearly 3,000 residents for every 100,000 over the age of twelve. The D.C. rate is a 22 percent increase since the end of 2006. As of 2007, over one million Americans were HIV-positive and over half a million Americans had died of the disease. According to the United Nations in 2008, thirty-three million people worldwide were infected with HIV/AIDS, and more than 95 percent of them were living in developing nations. Every day, 8,500 people die of AIDS and another 13,500 contract the virus. But it wasn't always everywhere and understood.

Not that long ago, there was a time when little or nothing was known about AIDS. Like most people in their forties, I remember when AIDS first became known in the early 1980s and became a reality in our news and daily lives. I was in college and there was this new disease in our midst. The media reported that there was a disease that seemed to strike gay men primarily, and at first, the disease was dubbed a "gay disease," which seemed like a derogatory term because it implied that that those afflicted were not really a concern for all in society. AIDS was also something whispered about.

The president at the time, President Reagan, didn't focus on AIDS until his second term, around 1986 or 1987. By then, tens of thousands of young men had contracted HIV and were dying—first ostracized due to ignorance and lack of acceptance about their sexual orientation and then this completely foreign and misunderstood, disfiguring disease. Ironically, out of tragedy, AIDS brought the gay community together and galvanized the rest of the nation, and helped make the gay community more accepted. It certainly made the gay community more visible and even more politically active.

In the mid- to late 1980s, community efforts began to take shape to help those with HIV/AIDS. Rock Hudson helped turn the tide of public opinion as he withered away before the world's eyes. In one long, painful moment, Rock Hudson bravely stepped forward and announced he was gay and was dying of AIDS. Seeing a longtime, stunning movie star look so ill was shocking. Keith Haring and countless artists and other stars died. Hollywood and Broadway were hit especially hard, personally and professionally. All communities, large and small, soon knew the pain.

Around 1990, one gay friend told me that he had been to so many funerals for friends that he had lost count. A whole generation was gone, he said, heartbroken and then furious and then sad again.

In the beginning, it was a disease out there, and then suddenly, it was the fellow in the next cubicle who was HIV-positive.

But it was not only the gay community. Young Ryan White, a brave boy who was a hemophiliac, contracted AIDS, became a spokesperson about AIDS and soon died. One of the all-time great tennis stars, Arthur Ashe, contracted AIDS through a blood transfusion during open-heart surgery and eventually died. The Arthur Ashe tragedy caused thousands of patients around the nation who had had blood transfusions to go get their blood checked immediately. That is when many Americans found out they were HIV-positive. My father, who had open-heart surgery around the same time as Ashe, was among those told to get their blood checked. It was a scary time for my family as we waited for the results of this one blood test. I remember the relief we felt upon hearing the good news, and I remember thinking that it was pure luck. The whole nation's blood supply had to be tested. To secure the blood supply, strict procedures were adopted. Back then, AIDS was definitely a death sentence, and in millions of cases around the world, it still is, even though there are retroviral drugs that now prolong life and manage the disease.

Though HIV/AIDS clearly affected the world and not only those who were gay, it was primarily the gay community that spearheaded efforts for all concerned and demanded better treatments and a cure. Their efforts paid off.

Food & Friends grew out of that dark time of despair. It was born out of necessity for those who were literally outcast and needing nourishment while so sick. It was pure outreach.

Most of us have been sick for a week or two with the flu or something. If we are completely sick, it is all we can do to maintain some measure of normal home life. Shopping for food, preparing a healthy meal, trying not to be nauseous in order to keep food down so we can take medicine, cleaning up the mess in the kitchen—all of that takes strength and real energy that the flu or other temporary illness strips away without warning. Then we are back in the pink. How quickly we forget how the day-to-day things require sustained energy. Naturally, we take it all for granted and move on.

Food & Friends serves people who are exhausted for weeks and months, perhaps years. Without concern for having to pay a dime, without concern for going to the store, without concern for preparing anything besides heating something up, those who are served by Food & Friends know that there is something they can count on.

And these are not just any meals. Designed for each patient's individual dietary needs, the meals from Food & Friends are nutritious and are specifically prepared for those with compromised or delicate systems due to illness and/or treatment. Everything is fresh and with the highest standards of careful attention to detail.

Like most programs, the history of Food & Friends did not happen overnight. Someone had a vision and the guts to get it going.

Launched in 1988, Food & Friends was developed by Carla Gorrell, who at the time was a parish associate at the Westminster Presbyterian Church in Washington. It all began as a social mission of the church. Carla saw a growing need and wanted to do something about it.

"There was a group in New York City that started a program in the basement of their church. It was called God's Love We Deliver. No one was doing it in Washington," Carla recalled in 2005. "I went to New York and worked in the kitchen to learn about how they were doing it. Our church saw the possibility of using the kitchen to feed people with AIDS. It is a congregation that had a ministry with the gay and lesbian community. That was in the '80s, and everybody knew someone with AIDS. It was spreading very fast at that time. We saw what was going on in New York City and made that connection with the need here in Washington. You can see a need and not know what to do. And when we saw a solution somewhere else, the possibility became real and it's pretty amazing. I volunteered to take the lead. No one could have developed a program of this scale alone. I always say that Food & Friends was started by *lots* of people whose vision and hard work made all the difference."

Many of the program's volunteers were members of the congregation, and the mission was focused on helping feed those who were living with HIV/AIDS. Soon, Food & Friends became a significant part of a growing community of compassion for those living with HIV/AIDS.

Carla had known unthinkable loss. "My youngest sister died of leukemia," Carla said, pausing. "She was twenty-five and I was only thirty years old. So I had lived with and cared for a young person who had an incurable disease. I knew firsthand about the treatments; some are toxic and make you sicker. It really prepared me and motivated me to work with people with AIDS and their families, because there's that hopelessness when they get diagnosed. So I can identify with people with life-threatening illnesses and their families. I knew what they were going through. The suffering is similar to the type of leukemia my sister had."

Out of tragedy came a commitment to ease another's pain. After her sister died, Carla became a hospice volunteer and finished her seminary education. Then in her early forties, while with the church, she developed Food & Friends.

Carla believed, "A visit from a caring volunteer and the food is a life-saving kind of thing to do. A lot of people with AIDS lived alone. And in those early years, people were nervous about visiting people with AIDS. It was a stigma back then. Even people with cancer find that to be true. Friends can disappear.

"I had never before met someone with HIV until we delivered food to our first client," she remembered. "People still didn't know what to believe about transmission then. I very quickly got over that and got to know people with HIV. No one from those early years survived. There was nothing to be done for them. There were treatments but nothing like today. Advocates for people with HIV/AIDS helped us see that people are 'living' with AIDS, so they won't be stereotyped as people who are sick and dying."

In those early years of AIDS, clients were often young. Some called it a lost generation. Parents buried grown children. Carla could relate and said, "Because that's not supposed to happen. It's not like losing your eighty-year-old grandmother. My sister was so young. So that need was very personal to me.

"I had a lot of experience [at hospitals] in terms of working with people who were living with life-threatening situations. In the late '80s, that is what AIDS was. People could live for two months after diagnosis. Some people would find us at Food & Friends, but they were far along and maybe only lived for a few days or weeks or months. That was in the early years of AIDS. Medicine has advanced since then."

As the executive director of Food & Friends for the first seven years, Carla shepherded and firmly established the nonprofit until 1995. That's when Craig Shniderman became the executive director. In the case of

Food & Friends, Carla and Craig could be dubbed the two visionaries. Sometimes that is what it takes to launch a nonprofit and keep it growing. The fact that Carla began it and stayed for seven years is a testament to her courageous determination and commitment. And from the get-go in 1995, Craig brought his own remarkable energy and vision to the organization. Much of an organization's success is determined by its choice of management and leadership. As with any business, succession is not always an easy transition. Food & Friends has benefited from choosing well.

At age sixty-one, Carla took a moment to look back on her life of giving. She is humble about all she has done for others. Through the years, she has ministered to a countless number of those suffering, and today she is busy as ever in her ministry at another church in the Washington area. Above all else, she said she is grateful. As she put it, "I have felt time after time that God has put me in places, and I'm always grateful and do what I can."

The growth of Food & Friends has been tremendous. Food & Friends grew sizably while in the basement of the church. Then in 1995, it moved to a location on L Street. Nine years later in 2004, it moved to its new headquarters in the Northeast section of the District. The facilities are a feat of architectural wonderment—a state-of-the-art, 25,000-square-foot facility, which will allow the nonprofit to double and potentially triple the number of meals they prepare annually. The architectural vision to have clean lines, exposed pipe, lots of natural light, and use of vibrant colors makes the space flow and seem open.

I arrived early to interview Craig at Food & Friends, so I had time to explore and chat with staff and volunteers.

First, I came across some students from Georgetown Day School, a local private school. I assumed the students were on a field trip. But one student said that she and a whole crew come all the time to volunteer at Food & Friends; it was their community service requirement for school. The students' enthusiasm for the organization was palpable. I asked if this was the only nonprofit they could help, and one student said, "No, we could go to others. But we choose to come to Food & Friends." They said they mainly get the bags ready and proudly showed me.

"The bags" are bags of specially prepared foods that get delivered like clockwork to an ever-growing list of recipients. Over 1,000 volunteers a month make Food & Friends' mission possible.

Another room in the building had more student volunteers, who were from Mamie D. Lee School, a special education school around the corner. The students were preparing a major mailing.

Despite the tail end of a bad cold, Craig insisted we keep our appointment. I thought his cold was somewhat ironic given that his organization helps those who are ill. But Craig didn't want any sympathy, for he would be the first to say that they serve those who are ill in a debilitating way. He knows the difference, sees it every day. Working with Food & Friends makes you treasure your health all the more.

With twenty years in social services in the Washington area, Craig was prepared to be a leader by the time he became executive director of Food & Friends. Originally from Michigan, he earned his undergraduate and a master's degree in education from the University of Michigan, and then he earned a master's in social work from Catholic University and worked as a fundraiser and then for the Meyer Foundation. As a program officer, health care and social work were his focus. He said, "AIDS is an epidemic in the United States. I don't have to go to Africa to work on an epidemic."

By 1995, Food & Friends had a solid foundation and mission. With Craig's guidance, the mission grew; the budget grew; the whole scope grew. Its budget in 1995 was $1 million, and it provided approximately 300,000 meals per year. By 2005, its budget was $6.2 million, and it provided meals for 1,100 clients per month in the area, serving approximately one million meals that year. As of that year, Food & Friends had provided about eight million meals since inception in 1988.

Craig summarized, "Food is provided six days a week/fifty-two weeks a year. If someone needs food on Sunday, then we double up on Saturday."

Back in February 2000, Food & Friends expanded its mission to include *all* debilitating illnesses. Craig explained in late 2005, "In the beginning, we could see a tremendous unmet need among people who were living with AIDS. Today, they just happened to be living with other illnesses. This year, 300,000 meals, or 30 percent of our meals, were for people with life-threatening illnesses other than AIDS." This is the group's fastest growing segment.

"All AIDS patients, all comers are welcome," Craig said. "With other life-threatening illnesses, we have twelve or fifteen referral organizations. We were at capacity at the old building. Now we have the capacity and building. We have to increase our operating funds so we can meet an unlimited need.

"We would like to be able to serve every person who qualifies, as opposed to just what we can handle presently. We built this building so that we're going to be here in one hundred years. There is no way of telling what health care crisis is coming. A lot of people have Alzheimer's and cardiac problems, and the population growth in the region is reaching further and further."

As always, being realistic about resources plays a crucial role in setting boundaries and guidelines for any nonprofit or business. But Craig still dreams of future possibilities.

"Someday, perhaps, we will be in the field of preventative nutrition. For the foreseeable future, we want to serve people who are life-challenged by disease. Optimally, to be successful, an organization is vibrant, imaginative, and fiscally healthy so it can move forward. Whether we will take people with other diseases like severe diabetes, or if they're at risk for diabetes, I don't know. Today, a client must be fundamentally disabled by the disease," he explained.

Being a part of the Food & Friends staff or team is also in keeping with the spirit of the mission. Craig said, "We're very committed to the American dream: equal opportunities, a place at the table for everyone. We provide a safe, nurturing, interesting workplace. We're diverse and inclusive because the criteria are commitment, devotion, dependability, and those things that are blind to race, gender, and sexual orientation. Creating a great workplace, you need to develop a consistent set of values." Food & Friends has approximately fifty-five staff, and almost half of the staff has been with Food & Friends for five years or more.

Top three things they always need more of: more volunteers, more financial support, and more canned food drives.

There are numerous stories of sacrifice and steadfast care that could be told. There is truly a team spirit among staff and volunteers. Something about them makes you want to be part of their world, be helpful. With over one thousand volunteers per month, many individuals have been part of the making of Food & Friends. There are regular shifts of volunteers, some of whom have been with the organization for years. Craig said proudly, "Dr. Graham Beard, a retired pediatrician, has been volunteering one day a week since we opened in 1988."

But one story stood out. Maybe it stood out because when Craig told me about Armando, his whole demeanor changed. His tone of voice lowered.

He took a framed photo off one of his shelves and said, "That is Armando Aguilar Rocha. He was an architect with the Washington office of Gensler, a large architecture and design firm that oversaw the build-out of our facility on L Street and then handled our new facilities here in Northeast. Armando died of AIDS."

Craig stared at the photo with me and added, "His life was a story of a successful young man whose parents emigrated to the United States. Armando focused on his studies and became a successful architect. He exemplified the best of any generation. He donated so much time and energy to Food & Friends. He and his partner, Ken Goss, gave so much of themselves to Food & Friends. Ken is still involved."

Craig recalled a phone call he had with Armando only a couple of weeks before he died. He said softly, "Armando was very sick but even though he was in the final stages of a mortal illness, he was asking about the expenses and interested in the welfare of how things were going with the final stages of the building. This fellow had a very big heart and was very concerned about this volunteer organization. He was only forty-two years old."

Craig's face said it all as he became quiet for a moment, as if he was thinking about his friend's selflessness and then remembering better times together. He knew the sense of loss in the Food & Friends community but he couldn't say anything more. It's always the people of the management, the staff, the board, and the volunteers who make an organization thrive. Quite a tribute to Armando, for the young, talented architect personified the giving spirit of Food & Friends.

In the end, Food & Friends is all about the same ideals it held when it started so humbly in the basement of a church. It's about the food and the friends. Friends like Armando and his partner Ken Goss. It's about a community coming together and doing something positive in the face of disease and death and sorrow. Ultimately, it's about life and love. Food & Friends sustains life with food and care. It's about the thousands of people they have helped, and about the thousands of people who give nourishment to the stomach and soul of those in need. It's about touching another's life, connecting with another human being, being there for them. Food & Friends is a beacon for friendship, a connecting rod that does good. And it all began in the basement of a small church.

UPDATE ABOUT FOOD & FRIENDS

THE NEED FOR Food & Friends continues to grow. From inception in 1988 to 2008, the nonprofit that originated in the basement of a D.C. church had served 18,000 clients about 11.3 million meals. In addition to serving D.C. residents, the nonprofit now serves clients in fourteen counties and six cities in Maryland and Virginia.

In the fall of 2008, with the nation's financial disaster on every newspaper's front page, Craig remarked, "The economic distress of our clients is definitely worse than it was. There are many people who are now making choices between food and medicine."

Contact information for Food & Friends:

Craig M. Shniderman
Executive Director
Food & Friends
219 Riggs Road, NE
Washington, D.C. 20011
Phone: 202-269-2277
Web site: www.foodandfriends.org

If you like Food & Friends, you might be interested in these organizations:

1) Casey Cares Foundation
   Baltimore, Maryland
   Web site: www.caseycaresfoundation.org
   Phone: 443-568-0064

2) Health, Hoops & Hope
   Chapel Hill, North Carolina
   Web site: www.healthhoopshope.org
   Phone: 919-425-2104

3) Metro TeenAIDS
   Washington, D.C.
   Web site: www.metroteenaids.org
   Phone: 202-543-8246

4) Open Hand
   Atlanta, Georgia
   Web site: www.projectopenhand.org
   Phone: 404-872-6947

5) Rock Against Cancer
   Durham, North Carolina
   Web site: www.rockagainstcancer.org
   Phone: 919-612-1166

MOBILE MEDICAL CARE

DRIVING THROUGH BETHESDA'S tony neighborhoods with their million-dollar homes and elegant landscaping, you might not guess that there is a need for a free or low-cost health clinic, that there are homeless, that some of the schoolchildren's families struggle to make ends meet. But there is such need. Real struggle exists beyond the inner city of Washington, D.C. It extends to some of D.C.'s wealthiest suburbs—from communities in Northern Virginia to Maryland. Bethesda and its surroundings in Montgomery County can be a shocker.

It was an early afternoon on an unseasonably warm, mid-September day when I drove into the parking lot of the Bethesda Library. The library recently had a multi-million dollar renovation and is a stunning state-of-the-art facility. I wasn't there to borrow a book. I was there to observe and photograph a van that provided free or low-cost health care to those in need in the library's parking lot once a week. When I told friends and family where I was going that day, they kept saying, "In Bethesda? At the library?" With over forty-six million Americans who are uninsured, the whole scene could have taken place anywhere in America.

As I drove in and looked for a parking spot among all the fancy cars at the library's metered spaces, I noticed about two dozen people loosely gathered in the shady parts of the lot—sitting on benches, under trees, or on a low brick wall.

It felt like early August, not early autumn. Yet, all these people were waiting, patiently. They wouldn't be there if they felt well. As I got out of my air-conditioned car, the heat hit me out of the blue, and I couldn't imagine waiting in this heat for long with a fever or a health crisis. One woman with a painful-looking limp went by my car. Maybe she had a bum knee. Where was the van, I wondered.

As I got my camera gear out of the back seat, a fellow in his mid-fifties sporting a worn blue baseball cap walked over to the car.

"Are you here for the health clinic?" he asked. He was wearing shorts and an old T-shirt with faded letters that read, "Long Island." His gray hair was long and tied up. His beard was gray, too. His rich blue eyes betrayed the rest of his look and I instantly wondered what he must have looked like in high school and what led him to this day. His name was Ian, and Ian looked me right in the eye when he spoke and sounded a bit like the comedian George Carlin. For some reason, even though I could tell he was going to approach me and say something, his words still startled me, and I suddenly felt a little out of sorts.

Before I could answer, he stepped closer and continued, "Oh, you have a camera. Are you some kind of reporter?"

"No, I'm writing a story about MobileMed, and I just wanted to get some shots. Do you know where the van is?"

"No. It's late. What kind of story?"

"About MobileMed," I replied.

"Oh, you work for a magazine or paper?"

"No. On my own."

"Oh, you're freelance. That's kind of up and down." He paused. "Up and down," he repeated, as if waiting for my answer.

"Yes. Up and down," I answered, wondering how he knew that and who was interviewing whom.

"We wouldn't have all these people waiting if we had some form of national health care plan. We're the only developed nation without major national health care," he said without prompting and continued for a bit.

I called MobileMed headquarters on my cell phone to see about the van, and they said the van had a mechanical failure. The backup was on its way.

As we all waited together, I saw the faces of those the medical team would serve. Many gathered under one tree now. One woman fanned herself; she looked about seven or eight months pregnant. One fellow, who I think was from India, was there with his elderly mother. People of all backgrounds were there. MobileMed illustrates perfectly what my book's thesis is: The Washington, D.C., metropolitan region is not only home to our nation's government; it is also representative of the rest of the nation, harboring both urban *and* suburban poverty.

What this day demonstrated was that despite being in one of the nation's wealthiest counties and home to a long list of well-known, successful professionals, Bethesda also has a growing under-served population. Fancy homes and expensive restaurants abound, and in the midst of all this wealth and comfort is a growing segment that needs health care.

Headquartered in Bethesda near the National Institutes of Health (NIH), Mobile Medical Care (MobileMed) is a clinic that is literally on the move. MobileMed has twenty-one different locations serving all of Montgomery County—from Silver Spring and Chevy Chase to Germantown, Rockville and Olney. MobileMed covers it all. Half of those sites are mobile vans; half are in existing medical offices like a medical clinic. Half are first-come, first-served, and half are by appointment. They serve those without health insurance and those without access to health care.

Their materials state, "Serving the critical needs of the medically under-served for over thirty-five years, Mobile Medical Care has been providing quality medical care to low-income, working poor, homeless, uninsured and under-insured individuals. With volunteer and paid providers, MobileMed provides both primary and preventative health care, referrals to specialty care as necessary, medications and vaccinations, and the diagnosis and management of chronic conditions for patients whose health conditions include but are not limited to diabetes, hypertension, obesity, asthma, high cholesterol, allergies, and various forms of cancer. More than 50 percent of their patients suffer from hypertension or diabetes or other conditions that require a consistent supply of medicine and ongoing case management."

A woman with a sense of purpose walked up to the expansive tree and the crowd gathered around. She apologized for any inconvenience, explaining the van's mechanical problem and assuring everyone that the backup van was on its way. On a piece of paper, she wrote down names in some kind of order. With about twenty-five names on the page, she walked back to her Honda. A nurse practitioner for MobileMed, Barbara Glassie is quick and decisive. I introduced myself and mentioned that I was there to photograph the team in action. Her eyes widened as if the situation were highly unusual, which it clearly was.

She chuckled and shrugged as we walked over to an elderly man standing in blue khakis, a striped polo T-shirt, and brown Birkenstocks. It was Dr. George Cohen, one of the original founders of MobileMed. Despite being seventy-eight, he looked like he could beat me at tennis any day of the week, or at least keep me running all over the court. I had spoken with him on the phone a few days earlier, and meeting him put a sweet face with the voice I had gotten to know. A more genuine fellow you could not find.

He and Barbara conferred briefly with a nursing student named Helen Cyr. The three of them went to their various cars to get their stethoscopes and set up working from the back of Barbara's Honda SUV, which had a ton of medical supplies.

"Well, we've worked without a van before," Dr. Cohen recalled. "In the old days in Ken-Gar, Dr. Meyersburg and I just hung some line in the church. And we hung some sheets across the line to give our patients some privacy. When we finished, we just took it all down!"

The whole thing was reminiscent of a *MASH* episode. And Dr. Cohen reminded me of Hawkeye Pierce, the Alan Alda character. Here was a true believer who lived his values.

As Dr. Cohen waited for his first patient, I asked, "I know you're retired now, but until recently, you had your own practice on top of MobileMed. Was that hard to juggle?"

"No. MobileMed was once a week. I volunteered once a week."

He volunteered once a week since 1970! More than thirty-five years! And counting. Humble about what he helped create, he epitomized the character of those involved in the nonprofit's growth—committed, giving, and caring.

As promised, a large van soon arrived—all shiny and white and named "Hummy" for one of the van's major donors, the Homer and Martha Gudelsky Family Foundation. It wasn't as big as the usual facility but it was large. The word "van" doesn't quite describe it. Hummy was more like one of those mobile homes that people take on a family trip to the Grand Canyon. A large, blue-and-white cross was painted on its side, a blue version of the Red Cross symbol.

Things were happening fast now. Bob Spector, MobileMed's executive director, drove over from the organization's headquarters just up the road and chatted with many of the patients. He explained that the main difference that day is that this van had one examination room rather than two. The medical team easily made do with grace under pressure and a touch of humor.

Another Barbara named Barbara Clark, MobileMed's clinical director, arrived with a box of medical files for those who are returning patients. The medical team quickly decided who would work from where. From the back of the SUV and a small desk inside the van, Helen and Barbara Clark decided they would do intake, triage, check vitals, and gather information about each patient's condition. After the basic intake, Dr. Cohen or

Barbara Glassie would handle the medical examination, diagnosis, and prescribing. In spite of the heat, Dr. Cohen chose a spot along the brick wall and handled everything there in the shade. Barbara Glassie was stationed inside the air-conditioned van.

At times, someone would go to the "master" list and yell out a name. Helen, the young nursing student who hopes to be a nurse practitioner someday, loves working with MobileMed, and stood in the middle of the parking lot and shouted the next name on the list, "Hector. Hector!"

"It is a bit surreal," she admitted.

And so it was. We smiled about the scene. There she stood calling out for Hector while owners of BMWs, Mercedes, and Lexus cars walked their young children to the library for the children's reading hour. Million-dollar townhomes and houses surrounded us, and some of the best restaurants in the region were within walking distance. All this while patients were waiting under a tree to be called, and Dr. Cohen was at his low brick wall examining a patient. It was amazingly efficient.

One of Dr. Cohen's patients was a woman whose right arm and back muscles were hurting her. Originally from Guinea, she came to the United States to live closer to her daughter and now has pain in her right shoulder and can't do her work as a secretary. Meanwhile, twenty feet away, Barbara Clark stood at the back of the opened Honda SUV and pulled out sterile gauze and alcohol and something to stick a finger of a middle-aged, African American woman. The woman had a history of high blood pressure and was complaining of pain in her abdomen.

Every patient was happy to speak with me. They all had a story. Some had been to MobileMed previously, but not everyone. All had heard about MobileMed from a friend or an acquaintance. Like any semi-underground entity, word of mouth was key. Nearly everyone there had some kind of work, often two jobs, but had no insurance coverage through their employer. They couldn't afford to get covered, or due to pre-existing conditions, they couldn't get health insurance coverage. Ian, the fellow who looked like George Carlin, explained that his disability involved asthma and rendered him unable to work.

Dr. Cohen went back and forth to the van where he could get certain supplies. The van also had a fax machine that sent back instant results of various tests. They had specialists standing by at a hospital looking at blood work, previous CT scans, etc.

The executive director for the past four years, Bob Spector has a clairvoyant way of describing MobileMed's work and mission and the overall health care crisis in Montgomery County and the nation.

Bob explained, "There are more than 100,000 people in Montgomery County without access to health care. They don't have health care, because they don't have health insurance; many don't qualify for federal programs. You have to live in the state of Maryland for five years to qualify for Medicaid. Then there is a whole group of illegal [or legal] immigrants who live and work here, but they're not yet eligible for any subsidy programs.

"*All* of the safety-net providers combined in Montgomery County might serve 10,000 people per year. MobileMed serves over 5,000 per year."

Assuming there are 100,000 without access to health care, and MobileMed and the other safety-net providers help 10,000, where are the remaining 90,000 going? Bob suggested the emergency rooms, or they simply do without and their health conditions get worse.

Bob surmised, "And the gap between capacity and need is growing, not getting smaller. There is increasing immigration, and the trend in the workplace is to provide less, not more, health insurance.

"Many people work more than one job, but none of the jobs has benefits. Also some of the growth areas like hospitality, nursing homes, hotel and food industry tend not to offer health care to their employees and those are significant growth areas in our community. And if you overlay that with the rising cost of health care, and the overall cost of living, you can see the nature of the problem. The cost of living in this region is around $60,000 for a single mother with two kids. The nature of the problem becomes even clearer.

"The problem is two-fold. First, it's an invisible problem. Second, it's a problem that moves in slow motion. It's invisible until you go to an emergency room and see all the people there. By and large, most of those people are uninsured. Their personal health plan is to stay well and avoid the emergency room," Bob said. "All of the provider communities, from politicians to community leaders and health care providers, say that the worst health care option is providing primary care in emergency rooms. It's not efficient; it's not good health care. It's not what an ER is set up to do, but that's what they end up doing.

"If the problem were visible, if everyone without health care had to wear red baseball caps, for example, you would see them everywhere—at the Metro, grocery store, etc. And that would be throughout the country. Besides being invisible, it's a crisis that moves in slow motion. There are people who lose their job and lose their health insurance. Eventually, when they get a job, they get covered again. But for those who get sick and diagnosed with diabetes or another chronic condition, they become visible when they visit the emergency room. People shouldn't have to choose between health care and the basic needs of daily living like food and so forth. The best preventative health care is to get people under care *before* they need it."

With twenty-one different locations throughout the county, MobileMed has a huge reach. Bob noted that all of MobileMed's locations are partnerships with community-based organizations that enable them to leverage their efforts. The nonprofit operates Pan-Asian, Hispanic, and French clinics that are staffed by doctors from Chinese, Hispanic, and West African communities. It has the county's only bilingual French clinic serving the West African/Haitian community.

As Bob put it, "Coming to our clinic is like going home; our patients see people they can relate to. We believe the best health care—the best human services—are delivered as close to the frontlines as possible, empowering the community as a result. We're opening a Korean clinic next month.

"We don't have to advertise; we work through other organizations and their newsletters, etc. The clinic's culture and the feel will reflect the community we are serving. Not only are there many barriers to health care, but many are cultural barriers. The best way for us to serve a community is for us to become part of that community," he concluded.

MobileMed reaches out to understand the cultural divisions and traditions of each community. At its core, MobileMed has its own version of cross-cultural communication. "The decision-maker in one community might be the husband, or the grandparents, or the patient themselves. People want to be served by people like themselves," Bob emphasized. "The children who bring their grandfather from China are comfortable bringing him to a Chinese service provider in their own neighborhood. In some cases, a male doctor is not acceptable. In some cases, a female doctor is not acceptable. We control the medical protocol, but we work through and with the local community. We have special training for people who treat victims of torture. We have two clinics that serve the homeless community, and they have their own culture.

"MobileMed began in the heyday of the late '60s and that idealistic time. Dr. George Cohen, a pediatrician, and Dr. Arnold Meyersburg, a psychiatrist, were the founders. They had heard there were some children in Kensington around an old, African American church who were malnourished or under-nourished. They said, 'We should go and help.' So they both threw their medical bags into their cars and drove over there. And what they found was children who were under-nourished. To their surprise, they found whole families that were in need of primary health care. They had no health care whatsoever.

"In the beginning, it's not that we had mobile vans. We didn't. The name of the organization came from the idea of throwing your bag into the back of the van, taking medical care to where it is needed instead of the other way around.

"They then recruited their colleagues and other kinds of doctors. They took more volunteer docs with them, sisters and wives and whatever, fifteen or twenty with them. The best they could do was like a MASH unit. Eventually, they needed a higher level of medical care. They realized that writing prescriptions that wouldn't be filled would be pointless. They needed follow-up care, medical records, malpractice insurance. So they needed to become a formal agency.

"This volunteer orientation is still a big part of MobileMed. We have over two hundred volunteers helping us—doctors, nurses, support staff. We have twenty-seven staff. Fourteen are full-time, thirteen part-time. The exciting thing is the quality of people working at our clinics is amazingly high. Our offices are right next door to NIH. A lot of volunteers are from NIH, and the head of emergency services from Johns Hopkins is a volunteer. A lot of military people. We have some volunteers who have worked with us for more than thirty years! Dr. Cohen still volunteers, and his sister has volunteered as a registrar for over twenty-five years.

"Many of the volunteers who just started recently are really the same," Bob continued. "People who want, as an extension of who they are, to make a difference. It's very real, very tangible. They're working in a clinic with people who otherwise wouldn't have health care. This is the way they're going to give something back. It's very rewarding, a very visible thing to do. In many ways, they're the same as Drs. Cohen and Meyersburg.

"Our board to this day still reflects those notions. Who would we not serve, not help? We want to screen people in and not out. We would rather serve a few people who could possibly be served someplace else than fail to serve people who have real need. That's what screening people in means. In thirty-five years, we have *never* turned anyone away because of their inability to pay.

"We have a negotiated sliding scale. We're the only clinic that charges on a smorgasbord model rather than *a la carte*. That is to say, if it's determined that a patient can pay $5, then that's what the fee is regardless of the intensity or amount of services that they receive.

"It's the same notion that we're doing the best we can with the resources we have. We're not compromising quality of care. Volunteers or any of our staff feel comfortable having their parent come to us."

MobileMed serves all kinds of people. Bob added, "People who are older, some who may not be qualified for Medicaid or Medicare, or they're new to this country and they have various problems. From MobileMed's perspective, this is a public health issue. If people are sick, they pose a risk to others. It's in everyone's best interest to have people under care.

"It's a public health question. We're leaving others to debate the issues of why people are here. The fact is they're here; they're sick and it's in everyone's best interest that they be treated. The fact is that over time we're facing a variety of public health issues in varying populations. Who knew two years ago that we would be dealing with hurricane evacuees, refugee groups, West Nile Virus, and the threat of avian flu?"

Noting the irony of the great wealth in the area, he said, "Though Montgomery County is one of the ten wealthiest counties in the country, Montgomery County does not have, like many big cities, large pockets of poverty. Poor people are scattered—so much so that we don't qualify for certain federal funds. Wherever you go, you are not that far from people who are poor. They're scattered from Olney to Germantown to Poolesville."

And what would be MobileMed's ultimate goal? With faint hope, Bob said in 2006, "The ultimate would be universal health insurance, and we would be out of business. Everyone would have access to health care. Montgomery County has taken a leadership role where the federal and state governments have let it drop, so the county has taken an aggressive role in providing quality health care. But this gap between capacity and need needs to lessen and not expand.

"And the recognition that these people without health care are not just unemployed. The vast majority are the working poor. They're working hard and raising their families. The difference between being a contributing member of society could be as little as a dollar a day for a pill to control hypertension. The fellow who can control his diabetes can work just fine, but if he can't?

"It's difficult to measure the impact of one man with uncontrolled diabetes. With diabetes under control, he is able to take a job and support his family and put his kids through school. Absent that, he becomes a burden on his family, on the community, and it impacts his whole extended family. His physical, mental and financial well-being brings down the whole family. So society has to ask itself, 'What is the value of one productive family?'

"One person at a time, one family at a time, one community at a time,"

Bob said, almost as a mantra that keeps him and his team going. With a master's degree in professional clinical services administration, Bob has been in the nonprofit human services field for more than thirty years. He joined MobileMed in 2002 after working for ten years at the Jewish Council for the Aging.

MobileMed, which got its start in 1968 and received its official nonprofit status in 1970, had a budget of $6 million in 2008, serving over 5,500 patients every year, which doesn't count the 1,500 Head Start children it also serves. Amazingly, $3 million of that $6 million budget is in in-kind contributions.

MobileMed began because professionals in the health field saw a growing need in Montgomery County. They were visionaries. One of those original health care providers, Dr. Cohen, still volunteers at least twice a week with MobileMed and loves the mission and the comradeship.

When I called Dr. Cohen to get his perspective, I said, "I'm sorry to call you at home."

Referring to his retirement from pediatrics, he said with a touch of wit, "That's the only way to reach me."

"You must be very proud. Creating such a tremendous operation."

"Oh, Dr. Meyersburg was the inspiration, the brain and the angel. I just tagged along."

In his early nineties and receiving care at home now, Dr. Meyersburg was a force in his day. Dr. Cohen told me about how it all began. According to Dr. Cohen, it was really Dr. Meyersburg's vision.

Adding to what Bob had said, Dr. Cohen recalled, "There was a program in the county in the 1960s when the schools were being desegregated. There were some women who were white in Garrett Park, and they knew some women who were black. Either they knew them or they met them at the grocery store or something. The women realized that there was going to be a big adjustment for the kids. One of the white women said to the black women, 'Your kids are going to be starting school soon at these new schools, and perhaps we can help with tutors.' There was a program called the Home Study Program. Dr. Meyersburg was the president of it at that time. A dozen and a half sites in people's homes—volunteers tutoring the kids. One of my patients suggested I come down and see what they were talking about. Maybe I can help? And I got involved tutoring.

"As it progressed, there was a number of us volunteers in the health field. One night, Dr. Meyersburg asked those of us in the health field over to his home for discussion. He asked if we noticed a need for health care.

Everyone had a sad tale to tell. These were working poor, who had little means and no benefits. If you got sick and missed a day of work, you lost pay. If you missed a couple of days, you could be looking for work.

"So we huddled and decided to provide health care. A family foundation gave us some seed money. We got some supplies from the Montgomery County Red Cross. And some volunteer physicians came to us from the U.S. Public Health Service, physicians who were assigned to NIH. They got lined up. There was a local citizens association in Ken-Gar, two neighborhoods near Kensington and Garrett Park in Montgomery County. They had an active chair, and he said, 'Let's get going!' He called a local church, and that church gave us some space. In the meantime, an old buddy of mine was a lawyer, and he got the legal paperwork and nonprofit status set up and organized for us.

"And so MobileMed got started once a week in Ken-Gar. And now we have all these sites and vans! Of course, there have been changes in personnel here and there, but the mission is there.

"It's funny. I remember what Dr. Meyersburg said when the first clinic opened on April 1st, 1970, on April Fool's Day. He said, 'We'll fool 'em.' People were saying it could never work and that it was pie in the sky."

At the time that this got going, Dr. Cohen had a medical practice and a family and an active life. He could have kept focused on his family and work, but he chose to volunteer one day and was intrigued not only with the need but also with the feeling he got from it.

"My parents were great believers in trying to help out. My father worked very hard all the time as an accountant, but he was always happy to help out. My mother did a lot of work with the Jewish organizations, and they taught us that people who need help need help, and it's worth doing some good. It came from early on. Not to be silly, but I took it rather seriously that the Boy Scouts' motto was that being helpful is a virtue. My grandparents, my father's parents, were very much in the realm of helping. They believed in *tzedakah* [meaning justice or charitable giving], and they helped family members in need, and sometimes total strangers and the Aid Society for newer immigrants. My grandparents came over in their late teens and early twenties. Whether it was conscious or not, it was certainly built into the family—a form of *tzedakah*."

Back at the Bethesda Library's parking lot, Dr. Cohen cajoled, "Go to Silver Spring tonight to see another MobileMed site. Or come tomorrow to Gaithersburg to see our work with the homeless." And then he was off to see another patient.

Update about Mobile Medical Care

In late 2007, MobileMed celebrated its fortieth anniversary. Dr. Arnold Meyersburg died in September of that year. He was ninety-three. Dr. George Cohen, at age eighty-one, continues to volunteer with MobileMed.

MobileMed has expanded its reach to meet growing needs in the community. In early 2009, MobileMed opened its first, full-service clinic, adjacent to Shady Grove Hospital's Emergency Room in Germantown, Maryland.

Partnering with the National Institutes of Health and the Suburban Hospital Heart Center, MobileMed opened a cardiac care specialty clinic for the uninsured. MobileMed believes it may be the first clinic of its kind in the world, providing world-class cardiac care for the uninsured.

Contact information for Mobile Medical Care:

Mr. Robert Spector
Executive Director
Mobile Medical Care, Inc.
9309 Old Georgetown Road
Bethesda, Maryland 20814-1620
Phone: 301-493-2400
Web site: www.mobilemedicalcare.org

If you like Mobile Medical Care, you might be interested in these organizations:

1) Alaska Native Tribal Health Consortium
   Anchorage, Alaska
   Web site: www.anthc.org
   Phone: 907-729-1900

2) The Bayou Clinic
   Bayou La Batre, Alabama
   Web site: www.bayouclinic.org
   Phone: 251-824-4985

3) Cabrini Clinic
   (Formal name: St. Frances Cabrini Clinic of
   Most Holy Trinity Catholic Church)
   Detroit, Michigan
   Web site: www.cabriniclinic.org
   Phone: 313-961-7863

4) Commitment to Underserved People (CUP)
   College of Medicine
   The University of Arizona
   Tucson, Arizona (with programs also in Phoenix)
   Web site: www.medicine.arizona.edu/programs
   Phone: 520-626-2351

5) The Floating Hospital
   (The vast majority of their work provides free health care
   to the homeless in the New York City metropolitan area.)
   Long Island City, New York
   Web site: www.thefloatinghospital.org
   Phone: 718-784-2240

6) The Free Clinic
   (Formal Name: The Free Medical Clinic of Greater Cleveland)
   Cleveland, Ohio
   Web site: www.thefreeclinic.org
   Phone: 216-721-4010

7) Haight Ashbury Free Clinics
   San Francisco, California
   Web site: www.hafci.org
   Phone: 415-746-1967

DOCS FOR TOTS

A s a young boy, all George Askew knew was that he wanted to grow up and help children. Then as a young pediatrician, George saw many children whose basic needs were not being met. He believed something could be done and envisioned Docs For Tots.

A voice for those who do not know how to ask and a voice for those who could not otherwise be heard, Docs For Tots epitomizes the good that can come about when an individual sees a better way to be of help to the most vulnerable. Unlike the other programs focused upon in this book, Docs For Tots does not provide direct services; rather, it demands support *for* direct services from government, business, and community leaders alike. George Askew saw many in need in his practice and decided to speak out on behalf of the children. From the get-go, his zeal and advocacy had such an impact that he engaged other physicians in his mission, and his program caught on nationally. Hence, George Askew and Docs For Tots are already sharing a roadmap for others to follow.

I t is fall now. The leaves outside my windows are shades of yellow, orange, and red. The ground is so covered by a potpourri of colorful and fading leaves that no one can possibly see the grass anymore. Autumn in Washington, D.C., with its crisp air and quiet splendor.

What does fall mean to others in the United States? For millions of blessed children and families, fall means a return to school, anticipation of Halloween and Thanksgiving, not to mention new toys in December. But for millions of American children, the fall season means a free or reduced-price breakfast and lunch at school, which often ceases during the summer months when school is out. During the summer, those same millions of children don't have a guarantee of a meal. They scrape by until school resumes in the fall. In California alone, in 2007, nearly 1.6 million children were poor, affecting their nourishment, health, and ability to read and excel in school. As mentioned in the introduction, according to Census Bureau data in 2007, over thirty-six million Americans lived in food-insecure homes, including twenty-five million children. The federal program for breakfast and lunch is literally the meal ticket for these children. It is not an exaggeration to say that millions of American children don't know where their next meal will come from, and they don't know enough to realize that that is not the way it should be.

In addition to food insecurity, poverty can be measured in terms of shelter. Nationally, as of early 2009, 1.5 million American children were either homeless or in transitional housing.

Poverty affects all children, regardless of race, but the impact on black and Latino children in the United States is notably worse. Marian Wright Edelman, founder and president of the Children's Defense Fund, referred to such a child's plight as "the dangerous intersection between poverty and race." Since early 2006, Ms. Edelman has repeatedly called attention to this crisis, saying that a black boy born in 2001 has a one in three chance of ending up in prison and that a Latino boy born in 2001 has a one in six chance. Yet, as she points out, our nation spends nearly three times as much on every prisoner as we do per pupil. She calls it "the pipeline from the cradle to prison." Organizations such as the Children's Defense Fund do their best to put out white papers and lobby Congress for more funds for children from low-income families. Yet, still the children suffer.

All Dr. George Askew really had to offer was a firm commitment to his ideals, a big heart, and a heaping amount of guts. He had an idea to augment long-established efforts. He is not an idealist, but rather an idealistic realist.

George likes to call himself "a children's doctor" rather than a pediatrician. As a children's doctor, he sees a myriad of unmet needs in the children he treats and as a result decided to be their advocate. But being an advocate wasn't enough. He wanted to engage others in effecting change. His good works embody that idea of setting forth a ripple of water and watching it form a tidal wave of change. In his early forties, George Askew created Docs For Tots, a nonprofit that is its own wave of change. George's idea is to make it easy and simple for doctors around the country to become advocates for children.

Launched in early 2003 in Washington, D.C., Docs For Tots' stated mission is "to develop, support, and grow a nationwide network of doctors able to respond to the requests of child advocacy organizations and others who seek doctor involvement in promoting policies and practices that will improve the health and development of infants, toddlers, and preschoolers. We envision a country where no young child lives in poverty; no young child suffers from disparities in health and development outcomes due to race, ethnicity or socio-economic status; all young children have access to quality early care and education; and children's doctors are actively engaged in bringing about these changes."

Highly effective, Docs For Tots is already attracting attention, harnessing talent around the country. Because of Docs For Tots, there are 454 doctors who practice medicine and are also active advocates throughout America: 454 ripples of water. Through regular communication, educational events, and media briefs, Docs For Tots reaches thousands of other doctors across the nation who have signed up to be part of their efforts. The Docs For Tots network is made up of children's doctors from various specialties in child health care, including pediatricians, family practitioners, psychiatrists, surgeons, obstetricians, and more.

George loves medicine and could have remained focused full-time on clinical practice, but he explained, "The reason I do advocacy for kids is because there were things that I saw in my office that I couldn't treat. I could certainly treat ear infections, pneumonia, and sore throats. But there were things that were happening outside my clinical walls that I think had a far greater impact on the children and families that I couldn't treat. Things like poverty, racism, and inadequate access to quality early care and education.

"I tell this story of a four year old, nearly five year old, who I was seeing in the office, who came in for a regular checkup with his three-year-old brother. And the mother told me about having to give up her job because her job wasn't paying her enough to afford quality child care. So that is issue one that concerned me but didn't really light a big fire.

"We finished our visit and they were about to head out. As I typically do, I give families a final opportunity to make sure we covered everything. I asked, 'Is there anything else you can think of that we didn't cover?' In this case, the mother said, 'I think my five year old needs therapy.' Of course, I was very concerned about that and wanted to know what she meant. And what she said was, 'He's been killing mice.'

"That sent off bells and whistles in my mind but maybe I didn't know enough. I asked, 'How does he catch them?' She said, 'That's easy. They're running all over the apartment and bed.'

"This kid has asthma. So I asked the mother, 'Why don't you move? Or get the landlord to do something about it?' And she said that she's tried but has had no luck getting the landlord to do anything. And she can't afford to move or any other kind of housing. And then, she topped this off by saying, 'And oh yeah, the five year old gives the three year old the mice to throw away.'

"And so I was distraught. She's a single mom who can't afford quality child care. Again, I can work on his asthma. I can send him to therapy or to a behavior specialist, but I was distraught because this mother felt so 'disempowered' by her situation that she felt the only avenue for help was to get the child therapy. In other words, she's living in a situation that is putting her children at risk. I was angry that we would live in a world that would allow this mother and children to live in this situation with a perception of having no other way of life.

"That was one of the most profound examples of the things I was seeing, but I was seeing other situations. There is a happy ending to this story. At the time, I worked in a hospital that had a legal advocacy program, which is something very unusual for a hospital to have. So I was able to have our lawyers draft a letter to the landlord. And that was very effective in getting the folks an apartment that wasn't mouse-infested.

"For her, it was a foregone conclusion that she had to live this way. This was her normal life, what she felt her life was about. We were able to have a greater impact on this family's life by addressing issues outside of the office setting. So I wanted to work beyond my clinical walls, so I could help prevent situations like this."

George likes to tell a story about two hikers. While the previous story about the single mother and her two young sons was true, the story about the hikers is simply told to illustrate his philosophy behind Docs For Tots and about getting involved in general.

"There are two hikers in the woods who come to a stream. And they see a baby in a basket floating down the stream," George started. "So one hiker goes in and pulls the baby out. Then before they're able to do anything more, another baby comes down the stream. So the other hiker goes in. Before they know it, they find themselves going in and out of the water, rescuing babies. And they're getting exhausted. So at one point, one hiker just bolts upstream, starts running up the stream away from the other hiker. So of course, the other hiker screams at him, 'Where are you going? We have to pull these babies out of the water or they're not going to survive!' So the other hiker says, 'I know but I'm going to go upstream and find out who is putting these babies in the water.' And that illustrates the work I do. The work I do is trying to keep the babies out of the water. Working further upstream—that's what I think the advocacy work I do is about.

"And so I came to Washington because I wanted to work further upstream and I thought Washington would be a way to do that."

He left his faculty position at Boston Medical Center, and came to D.C. as a Soros Physician Advocacy Fellow to work with ZERO TO THREE, which is officially called ZERO TO THREE: The National Center for Infants, Toddlers and Families. He worked on trying to develop policy language around infant mental health that would resonate with policymakers. He did that for a year and was asked to become the chief of the Health and Disabilities Services Branch of the national headquarters of Head Start within the U.S. Department of Health and Human Services. He explained that essentially he was the pediatrician for the Head Start Program and was there to determine the medical and disabilities services needs and delivery for the 900,000 kids in the Head Start and Early Head Start programs. That was 2001 to 2002.

"Then I reestablished myself with the Soros Physician Advocacy Fellowship—again working at ZERO TO THREE and this time on a project called The Better Baby Care Campaign," he said. "I was supporting their advocacy around improving out-of-home care for families with infants and toddlers who needed the care either because they were working or in school or otherwise. It was during that year, from 2002 to 2003, that I developed the idea for Docs For Tots.

"One of my mentors, Dr. Barry Zuckerman, is the chair of the Department of Pediatrics at Boston Medical Center, which is at Boston University. One of the things he said is to have your advocacy or your programmatic life grow out of your experiences, if that's part of what you want to do as a doctor.

"And in this case, my experience was that people were calling me as a children's doctor to attend different venues and to talk about the impact of social policy on young children from the perspective of a children's doctor. I was seen as a nontraditional advocacy voice for kids on social policy issues. Nontraditional because I was addressing issues that doctors didn't normally talk about but they could be very effective advocacy voices. Things like paid family leave, quality foster care, quality child care, Head Start, abuse, neglect, hunger, food security, school readiness, etc. My thinking was while it was nice to do these talks and make these appearances around the country, it really should be local docs, and that doctors would be very interested in getting involved in advocacy in these areas. And it turns out that I was correct!"

Within two years, George Askew knew he was very right. After incorporating as a nonprofit in early 2003, Docs For Tots received a substantial grant from the Kellogg Foundation and an anonymous foundation in Massachusetts. By late 2005, Docs For Tots had an annual budget of $500,000, a modest staff of five administrative and programmatic professionals, and a handful of consultants. With their 454 doctors around the country who are volunteering to advocate for children, Docs For Tots shows that you don't have to live in Washington to work upstream.

Thus, the mission for Docs For Tots is to build "a nationwide network of doctors advocating for young children." The two-part vision includes working on social justice issues for kids and changing the nature of professionalism for children's doctors by increasing their civic engagement beyond clinical practice walls. Docs For Tots makes it easy by providing training and technical support for advocacy, and they broker relationships between doctors and child advocacy organizations. The doctors act as messengers and medical experts for child advocacy groups.

George knew that he wanted his practice to include advocacy and said, "I encourage anyone who considers themselves to be a children's doctor to get involved, including surgeons, ob-gyns, family practitioners, psychiatrists, etc. I would much rather just have to deal with an earache in my office. It would be much easier to just treat the earache in that short time I have with a family in my office and not have to deal with a myriad of other social problems that could be prevented before the family gets to the office."

Docs For Tots is what I call expansive engagement—engaging others in your cause. Looking at the nonprofit's dynamic reach, George agreed and said in 2005, "We've given an avenue for over 450 docs to do advocacy work. Organizations are seeking us out more to help as advocacy partners in promoting policies and practices that are crucial to the well-being of young children. Organizations contact us from all over the country—from California to Massachusetts. I would love to see advocacy work more included in medical training. We don't use social workers, nurses, or teachers because they're considered to be more traditional advocates."

George's dream of building a national network of doctor advocates is clear. He said, "I would love to have a substantial number of docs in each state. I don't know what that number is, but I want to be able to be responsive to all organizations that seek out our help, which means you have to have a large number of doctors with a large spread of interest. I also see this as a model for other professional groups, sort of a network for social justice for young children."

Originally from Cleveland, Ohio, George was the first from his family to go to college and medical school. He explained, "My parents left high school to get married. My mom had me when she was nineteen; my dad was twenty. So they were young parents. I grew up as an only child. I grew up in an urban area in Cleveland. My parents did eventually finish high school. My dad was a machine operator and my mom a secretary. And they did go onto second careers in real estate after their retirement. And they've been married for forty-four years."

George and his wife Katherine, who married in their twenties, have a boy and a girl. In addition to his nonprofit work, he continues to see patients and is busy juggling all aspects of a full life. He has prepared well for this moment and worked hard to get where he is. He studied psychology and social relations at Harvard University and then went to Case Western Reserve University for medical school. In 1999, he was one of only fifty professionals from a wide range of disciplines identified as a "Future Leader" and invited to participate in the New Leadership Program of the American Academy of Pediatrics' Child Health Research Center.

"From the time I was in high school, I've wanted to work with kids. I studied psychology in college," he recalled. "When people asked me why I became a doctor, my calling since high school has been working with and helping children. Medicine is one of the most important and fulfilling ways to do that in my mind. My parents say I've always been pretty independently-minded," he chuckled almost to himself. "I don't tend to follow in the footsteps of others. There are people I admire, but I really always try to set my own course."

And so he has. Someone like George might not take the time to look back and see all the good he has created. After all, he is not finished creating yet. Clearly, George Askew has high hopes for Docs For Tots. But mainly, he has high hopes for children across the country, children he may never know but who will benefit from his commitment—that they should have a blessed life.

UPDATE ABOUT DOCS FOR TOTS

IN 2008, Docs For Tots formed a strategic alliance with Voices for America's Children, a twenty-five-year-old nonprofit based in Washington that coordinates and spearheads advocacy efforts across the nation on behalf of children. Docs For Tots remains an autonomous nonprofit. George now serves as the Deputy CEO of Voices for America's Children while remaining an active board member of Docs For Tots.

Dr. Dina Lieser, a pediatrician who has been a children's advocate for fifteen years and had been head of Docs For Tots' New York office, now serves as the nonprofit's executive director. As Dina put it, "In addition to public policy advocacy focused on young children, Docs For Tots is expanding its capacity and outreach by concentrating on the following areas: ensuring that all children are reached early with screenings and referrals; helping doctors address issues, including early learning and mental health, through their clinical venues and direct care; supporting local, state, and federal initiatives that build comprehensive systems for young children; using research to demonstrate critical public health returns on early childhood investments; working in concert with advocacy organizations; hosting educational programs to give doctors a forum to address social justice issues; and giving doctors concrete steps and a clinical toolbox to help them interact effectively with patients, legislatures, policy makers, and the media."

Contact information for Docs For Tots:

Dina Lieser, MD, FAAP
Executive Director
Docs For Tots
1000 Vermont Avenue, NW, Suite 700
Washington, D.C. 20005
Phone: 202-589-0103
Web site: www.DocsForTots.org

If you like Docs For Tots, you might be interested in these organizations:

1) Children's Defense Fund
   Washington, D.C.
   Web site: www.childrensdefense.org
   Phone: 202-628-8787

2) D.C. Action for Children
   Washington, D.C.
   Web site: www.dckids.org
   Phone: 202-234-9404

3) Youth Advocacy Center
   New York, New York
   Web site: www.youthadvocacycenter.org
   Phone: 212-675-6181

THE ARRIBA CENTER
FOR INDEPENDENT LIVING

THEIR FACES SAY it all. The faces of those at Arriba. Lovely, open faces. Some smile easily. Some not as easily. A few are reluctant to smile at all. Some cannot look me in the eye for too long. One sits in a wheelchair that is too big for him. He doesn't seem bitter but he's been through something. Some have survived torture; a few have diseases or suffer from depression. Almost all are welcoming. They're sitting in a small classroom trying to learn how Americans handle matters like Social Security and other benefits. As I photograph the group, a tall gentleman is standing at the front. His voice bellows as it ricochets around the room. His enthusiastic belief in the work fills the room as well as the hearts of those sitting there. Each day, he gives them hope for a better tomorrow and the tools to make things happen. That's Dr. Cristobal Covelli. His Arriba Center makes life possible again.

Later in the day, Dr. Covelli quietly described how one client was a young man who had been trying to catch a ride on a train and was running alongside it and slipped, losing his legs under the wheels of the train.

"The man didn't know how to live, what to do. So these people need the same attention," Dr. Covelli said of the immigrants who are helped at his center. Arriba gives people a way to live, a way to get their lives back.

It's one thing to be an immigrant in our nation, to come here with high hopes for a better tomorrow. No matter what background, it is a rough journey to assimilate to a new land—trying to fit in and learn the language and customs of a people while maintaining some connection to your homeland's traditional ways. Finding consistent work is one of many hurdles. There are concerns about food, housing, and health care. But what if an immigrant is also disabled? What if an immigrant is traumatized by what he/she saw as they left or fled their homeland?

No matter how you feel about the controversies regarding the nation's evolving immigration law, the reality is that immigrants arrive in the United States, get jobs and some then become disabled while on the job. Usually, there are no protections or benefits. They have no support system or way to become whole again. It can be frightening and overwhelming. The Arriba Center for Independent Living, better known simply as Arriba, is a nonprofit in the heart of Washington that is committed to helping immigrants become whole again and find work. Their astounding success rate for employment is over 90 percent.

As Dr. Covelli explained, "Arriba means up, and it can also mean, 'Cheer up,' or 'Rising up,' or 'Moving up.'"

As the founder and executive director of Arriba, Dr. Covelli had a vision for a way to help Latino immigrants who have physical or mental disabilities. If implemented elsewhere, Arriba could be the basis for success for immigrants in other communities across the country.

Founded in 1999, Arriba's official mission is to "serve a community of Hispanic individuals with severe and chronic disabilities in Washington, D.C., age fourteen and above. Arriba offers employability skills training to the large population of mentally and physically disabled Hispanics in D.C."

As of 2005, Arriba had helped over 1,100 people, and these were unduplicated clients. Before entering Arriba, the average income of the clients is below the federal poverty line. After receiving Arriba training, their income more than doubles. For example, before Arriba, if they were working, they were typically making the federal minimum wage, which was $5.15 until 2007 when the U.S. Congress passed legislation to raise the minimum wage to $7.25 over the next two years. (Until 2007, the minimum wage had not been increased in ten years.) The D.C. minimum wage is one dollar higher than the federal minimum wage. With Arriba's help, the clients earn between $10 and $15 per hour with benefits. Arriba looks for job placements for its clients that offer benefits, especially health insurance. Before entering Arriba, a client on average earned between $9,000 and $10,000 per year and sometimes without any benefits. Sometimes, they were on welfare. About half of the clients are male and half are female. Arriba conducts screening, counseling, and referral interviews for at least 140 individuals per year. They also teach the Arriba workforce development program called Arriba Center Training the Disabled for Employment Adjustment and Reintegration (or ACTDEAR) program to 100 of these people.

With only two full-time staff members, a few part-time staff members, and some volunteers, Dr. Covelli and Arriba do a great deal with very few resources. In fact, the first three years of Arriba, Dr. Covelli said that he didn't even pay himself. He added, "For the next year or two after that, I was paying myself a lot less than I was paying the employees. I was working on my own money, maxxing out my credit cards and putting a second mortgage on my home."

In 2005, its annual budget was about $200,000. By 2008, its budget had grown to $240,000. More dollars will mean being able to help more clients find work.

Arriba works in a space of 2,000 square feet in the heart of downtown Washington. Dr. Covelli believes, "The clients need to come to a dignified location, and it's helpful for them to be around a place similar to where they would be working."

Dr. Covelli's remarkable success record speaks for itself. Brimming with pride about the nonprofit's "graduates," he mentioned a few, "One of the ladies is a secretary with the D.C. public schools; she's one of our disabled clients. Another one will be a secretary or office assistant in the D.C. government and she's in a wheelchair. And another graduate is a graphic designer for a local newspaper. A number of our clients go into custodial work. Remember these are people who come to the U.S. and become disabled here as a result of work injury or degenerative disease. They got degenerative diseases that went untreated because of a lack of access to health care, and thus rendering them disabled. They have no education from back home; a number of them are not even literate in Spanish. They were displaced people of the wars in Central America, for example. They come here with no education. What they can do is custodial work. That is their goal, to work as cleaners."

He explained further: "The disabilities range from degenerative disease—disease that causes partial or total loss of limbs. Maybe they wear a prosthetic. Maybe they have advanced arthritis, cancer, diabetes, loss of body function, muscular degeneration. The great majority has varying degrees of clinical depression. Some of them have depression, and that is their disability. And some of them have depression *on top* of their physical disabilities. In order for a client to be part of Arriba, they have to have a medically diagnosed disability, physical and/or mental.

"Some of our clients have had a head injury or trauma to the head. You wouldn't know they're disabled to look at them, but their disability is functional. One fellow was hit by someone on the street, hit his head and is now paralyzed."

As I photographed some Arriba clients, I realized I could not identify their disabilities. I was told their disabilities ran the gamut from various diseases to head trauma to torture victim.

Dr. Covelli said, "Some are diagnosed with post-traumatic stress disorder [or PTSD]. Remember these are victims of war. They have seen family members maimed and/or killed, or [they] disappeared. Many of our clients were also maimed or threatened, and they had to run from their homes and villages and run for their lives and leave behind loved ones being tortured and/or killed. So they become very depressed. Some clients from Central America or Cuba have been victims of torture, either because of the government or some group. These are the same conditions that appear in those who are ex-soldiers of the Iraq wars or of the Vietnam War. With Arriba, they all end up with the skills to find employment and over 90 percent end up with a job!"

As mentioned in my essay about Mary's Center, many women had to flee from Central America and come to the United States without their husbands. They paid a guide, known commonly as a *coyote*, to show them the way through treacherous territory. Some of the *coyotes* threatened and raped the women all the way to the U.S. border. Thus, the women arrived traumatized, pregnant by a man not their husband, and in a new land without language skills or health care. Dr. Covelli has worked with some of these women.

"No matter what nationality they have, they are admitted to Arriba when they have a work permit," Dr. Covelli elaborated. "An increasing number of U.S. citizens are coming to us at Arriba for medical treatment and/or psychological treatment, and we refer them to other community-based organizations and/or make them become self-advocates and use their own resources to get the coverage they need.

"There is an increasing number of U.S. citizens who are also members of ethnic minority communities. They cannot find the services readily available or accessible to them from other agencies, so they come to us at Arriba. These community-based organizations in the Hispanic community are a network. Some of our clients go to Mary's Center or La Clinica [del Pueblo] for health care. Some go to a place for the children to be tutored. Or they go to the Hispanic Catholic Center and Bread for the City. They could be clients of a number of agencies at the same time."

Dr. Covelli explained, "We advertise in local Hispanic papers, and we send flyers to the different Spanish churches. We post flyers in the community and distribute them at local events like health fairs and in stores in the Hispanic community. And word of mouth is becoming a very powerful vehicle also."

Wearing a lot of hats like any fine executive director, Dr. Covelli is the fundraiser, does part of the training, and supervises the team. He said, "Everybody who works here does everything that they can because we are such a small agency. We have two very committed volunteers plus five more board members. One of our graduates is now a board member and volunteers as a clerical worker for us. There is another volunteer who does grant proposal writing and bookkeeping for us. I'm grateful but we need money to pay a professional. I'd rather have a staff member who can do all those things who is here all the time."

Dr. Covelli said there was one other very important staff member, and her name is Nelli Covelli.

"Nelli Covelli?!" I asked. "Is that your wife?"

He chuckled and said, "Nelli is a blond lab, a seeing-eye dog. She's the best thing that ever happened to me. I got her six years ago."

Talking about Nelli was a sweet part of our initial conversation before I met him in person. Frankly, Dr. Covelli's work is of such a serious nature where everything is at stake for his clients, but our chat about Nelli was pure delight. His voice also took flight when he spoke of how proud he is of their clients, almost all of whom have taken control of their lives and have gotten steady jobs thanks to Arriba's efforts, thereby regaining their dignity in their new land.

In an endearing and humble way, Dr. Covelli insisted that Arriba be the focus of my essay, rather than himself. Though he didn't want to speak about himself, the success of Arriba is also about Dr. Covelli and his vision for a better way.

He finally relented and said, "I'm one of those people who discovers a cause, a mission, a calling, and then embraces it with a passion. I created Arriba. My passion was to help immigrants with disabilities because no one was helping them, and they wouldn't fit into any other mold that existed here. I discovered there was a need here and therefore founded Arriba as the vehicle by which these people could be helped, the same way as I discovered I could help myself."

As a young person, Dr. Covelli recognized that he was blessed with certain advantages in life, namely his ability to seek a fine education. "I'm an Italian from Colombia," he said. "I was a professional in South America and decided to come here. I had education and come from a cultured background. So I didn't need too much guidance."

It's more than that, however. Dr. Covelli is the visionary in our midst who saw immigrants like himself and wanted to be of help to them. In this case, this visionary in our midst is blind. He knows quite a bit about overcoming challenges. Having earned his Ph.D. in educational administration and higher education from Southern Illinois University, Dr. Covelli was also a Fulbright scholar and received his M.S.W. from Washington University in St. Louis.

Trying to summarize what motivates him, Dr. Covelli said, "It's not a religious, spiritual thing. It's a thing of justice, to create social justice. It's not fair for these people to be disabled and not have access to services that other disabled people have. They come to this country in good health condition. They become disabled here in this country. Because they're immigrants and their legalization was pending, they had no recourse. For whatever reason, they become disabled. They lose their job, and they become outcast and so they come here to Arriba.

"I saw it as a national social problem. I got involved way before that. Before Arriba, these people were going into emergency rooms, and I knew that if only a few things would have been in place, they wouldn't have such problems. I got involved with the Americans for Disabilities Act, but they left out immigrants with disabilities. Nothing is perfect, always room for improvement. I was also one of the creators of the Hispanic Agenda, which is a document created after the Mount Pleasant riots of 1991. That agenda called for programs for immigrants in Washington, D.C.

"I got involved as an advisor during health care reform in the Clinton years. Nothing was implemented; Hillary's health care plan failed, and the people kept suffering and living on the margins of society. Many became homeless and had no access to anything. That is when I conceived the idea of starting Arriba." He emphasized, "That's a vehicle to be part of society. It's a thirst for justice not for me—a thirst for justice for others."

Daniel Jones, Arriba's employment training specialist, helps the clients with job training and job placement. Everybody calls him Danny, and he loves his job and said of Dr. Covelli, "He's a pioneer in the disability arena. And he has a big heart, really cares about the people he serves."

Describing his job, Danny said, "Sometimes one of our clients will call about something other than their employment. But we don't send them away because we only deal with employability issues and it's not our job to help with their living arrangements or medical care. We help them, period. We want them to succeed."

Arriba's clients are Hispanic and Caribbean. They are from the Dominican Republic, Puerto Rico, Cuba, Virgin Islands, Haiti, Philippines, and all other Spanish and Portuguese-speaking countries. Arriba started as an agency with a program called Community Adjustment Training (or CAT) and evolved to include job employability.

Arriba's success rate with employment is off the charts. Dr. Covelli explained, "Nationally, the U.S. Bureau of Labor Statistics shows unemployment among Hispanics with disabilities is higher than 70 percent. Nationwide, among all Americans with severe disabilities, unemployment is higher than 82 percent. From that, you can assume that the success rate of employment programs to help these people is very low. Therefore, the Arriba program's 90 percent success rate is tremendous."

Unemployed and hopeless are the words that best describe their clients *before* they come to Arriba. Dr. Covelli summarized the beauty of the program by saying, "They've been disabled for years and without a job, without any hope, desperate, and wishing for death. Some of them have attempted suicide. And they come to Arriba, and their lives change completely. They have renewed hope, and they have life itself. To see their faces of desperation and despair when they start our program and then to see their faces at graduation is amazing. Their whole spirit has changed. Our concern is to employ them at the living wage, which is about $10 an hour. All our clients, who get placed with employment, get to be employed at that or at approximately that level."

One key to its success is that Dr. Covelli, Danny, and the volunteers work with their clients one-on-one, and they recognize the different levels of impediments, which may include language, cultural, and/or trauma. Dr. Covelli added, "Also the key to success besides helping them one-on-one is that we assist them every step of the way from intake to placement. We know them personally. I do counseling with them, and Danny helps them fill out applications, and he goes with them to interviews. We provide them all the support that they need."

Envisioning a better tomorrow, he said softly, "Someday, I would like to have our own facility for our programs. Expand the facilities. Once you discover a need, and the need is met, then the need grows and you want to help them all. We need more than one instructor; we need three or four support staff in the office. Choosing a location that is accessible by public transportation and physical accessibility has to be a factor."

Then with gusto, wanting to help more and more clients, Dr. Covelli added, "I'm not going to be satisfied until we have a million dollars in the annual budget. I am working day and night and with a bunch of volunteers. We need more money to give shape and form to assign these tasks to staff. We would like to have a facility with a workshop where we would be able to employ people here, people who cannot be hired elsewhere due to their very low functioning skills and/or due to multiple disabilities. The need is enormous!"

Working directly with the families, Arriba is committed to saving the family unit as well. If the adults are not helped, then their children are that much more susceptible to problems in school and possibly becoming part of a gang. Investing in programs like Arriba gives immigrants a fighting chance to assimilate and succeed, thereby saving society money it does not have to spend on incarceration and rehab.

Arriba exists because an immigrant, who happens to have a disability, saw a need and decided to make a difference. Dr. Covelli and the story of Arriba touch a chord as he describes those who are among the most vulnerable in our fast-paced world. What he does not say is how all of us are not that far removed from the plight of his clients. From my point of view, we are all immigrants in this nation of plenty. After all, except for the Native Americans, once we were all immigrants. Dr. Covelli probably thinks I have forgotten what that means, or perhaps that I have never known. But I know my family's struggles.

It was not that long ago that my mother's family came to the United States in 1904. One of seven children, my mother's mother was a toddler when she arrived in Boston. My sisters and cousins and I called her Nanoo, and we were incredibly close. When I knew Nanoo, she was elegant, beautiful with stunning white hair; she was a wonderful grandmother. With a heart of gold, she made us all quilts and booties to keep us warm, but her early life was not easy. I knew she never had very much money, and yet, she was generous and always enjoyed life, especially when playing the piano. For a short time, she lived with us in our home when I was around five years old. Even when she didn't live with us, she was often at the house and ate dinner with us.

But when Nanoo was a child, her parents struggled to put enough food on the table. Nanoo was about three years old when her family was living in Poland, Lithuania, and Russia. The boundaries kept shifting, so her parents were forced to move now and then. In addition to poverty, the Cossacks on occasion ravaged villages, burning homes and killing Jews, something very similar to what was going on in Central America when many fled to the United States and very similar to what is going on right now in the Darfur region of Sudan. Nanoo's parents decided to flee all that they knew for a better life in America. Her father barely escaped conscription in the Russian-Japanese War in the early 1900s, a war in which almost all the Russian soldiers were killed. Nanoo's father somehow managed to escape the war and fled to Boston where he found some menial work and shelter. He sent word, and Nanoo's mother immigrated to Boston with two toddlers. Soon they would have five more children.

Nanoo's father became a peddler in America, one day selling rags and another day carrying a block of ice up to a customer's fifth floor walk-up. Once they were old enough, some of his sons would accompany him. Nanoo's brother, my Uncle David, told me they got a nickel or a dime for each block of ice. Other days, Nanoo's father sold apples out of his wooden cart that he pushed down the streets of Salem or Boston. My Nanoo's mother might have worked as well, but she was clearly quite the community activist, working for women's suffrage and organizing the poor in her neighborhood of Boston. She registered poor people to vote and urged them to vote for Mayor Curley, a man who had his share of corruption charges but who also fought for programs for the poor of Boston. If a new immigrant had nowhere to go, Nanoo's mother helped the stranger with some food and with a place to stay for a night. All this even though she and her husband had seven children to feed.

Nanoo's mother was around my age, in her early forties, when she had her gall bladder out. The surgery went fine, but according to a cousin, she got an infection in bed and died. This was long before the miracle of antibiotics. Nanoo's father died about a year later. Nanoo always said he died of a broken heart. Her parents left behind seven children from ages twenty to ten. When Nanoo's mother died, the funeral cortege for this peasant woman was large. This woman from Poland and Lithuania, who had very little but gave much to her adopted city of Boston and her adopted nation, was truly mourned by the community. In fact, they stopped the funeral cortege at City Hall, a great honor of its time.

In her later years, even though she did not have a great deal, my Nanoo did what she could for the community, and my mother has been involved a great deal with the Jewish and non-Jewish community and continues to be active in public service. Today, my sisters and I are involved at different levels. The acorn doesn't fall far from the tree. I have heard about Nanoo's mother all my life, about caring about the stranger in your midst, about creating a giving life, about doing the right thing.

All of us, except the Native Americans, are merely steps ahead of the immigrants who Dr. Covelli and Arriba serve. We are not that far removed from immigrant status ourselves. Yet it seems so long ago that we don't think about it that way. And even if our families have been here since the 1700s, there but for the grace of God go I.

Our nation of plenty was built on the backs, the sweat, and the dreams of immigrants. As the Statue of Liberty reminds us, the huddled masses have a home here—free from persecution, free to realize their potential, and free to make a better life for themselves and their children.

No one said it would be easy, far from it. But to have a disability on top of immigrant status is too much for anyone to bear alone. Arriba is a refuge for that immigrant, a place to launch a new chapter of their lives, a place of friendship and hope. Dr. Covelli had a vision for a better way and made his dream part of the American dream so that other immigrants may have a chance.

Like millions of Americans whose families came to these shores about 100 years ago, I know the stories of my family's struggle to make a life here in America. I can't forget and don't want to forget. When I met some of Dr. Covelli's clients, I could see the hope and fear in their eyes. They reminded me of the struggle my family knew not that long ago, and it made me wonder, Why does it have to be so hard? Dr. Covelli says it shouldn't.

UPDATE ABOUT ARRIBA

THE CATALOGUE FOR Philanthropy selected The Arriba Center for its 2007 catalogue.

After three years, Danny Jones left Arriba in mid-2007. Marleny Diaz joined the staff as a full-time training specialist. Volunteers help with fundraising and reception duties. Many of the volunteers are former clients.

After an illness, Nelli Covelli, at age ten, died in 2008. Ruby, a young Golden Retriever/Labrador mix, is trying to fill Nelli's shoes.

In early 2009, Arriba celebrated its tenth anniversary, and Dr. Covelli and his team marked the occasion not with a big bash, but by reaching another milestone: having worked with more than 2,000 clients in the past decade.

As Dr. Covelli surmised in February of 2009, "Of the 2,000 people we have helped, many of those lives have totally changed because of our intervention, because we helped get them jobs and helped them get back on their feet and become productive members of society who pay taxes. We rescued them from welfare and a possible life of crime. When they become better providers, their children relate better to them. The parent regains that provider role.

Barnes & Noble Booksellers #2867
3651 Jefferson Davis Hwy
Alexandria, VA 22305
703-299-9124

STR:2867 REG:007 TRN:8535 CSHR:Robin B

Visionaries In Our Midst: Ordinary Peopl
  9730076184/199   T1
  (1 @ 19.95)   19.95

Subtotal   19.95
Sales Tax T1 (6.000%)   1.20
TOTAL   21.15
AMEX   21.15
  Card#: XXXXXXXXXXX5000
  Expdate: XX/XX
  Auth: 504313
  Entry Method: Swiped

A MEMBER WOULD HAVE SAVED   2.00

             Thanks for shopping at
                Barnes & Noble

101.32A   10/06/2013 03:02PM

CUSTOMER COPY

title and only if defective. NOOKs purchased from other retailers or sellers are returnable only to the retailer or seller from which they are purchased, pursuant to such retailer's or seller's return policy. Magazines, newspapers, eBooks, digital downloads, and used books are not returnable or exchangeable. Defective NOOKs may be exchanged at the store in accordance with the applicable warranty.

Returns or exchanges will not be permitted (i) after 14 days or without receipt or (ii) for product not carried by Barnes & Noble or Barnes & Noble.com.

Policy on receipt may appear in two sections.

Return Policy

With a sales receipt or Barnes & Noble.com packing slip, a full refund in the original form of payment will be issued from any Barnes & Noble Booksellers store for returns of undamaged NOOKs, new and unread books, and unopened and undamaged music CDs, DVDs, and audio books made within 14 days of purchase from a Barnes & Noble Booksellers store or Barnes & Noble.com with the below exceptions:

A store credit for the purchase price will be issued (i) for purchases made by check less than 7 days prior to the date of return, (ii) when a gift receipt is presented within 60 days of purchase, (iii) for textbooks, or (iv) for products purchased at Barnes & Noble College bookstores that are listed for sale in the Barnes & Noble Booksellers inventory management system.

Opened music CDs/DVDs/audio books may not be returned, and can be exchanged only for the same title and only if defective. NOOKs purchased from other retailers or sellers are returnable only to the retailer or seller from which they are purchased, pursuant to such retailer's or seller's return policy. Magazines, newspapers, eBooks, digital downloads, and used books are not returnable or exchangeable. Defective NOOKs may be exchanged at the store in accordance with the applicable warranty.

"There are two days of joy at Arriba that happen frequently. One is when we graduate a new class, and the other is when we find a job for one of our graduates. It is estimated that in D.C. alone there are between 12,000 and 15,000 Hispanics with disabilities. At the pace we are going, it would take us at Arriba fifty years to help all of those people. We would need to double or triple our budget to grow and advance our cause to make a real dent. We do what we can, but we would like to do more. What if we could help more people? That's what I reflect upon and hope for."

Contact information for Arriba:

Cristobal Covelli, Ph.D.
Founder/Executive Director
The Arriba Center for Independent Living
1010 Vermont Avenue, NW, Suite 516
Washington, D.C. 20005
Phone: 202-393-7490
Web site: www.arribacenter.org

If you like Arriba, you might be interested in these organizations:

1) Casa Latina
   Seattle, Washington
   Web site: www.casa-latina.org
   Phone: 206-956-0779

2) CentroNia
   Washington, D.C.
   Web site: www.centronia.org
   Phone: 202-332-4200

3) Focus: HOPE
   Detroit, Michigan
   Web site: www.focushope.edu
   Phone: 313-494-4300

4) Neighborhood House
   St. Paul, Minnesota
   Web site: www.neighb.org
   Phone: 651-789-2500

5) Towards Employment
   Cleveland, Ohio
   Web site: www.towardsemployment.org
   Phone: 216-696-5750

6) Upwardly Global
   San Francisco, California
   Web site: www.upwardlyglobal.org
   Phone: 415-834-9901

LIFE PIECES TO MASTERPIECES

Creating Art...Changing Lives

LIFE
Something that we all experience
But can't always control...

Like a box of chocolates
OR
a raisin in the sun...
Ready to explode!

I'm too young to know.

PIECES
The good, the bad, the unspoken...
The joys, the pain, the broken...
Frag-ments of some-thing once whole...

TO
A preposition whose purpose is making a connection...
Somehow incomplete without a direction...
The glue...

MASTERPIECES
Our lives in living color...
Our blood through a kaleidoscope...
OUR EXPRESSIONS OF HOPE!

— A Life Pieces To Masterpieces poem

OOK AT THINGS differently. Achieve something beautiful together. Be part of something that believes in reaching higher. The boys in Life Pieces To Masterpieces (or LPTM) are doing all of those things. They cherish Life Pieces and are in a different place because of it.

To know the impact of Life Pieces To Masterpieces, all you have to do is meet the young black men of the program. Their words, their facial expressions, their gratitude say it all.

When I walked in, a group of eight young African American men was hovering over a laptop, in serious discussion at a long set of tables with their fearless leader, Mary Brown. They all stood to introduce themselves, and each welcomed me with a warm handshake. That room and their headquarters were orderly but not fancy. Life Pieces rents the top floor of a dilapidated, dusty, old building, which sits on a hill in a troubled part of the District. Displaying obvious defects, the walls and ceilings were in need of a fresh coat of paint. The different-colored curtains were a bit tattered and barely hanging onto a rod. The lighting in the hall and the rooms was inconsistent and reminiscent of an old Gene Hackman movie like *The French Connection*. Despite the flaws, everything was serene, beautiful, and warm. The people in the room made it so. The large, colorful paintings on the walls told a story of hope.

Mary Brown, the co-founder and executive director of Life Pieces, smiled broadly as she watched each young man shake my hand. She was in the process of meeting with this group about being mentors for the young boys in the new class. Back in 1996, most of these young men were the young boys who needed a mentor. Now, eleven years later in 2007, they were on the cusp of becoming mentors themselves. They had made it and were eager to give back. I soon learned that there was one thing they all have in common: Today, they are men with a plan.

One by one, the young men opened up about the importance of Life Pieces in their own lives. Seneca Wells, now twenty-six, got involved with Life Pieces as a senior at H.D. Woodson High School in the District. He went through the Life Pieces program eight years ago, became a volunteer, and then started working there. Recently, he directed an impressive Life Pieces exhibit at the ARCH Training Center (or the ARCH), which provides support and vocational training for young people and adults in Anacostia. One large piece of art had sneakers cut in half and attached to the canvas. As Mary explained, the sneakers represent a life cut short in the streets. That's why you often see sneakers tied together and thrown over a wire. Devoted to Life Pieces, Seneca is thrilled to be a fine arts student at the Corcoran College of Art and Design in Washington.

To him and all of those gathered, Life Pieces is much more than a non-profit with a mission to help them realize their potential through artistic expression. For Seneca, it runs far deeper. Life Pieces showed him how to focus on his interest in the arts. Getting into the Corcoran's famous and competitive art program was no easy feat. Larry Quick, Life Pieces' other co-founder, made an introduction for Seneca to help make that possible. Usually a man of few words, Seneca wanted to ensure that I understood what Life Pieces had done for him, his art, and his education. The gratitude was immeasurable.

Another participant in Life Pieces was James Wise, who was on his way to Carolina to see his mother preach at a church over Labor Day weekend. He walked into the Life Pieces headquarters with a suitcase, his trademark exuberance, and positive outlook. With a sense of confidence at fifteen, he is tall for a tenth grader at Suitland High School in Maryland. This is his third year in Life Pieces, and he says that he "hopes and plans to go to college in New York to study the arts and culinary arts."

James explained, "I joined Life Pieces To Masterpieces because it kept me out of trouble. I heard about it from word of mouth from another organization, Kiwanis. A lady from Kiwanis introduced my grandfather to Life Pieces, and I've been going here ever since."

"Any lessons for life that you will carry with you?" I asked.

"Always be yourself. No more masks."

"Did you feel like you were wearing a mask?"

"Oh yeah, you know the Alpha Male thing trying to be tough, old. Lots of pressure everywhere. Life Pieces showed us things and helped me experience lots of things. Without the grades, I can't experience anything. I can't go to things without grades. They'll take us to a national park. Without grades, I limit myself from getting places."

James lives with his father and says that he sees his mother all the time. He is the oldest of three kids in his family. Of his brother and sister, he said, "They have experienced Life Pieces, but they live with my mother and can't get over here all the time."

James is unusual, I would soon learn, because he is one of the only ones in Life Pieces who still has a father.

Then, Terry Johnson, age eighteen, stepped up. A graduate of the Friendship Collegiate Academy, he is now studying music production at the University of the District of Columbia (or UDC). Wearing glasses with incredibly thick lenses, Terry has a sincerity and ease about things in his voice. Mainly, he is eager for his future to happen. He has been in Life Pieces since the fourth grade and he's now a mentor.

"But why get involved in Life Pieces?" I asked.

"It kept me out of trouble, 'cause at first I was just in fights, altercations. When I came up here, I just saw my dream. I wanted to be into music. They encouraged that dream."

Terry seemed so at peace and thoughtful; it was difficult to see him as troubled. His sister, Monique, and cousin, Andre, also became attached to Life Pieces. He explained, "Monique and Andre came up here to look for me. They followed me up here and that's how they got involved. They just kept coming ever since."

Explaining the essence of the teamwork and life lessons at Life Pieces, Terry said, "Some people draw what they experience. Some people paint or sketch. Some people are cutting art pieces. All kinds of roles in the art."

To Terry and all of the boys and men of Life Pieces, the art has become a metaphor for working together in this world and making things happen—together. Terry hopes he can make things happen and hopes to transfer to Howard University.

JaVan Precia has been involved with Life Pieces since he was fourteen and at Eastern Senior High School in the District. He graduated in 2000, and now at age twenty-five, he works as a graphic designer and exhibit specialist at the National Geospatial-Intelligence Agency. With his security clearance, JaVan works on Web and visual media. The job starts at 6 A.M., and he's at his desk by 5:45. He said he wakes up at 4:30 every morning and has been working there for seven years. He's full-time there with benefits.

"I love computers," he said. "My dream job would be dealing with video games because that combines computer and art. My first love is art."

Somebody razzed JaVan about something and everyone cracked up, including JaVan, who looks like he could be a linebacker for the Washington Redskins. He explained, "I'm a comedian; I like to keep everybody laughing." He paused and added quietly, "I'm now a mentor and giving back. Life Pieces taught me how to be a leader. It means a lot. It taught me how to be a man, to change my negative energy into positive energy and just dealing with the public in general. It helped me grow and exposed me to a lot of new things."

Every one of these fellows has a raw authenticity. It seems to come from Mary. She has a presence, a way of seeing the best in others and helping them see it as well. She does more than believe in someone; she shows them the way—gently. The boys/young men need that. In addition to not having a father who is in their lives, they don't always have a guiding force at home, someone to watch over them. Some of them raise themselves.

For a young man who has no father, questions hang in the air. At times, there is anger that at times morphs into guilt and back again to anger; sometimes it's anger at themselves and other times, their lot in life and what they could have done differently. They blame themselves. One young man has to cope with a father who committed suicide. He wondered aloud to Mary, "If I had been better, there would have been no way he would want to leave me." He was a toddler at the time and yet he wondered if there was something he did wrong, if he could have been better in school or at home, if he could have kept his room neater or told his father he loved him more often. The fact is that most of the boys in the program don't really know their fathers. Yet, still they wonder, because maybe their dad would have stayed. Sometimes there is abuse, neglect, or both. All this and living in subsidized housing and dealing with the rough streets of Washington. Each young man has a story that is complicated and at times tragic through no fault of his own. They're just trying to make their way. The more I hear from the boys and young men, the more I realize that Life Pieces has become their family. As Mary said, "They're with all kinds of parents. And those parents are not always present, emotionally or physically." Mary takes the scattered pieces of the children's young lives, and together they create a life that is a masterpiece.

Maurice Kie (pronounced like "pie") is a big brother in more ways than one. First, he is a big guy who is more like a teddy bear. He is not only a big brother to many of the boys at Life Pieces; his little brother, Donnell Kie, is in Life Pieces. One of the original boys in the program in 1996, Maurice was one of the four in the room when Mary and Larry came up with the idea and name of Life Pieces. At that time, Maurice was twelve. Now almost twenty-two, he is a sophomore at UDC studying elementary education. He plans to teach and then go into administration.

"My mother was in some of the community programs, and she found out about Larry. And he started working with the boys, and I was one of those original six or seven," he began.

"Now you're a mentor?" I asked.

"A great mentor!" Malik Fitzgerald, sitting nearby, chimed in.

Maurice beamed with a smile and looked down for a second and then over at Malik, who is fifteen and in the ninth grade at D.C.'s McKinley Technology High School. Malik has been in Life Pieces since he was six years old. Now he is a mentor-in-training, and he cannot wait to be a mentor and recalled, "At my school, they picked two boys from each grade level [to be in Life Pieces]. I started coming and it became part of my life."

Planning to be an entrepreneur, Malik plans to go to college and go into broadcast and technology and media arts.

Maurice's little brother, Donnell, walked into the room. Maurice, who is Donnell's guardian, explained, "He started hanging out and saw I was having fun. He was one of the youngest."

To Maurice, it's all about respect and exposing yourself to different things. As if he were a young philosopher or counselor, he said, "There's something different besides the environment you're living in. There are different types of neighborhoods all over the world. If you're truly happy with your situation, then stay there. But if you think there's a chance you can improve it, then do that."

Originally the baby of the group, Donnell is now sixteen and in the eleventh grade at Ballou Senior High School in Washington's Anacostia neighborhood. Tall and wiry, he gets very good grades and has been part of Life Pieces since he was four. With a full heart, Donnell said without hesitation, "Life Pieces is like a second family. I've been coming to the program for so long. It fits into my daily regimen—like everyday things like brushing your teeth or taking a shower. It's every day. Good to have an additional family support. I try to be here every day. Now that I'm in high school, I'm involved with community-based organizations and college prep and all of my volunteer experiences.

"When I grow up, I want to be a fashion designer and also a businessperson. I want to also own real estate. That'll be part of my business. As soon as I turn eighteen, I'm going to go for my first property while I'm in college and have money coming in."

"So you're a man with a plan."

"Yes, I have to have one," he said with conviction. I got the feeling that in ten years, Donnell Kie will be established. All of the boys had that same determination and steel core. It was palpable. And it goes back to Mary Brown, a woman of forty-three. Looking at her face is like looking into a majestic being, a face and voice akin to Leontyne Price, an energetic demeanor that is one part Whoopi Goldberg and one part Oprah. Being around Mary is like being pulled into a force for good.

If one word had to be chosen to describe Mary Brown, it would have to be *determination*. She is literally fighting and demanding for these boys to seize their chance at life, for the world to see the beauty they can create for all to share. She is more than a mentor; she is a beacon.

To be in Life Pieces, each kid or young man must agree to the core principles of the program. First, he must be a gentleman, which means respect for yourself and for others. Are you caring? Second, he must be an athlete, which means taking care of your body and being a team player. Third, he must be a scholar, which means hungering for truth and knowledge. And fourth, he must be an artist, which means knowing that we all have the power to create our future and to look at living as an art. Life Pieces has a motto, "Thoughts, words, actions determine destiny." Whatever you can control, Mary says to them, you need to control that. In other words, take responsibility for your life and then you will control it.

Life Pieces emphasizes a four-part process: connect, create, contribute, and celebrate. Mary says they have this process so that the boys won't have that feeling of being a victim. She explained, "Connect. That means going inside yourself and being introspective and listening to your heart and to the stories of others. That leads to empathy and that feeds your creativity. Create. Through visual arts, give voice to all the things you've experienced, the stories in your life, your dreams. Can you express yourself? The deeper level of this is to teach the boys that their thoughts create their destiny in life. Our boys experience so many horrific things. We try to help them. So we use whatever their challenges are as fuel to create something positive in life. Acknowledge the pain. Teach them to talk about it. Don't allow it to consume you. Communication is a positive attribute. Young black men are having trouble expressing themselves. On a daily basis, most are born without male role models. And most who are there, well they don't have *real* role models. Next is to contribute. Share your voices with the outside world through visual arts. No matter what, you always have something to share. This is where we teach the boys about community service and helping in the family. Celebrate. Have gratitude. Be grateful for the sharing. Acknowledge what everyone brings to the table. The deeper level of this part is to look at every challenge or obstacle in life as an opportunity and always have gratitude. Every situation is an opportunity to grow. Be thankful for everything. This goes right back to creativity. It all comes full circle. We have a saying at Life Pieces, which is: There's no such thing as failure—only opportunity."

Mary doesn't do all the work by herself. Her right hand, as she calls him, is Ben Johnson, the nonprofit's director of development. In 1999, Ben was interning at a rehab center as a counselor. His D.C. friends told him about Life Pieces, and he started volunteering and it turned into a full-time job.

"It's meant a great deal. I've learned a lot," he said quietly. "It's like a family. That's the best part."

Hearing his last comments as she walked into the room, Mary sat down and added, "Let me tell ya. When Larry was making a decision to move on and be an artist, and he has every right to be an artist, here was Ben and he literally took on the fundraising, then mentoring of the boys, cleaning up, being here to open and close, fixing lunch, etc. And then he connected his family and they got involved."

"I have three brothers and a sister, and they volunteer and help [here] as they can," Ben interjected.

"So just boys in the program?" I asked Ben, knowing that I had seen a few girls running around.

"Yes, technically, but we often have brothers who are supposed to look after their little brothers and sisters."

Today in 2007, Life Pieces serves a total of two hundred kids. Around twenty-five to thirty of the kids/young men are part of a core group. Life Pieces has two main year-round programs. Mary explained, "Life Pieces To Masterpieces Central, or LPTM Central, is where our boys come here every day after school and they receive homework assistance and tutoring. We also expose them to yoga, meditation and leadership training with art expression being the core to everything just mentioned. Life Pieces To Masterpieces Express, or LPTM Express, is where we bring part of the curriculum to elementary, middle and high schools, and we've been piloting our program at the Maya Angelou Public Charter School in Washington. We have about twenty-five boys in that program with about fifteen we can track. We are also at Oak Hill on Saturday. Oak Hill is D.C.'s juvenile detention facility. We're one of the elective courses there. LPTM Express is also being piloted nationally with NeighborWorks America. Basically, we have young people who are apprentices in the LPTM Central program, and then they become senior apprentices. We train them to facilitate and co-facilitate the training. They learn to create a power-point presentation for our workshops with other youth. The workshops are also for teachers, community organizers, and adults."

Back in the mid-1990s, Mary Brown knew that there had to be something just for boys. It had to be something that involved the arts. And not just observing the arts but also creating it. So in 1996, she and Larry Quick, her beau who became her husband, founded Life Pieces To Masterpieces. Though the marriage did not work out, together they formed something that has lasted.

With a staff of eight now, Mary has watched the tiny nonprofit blossom. It's all about the children, the arts, and trying to show the kids a way to dream of the possible. With the energy of a freight train, Mary's commitment to the boys and young men of Washington is clearly in the marrow of her bones. She can make anyone, who is willing to listen, believe it, too. Without any pretension or awareness of her compelling words, Mary tells it like it is and runs the nonprofit with grace and humor.

She recalled, "At the time we started Life Pieces, I was working as a consultant for nonprofits in the District in conjunction with something that was called the Children's Trust Neighborhood Initiative, or CTNI. Larry was at the Corcoran College of Art and Design. Later, he graduated from the Corcoran with a degree in fine arts. His roots were in Kenilworth [the public housing complex in Southeast D.C.]. He was eight years younger than I and had a completely different life experience.

"As a boy, he had to deal with the domestic abuse of his mother, having to understand being called the man of the house," she said. "Early on, you're being called a man and having no idea what that is. If I'm the man of the house, and yet I'm in my room with thin walls in the public housing apartment, and I can hear my mother being beaten to a pulp in the next room. And then in the morning to see your mother bruised and battered and worn out. And then you go to your mother and say, 'Let me set him straight. Let me get back at him.' And then, in turn, you get beaten by your mother. Dealing with scenarios like that. Throw in substance abuse. The whole history in their own individual lives growing up in abusive settings.

"At first, Larry was a boxer who was a seven-time Golden Glove champion, but what he would keep secret is his love of art. The boxing kept him positive, but his secret was that he loved art and drawing. He didn't tell anyone because in the neighborhood, they would call him 'soft.' So he would kind of hide it. What art would do, it would create an expression for him. Whatever he didn't have, a house with a mother and father, he would draw it. And by drawing it, he would have everything he could imagine. He was talented. He really is an amazing artist. He tried for the Olympics as a boxer! But he didn't get selected. After that, he decided to throw himself into art and went to the Corcoran. And that's when I met him. I enjoyed his story and I found him so magnetic.

"I knew what it was to have a loving mom and dad, to sit down at a family dinner table every night, the one time every day everybody would gather and share about your day. You talk about your challenges and you get a feel for everyone's moods. I knew what it was to know that kind of care. It was the first time for me to experience someone who didn't have that kind of upbringing. In my home, we said goodnight to each other. It was a nightly ritual. Have dinner, clean up the dishes, finish our homework, do our chores, and then our dad, who was a high school biology teacher, would go over our homework. And once that was done, we did our nightly prayer and then went to sleep. That was my life growing up.

"The thing that would wake us up every morning would be the smell from the kitchen. My mom would be in the kitchen making bacon, or eggs, home-made biscuits. My mom made the best buttermilk banana biscuits and cinnamon buns. That's why we were all so chubby. She would be in the kitchen, and she would be singing in the kitchen, 'Wake up you sleepy heads. Time to get out of bed.' Everything was always fresh and clean and organized."

Mary chuckled to herself, for she hadn't thought about her mother's morning singing in years. She had a golden time growing up in New Orleans. There were six siblings in all, and Mary was the baby. Her voice suddenly lowered as she said that two of her siblings had died of cancer in recent years. Like the boys in Life Pieces, she knows loss.

"My siblings and I say the same that we were probably the most fortunate kids on the planet, the best parents on the planet. To have the parents that we had—it was amazing. I would see how my dad would treat my mother and how my mother would treat my father. I know that they had disagreements but never in front of us. Whatever event we had, they were there. If you had an event, you knew you could look out and see a big smile. That was our reality.

"So when I met Larry, my heart went out to him. He was extremely handsome. I was very moved to meet someone who had overcome so much, working towards overcoming so much. His artwork was so amazing. That's how we started.

"I was working with older teens at CTNI, and there were younger boys who would come around and act out, and I wondered, Why are they doing that? Larry said, 'They're bored. They want to be a part of whatever the CTNI Center had going on, the activities with the older boys.'

"When Larry would come to pick me up, he would actually entertain the younger boys. He would take them to McDonald's. I observed what he was doing with them.

"First, he made a connection with the boys and they trusted him. It just so happened that he was this young, budding artist at the Corcoran. Young people will learn anything. If he had been an accountant, they would have been interested in that. But here he was this artist, and they looked up to him. Keep in mind the culture about art.

"They would all get on the Metro and go to his studio at the Corcoran. So you would have Larry and these five or six boys from the neighborhood walking through the Corcoran and learning about art. They loved it; they absolutely loved it. And you don't often see little boys, ages eleven or twelve, walking through the Corcoran, not like that and not back then.

"Larry and I were living together, and the boys were coming over during the weekend. Larry began to share his art form with them, using canvas and acrylics with them to show them how to use it. It wasn't kiddie art like Crayolas. He was teaching them how to sketch out their ideas, using canvas as fabric, and he would use his grandma's sewing machine to sew the canvases together.

"That's how we got the name for Life Pieces. We were brainstorming. Larry, myself, Maurice Kie, who was one of the boys, and Marlene Foltz, a friend. 'Let's do a nonprofit! We can do it,'" Mary chuckled at the innocence of it all. "My brother, Robert, suggested the development of the nonprofit. He was head of CTNI, and they actually incubated the idea of Life Pieces and got us going.

"It was Larry's art form that inspired the name. It was the way he created art that was a metaphor for life. It's that we all come in as blank canvases. We don't choose our family or our culture. We randomly have color applied to us. Different experiences we have in life could be likened to splashes of paint, and then sometimes you have things that cut you or rip you. Why did that happen to me? These cuts in life—whether it be divorce, abuse, or neglect—life pieces to masterpieces. It's saying that you can take this hand that has been dealt to you in life and you have the innate creative ability to transform it to be whatever you want it to be. You can make life pieces to masterpieces. You have that power. You can make masterpieces out of your life pieces. That is what inspired the name...in our little apartment in Southwest [D.C.]."

Together, Larry and Mary wanted the boys to know that you don't have to be a victim.

As Mary put it, "The boys felt like we were a family. That's how it felt. Life Pieces focuses on young men and boys. It's from Larry's life and his experiences as a young black male growing up in public housing in Washington, D.C. Plus my part of it is that I knew what love was and how love looked in a family setting and knew how to create that for the boys, that sense of security for them. I think that was very healing for Larry. Larry's life showed me how to be more compassionate, gave me an opportunity to share what my parents had imparted to me all my life.

"We began to grow and Life Pieces began to grow. Larry was serving as the executive director, but all along, he was saying, 'I'm an artist.' And it kept growing. It wasn't just the seven boys anymore. And there were art presentations and then more boys wanting to come.

"My focus was building organizational development. While Larry was serving as a role model, I was putting the organization together, fundraising, creating materials, etc.

"We were having some challenges. I think it was too much. At the end of the day, we felt the mission was central. The mission of Life Pieces is bigger than either one of us. We may have to step to the side, so it can continue. Larry was still finding himself and still exploring, and he was feeling like a role model and yet not perfect. He can make mistakes.

"He moved on. He now has remarried and has a wonderful marriage. He still comes in and works with the boys who are really interested in the visual arts."

Running a nonprofit requires passion with a large dose of reality and commitment to running a nonprofit "business." Ultimately, Larry wanted to share his love of art with the boys. He didn't really want to run a nonprofit. In retrospect, if he could have become the artistic director or artistic consultant, then he might have been happier. But running a nonprofit is like being one of those people at the circus who is keeping a bunch of plates spinning on a bunch of thin sticks all at the same time. It's a lot of juggling.

Mary suddenly had to rethink her own role. She said, "I was raised this good Catholic girl where you stand by your man. Because of my upbringing, you stick to it to the end. After Larry and I decided to separate and divorce, we had to try to explain it to the boys, and one of the boys said, 'So, Ms. Mary, you're going to leave us, too?'" She paused. "We had to explain that Larry wasn't really leaving Life Pieces. It was tough. It's almost like being a single parent. A few of those apprentices that learned Larry's art have stayed in touch with Larry and Life Pieces. That was about five or six years ago. At the time, we had twenty-five boys. I stuck with it and pulled it together. I learned about how an organization can be defined by an individual."

Mary soon learned the pluses and minuses when one individual dominates the scene. Without Larry out in front, things suddenly had to change. As Mary recalled, "I had always worked in the background. Larry was the one doing the media, and I was in the background. Then I decided that the mission is first and foremost. I still like to be low-key and let the work speak for itself. So much of the organization was tied to Larry's personality, which is crazy because nobody's perfect.

"Today, I have a great board and a great advisory board. We have a finance committee that handles the development. We have a strategic communications plan.

"We put our mission and the boys out front with the entire team and a family approach. So it's not just one person. It's normally a group of boys with mentors and board members. Now we are developing a written curriculum and intergenerational training with mentoring.

"I could work with youth development elsewhere. People call and ask, 'Can you start a Life Pieces here?' If we could somehow create a curriculum, then others could use our methodology and keep their identity and apply it to their program. We want to stay committed to our area in D.C. We are really just scratching the surface still. We would love to share what we do. Our approach is very humanistic. Any group could use what we do, but we don't want to franchise."

Looking back, Mary surmised, "Years ago, we were working out of a shoebox, and it kept growing. Ensuring that the work was being used well for the boys, I knew I needed a team, especially after Fair Chance." (As mentioned in the chapter about The Fishing School, Fair Chance is a successful, local nonprofit that selects a few D.C. nonprofits each year and gives those organizations, free of charge, a year of intense nonprofit capacity building and lessons in management and strategizing.)

"Fair Chance really invigorated me. That helped me tremendously," she said enthusiastically. "It helped me to see the mission and have the whole team involved. It was good for me, and I now have a wonderful finance committee."

At first, Mary's background would not seem perfect for nonprofit management, but the one thing that is always critical she had down pat. She had a committed heart, and she credits her parents for her moral compass.

Shrugging, she laughed, "I have a biology degree and here I am running Life Pieces. The reason I know so much about youth development was more [about] the volunteerism over the years. My parents always volunteered ever since I was little, and my siblings and I would see hungry people and we would give blankets and go to meetings and learn how to make a difference. My parents would be involved with campaigning, and I was licking envelopes in elementary school for candidates. I couldn't wait to grow up and vote. 'I want to do that,' meaning vote. That's how I learned about working for nonprofits. There was on-the-job training, and I had responsibility for different roles."

Mary's networking skills with the major foundations in the region have helped her nonprofit. First, she credits Kathy Freshley at the Meyer Foundation. (The Eugene and Agnes E. Meyer Foundation is a major Washington foundation named for the parents of Katharine Graham, the now-deceased publisher of the *Washington Post*.) Mary insisted, "Kathy is the one who gave Larry and me the steps for managing an effective and responsible nonprofit. She was a *huge* support for me, and that particular foundation has a lot to do with Life Pieces To Masterpieces."

Another big supporter, the Cafritz Foundation, also believed in the importance of incorporating the arts into a mentoring program and gave significantly.

Through the years, Mary has learned to delegate and build a team so she doesn't feel so overwhelmed. But at times, it can still feel overwhelming even though there are so many successes. As she admitted, "It's like being on the front line. Our children are surrounded by a lot of drama. This one was murdered; this one was raped; this one was abused. A lot of drama.

"We had one," she began and then had to pause. "He was the inspiration for an art show currently on exhibit at the ARCH Training Center. His name was Miguel, and his body was found at Lincoln Heights. It was a few years ago. You know the sneakers thrown over the wire? That can mean different things. Shoes are a big thing—a high value on shoes. That inspired the show, *Mile in My Shoes*, our poetry and visual arts exhibit. The boys took tennis shoes and cut them in half and mounted them on canvas. We have a few tennis shoes on wires. And the other side, we have images of different boys in our program. Miguel, he was a child who kept making the wrong decisions," she said softly and with regret in her voice.

"A lot of us make the wrong decisions as a kid," I said. "But in most neighborhoods, that doesn't mean that we'll lose our lives."

Mary agreed, having seen her share of loss in the inner city. She sees how far so many of the boys have come, and she stays focused on those achievements. Her nature is to be hopeful and up, realistic but up. But at times, the losses can grip her.

"It's a feeling of being on that front line. For me, it opened compassion in my heart. Because of a lack of resources, we have to do more with less, but now I have folks working on development because of Fair Chance. I'm now able to use the board more, so we achieve more together. As I said, Ben Johnson is my right hand.

"Twelve years ago, we started off with a $2,000 from my pocket. Our first two grants were from the Hitachi Foundation and the Meyer Foundation, and we now have a reserve fund, thanks to the Meyer Foundation. Today, we have a very aggressive fundraising campaign."

They need one. Their annual budget is now $650,000, but Mary still makes $45,000 a year. More fundraising will hopefully increase that salary so she can stop working "side" jobs to make ends meet.

Mary thinks about all the blessings that the organization has. The Georgetown Law Clinic helped Life Pieces set up something called Individual Development Accounts (or IDAs), which are accounts for college or other training. That way, the kids have funds set aside for their books and living expenses. These resources can help the kids go to college or get training to be a plumber, mechanic, or some other trade.

Citing one recent blessing, Mary was moved by the generosity of a group called the Jewish Youth Philanthropy Institute, through which Jewish youth donated their time and resources to Life Pieces. "The Jewish youth are learning about giving responsibly, getting connected to community. It creates a dialogue around giving, caring, compassion. This is the third time the Jewish Youth Philanthropy Institute has done a community project at a school, and they chose to come to Life Pieces," Mary said, really touched. "All of our young people need to grow up to have compassion and care for others."

"We all need to have a sense of value and worth to create better outcomes for our lives," she surmised. "We need to find better role models for them. A diverse team of mentors would be good so the boys can see manhood from different perspectives. Ben tells the mentors, 'Bring things that you like. Don't come in and be what the kids want.' A man from any background can work with us. The kids enjoy the music and the differences of the diverse group of mentors. We got slapped on the wrist at first, because old school said that brothers should raise brothers. Maybe it's because I'm a woman, but every day, women are raising boys by themselves. I have different people mentoring the boys. I'm working with who I have. The diversity works for us. This summer, I had a group from Georgetown, a total mixture of backgrounds. This works for us. What was done in the past doesn't necessarily work now. For us, we look for the best super-stars.

"Right now, we're learning how to develop a mentor team. The young men I hire to mentor the boys have to have the right skills. We can't just have anybody.

"In my youth, education was a given. 'You are going to college. Non-negotiable.' With my guys, ultimately I want them to have good values, to be able to provide for their family, and to give back." And what is the endless source of her drive, her vision?

As the baby of six children in her own family, Mary is someone who thrives on the many voices in the room. Watching her maneuver around the table and get everyone focused on their action plan is second nature to her. Originally in her family, there were three boys and three girls. Now, with two siblings gone, she has two brothers and a sister left. Through it all, Mary is grateful for her many blessings. But she thinks often of her idyllic childhood. Maybe that's why she is able to share so much with the children of Washington's inner city.

As she recalled, "My dad taught in the New Orleans public schools for forty years. Back in the day, my mom worked at the switchboard at Xavier University so we could go to college for free. And she went there, too! When she died, she was a senior in sociology. Because of her work, all six of us went there. And my mom could really cook. She cooked gumbo and etouffee."

As Mary and I chatted about her mother's favorite dishes, it was the second anniversary of Hurricane Katrina's treacherous course through the Gulf, all but destroying New Orleans. For the past two years, a family from New Orleans has been sharing Mary's home in Northern Virginia. She and her siblings still own their childhood home they and their parents lived in, but Mary said that there was a great deal of damage. After the hurricane and the levees broke, unleashing the deadly water, their New Orleans home was ruined. The shell remains, and they're hoping to rebuild. A nephew was living there at the time of the hurricane, and he escaped in time. Mary said they were also lucky because all of the family heirlooms and photos had been moved out of New Orleans a few years earlier. But the storm's destruction was deeply felt; some of her parents' friends were in a nursing home in the Ninth Ward and perished.

"My mother and dad marched for civil rights. All the different groups—Catholic, Jewish—they all pulled together and walked hand-in-hand," she said, relishing the memory.

"I remember my mother and father being involved. They would always tell stories. My father grew up in Natchez, Mississippi, and my mother in New Iberia, Louisiana, which is just south of New Orleans. They would tell the stories of the whole Jim Crow era. My dad would talk about going to school. The family that his family worked for as sharecroppers liked my dad and they were very nice, but you were still black. It wasn't the N-word. It wasn't negro. It was *nigra*. It was very comfortable and you got comfortable with it. It was *almost* as if it wasn't offensive because it's how you grew up. The family liked him and allowed him to ride to school on the outside of the car on this floorboard or sideboard. He would talk about his hunger for education. He knew that would be the key for him, and he read books on top of books. He was a big reader, and kept us reading, read the newspaper every day. He had many books on civil rights issues. He loved *Invisible*

Man. He would use metaphors from that book to teach us about being connected to people of different backgrounds rather than focusing on how separate we are.

"For some reason, my parents were always open. The nuns that would come to our house were white and sometimes Germanic. And these rabbis would come to our house. They were talking about this movement in terms of education and the schools. My parents were involved with part of the planning of the marches after the bombing of that church where those little girls died."

Born in 1963, Mary was five in 1968—the year that changed many lives.

"And then what I do remember, I remember being in my room," she said, pausing. "And Dad was in their bedroom, and my mother was in the living room where our television was, and she screamed this horrible scream. I'll never forget that. It was like nothing I had ever heard. Dr. King had been killed. The phone ringing and everyone coming together. And then after that, the riots. My dad said everyone is going to go crazy. Those were some somber times. The energy had shifted in our house for several months. We knew something had shifted in our home. My parents wanted things to be the same, but it took a while to go back to normal."

One memory has stayed with Mary all these years. She recalled, "I was going to a Catholic elementary school in New Orleans. It was predominantly white, and some Cubans went to that school. I might have been in the second grade, and my dad was picking me up in our new green and white Plymouth. And I remember a siren going on behind us, and my dad said, 'Don't say anything.' He knew I liked to talk.

"A very young white police officer, who was younger than one of my brothers, came to the car and referred to my daddy as 'boy.'"

Mary paused and changed her voice, saying, "'Boy, you got your driver's license? Do you know how fast you were going on Franklin Avenue, boy?' I watched my dad and saw the side of his jaw move, clench really. 'No suhr,' 'Yes, suhr,' 'I didn't realize, suhr. I'm sorry, suhr,' he was responding to this young white guy.

"What is this? I wanted to fight. You don't call my daddy, 'boy.' Keeping in mind that this is the one who provided for our family, who would go over our homework, who taught at school, who would teach us not to hate. He would say, 'People are people.' It's what King said about the content of character, not feel any form of hatred. And then to be sitting in this car with this young man referring to my dad as 'boy.'

"He didn't cry. But I was sitting to his right, and there was a single tear on his right side of his face.

"That was just something I carried with me. It wasn't until high school that I finally asked him about it. 'Well, Mary,' he said, 'You have to remember I had my little girl in my car, and I didn't want to give anyone a reason to hurt you. So it wasn't about lashing out. I had to make a decision, because I was very angry and very hurt, but I had to think about that you were in that car. If I had tried to argue, I wouldn't have been protecting you.'

"My dad always used to say, 'If you don't stand up for something, you'll fall for anything.' I was fifteen or sixteen, and I felt he had not stood up against that officer. Yet, he had remembered what had happened to those little girls at that church and all the other injustices."

Her dad said she didn't understand. "When he broke it down for me, I understood and I apologized. He was a very courageous person and spoke out about not allowing things to happen. And then my dad set me straight. He didn't have any trouble from me after that. He taught me the difference between knowledge and wisdom. That's how we have the definition of wisdom at Life Pieces To Masterpieces. You can know someone is being racist, and you may have knowledge of the whole reason why racism exists. The question is what are you going to do with that knowledge. Knowledge is based in the past, but wisdom is what carries you into the future. 'Because I care for you as my daughter, I could have fought, but it was that combination of knowledge and wisdom, I made the right decision at that time.' Then Mary added, "That officer probably wanted my dad to fight.

"No suhr, yes suhr, I'm sorry, suhr. I didn't realize, suhr. The officer said something, 'Well, this time, boy, I'll give you a warning.' I had carried that around until I was fifteen or sixteen and he set me straight. That was my only major experience with that direct form of racism."

Except for that moment, Mary's youth sounded golden. She recalled proudly, "I was the president of my eighth grade class. I got along with everybody. I had great friends in Catholic school, which was first through eighth. Then I went to Xavier Prep for high school, also a Catholic school and all girls. My sisters and I went there. In fact, my dad retired from teaching in the public schools and my senior year, he taught me physics at Xavier Prep. That's when we ended up spending even more time together and growing closer. He would wait for me after school to go home. Then I went on to Xavier [University], and I was pre-med. I knew I was going to practice medicine. But I got interested in the community side of things. After college, I got involved in Spa Lady, and someone there introduced me to WAVE, or Work Achievement Values and Education. I went in as a program development associate and a curriculum salesperson. They taught me to handle workshops. I did well with them for seven or eight years. That was when my father was diagnosed with Alzheimer's, and my mother began caring for my dad."

Mary and her sister, Loretta, spent the better part of a year in New Orleans trying to be of help to their parents. She recalled being home and said, "It was the day before Valentine's, and earlier that day, my mother was complaining about not feeling well. She had made a lemon cake for the nurses. We were walking down the hall, and my mother fell down and seized. She hadn't gone to work for a month or so. She had been at the hospital with my dad and wasn't sleeping. Earlier that day, she was crying and was so worried about Dad, but she went to work. After work, we were at the hospital. She kissed my dad on the forehead and then a few minutes later she was gone. The doctors and nurses rushed me into a room while they helped my mother. Then a doctor came in and I'll never forget, he said, 'We did everything we could.' And that moment I realized it's the spirit that makes us who we are.

"Dad knew when we told him what had happened. His face filled with tears. He wanted us to handle the burial quickly. He stayed in the hospital a few more days and then when we were wheeling him into our home, he cried. Fifty-five years of marriage," Mary said, her voice trailed off. Not a year later, Mary and her siblings buried their father.

Mary's parents gave her a strong foundation on which to live a life. She has found the fortitude to give that same foundation to the boys of D.C. Who knows how many of those boys will help others in the future? One young man in Life Pieces, Maurice Kie, recently formed a program that creates opportunities for dialogue between the African American and Latino communities in Washington. So it's already begun. The ripple effect, it keeps going. That's quite a legacy. She's living her life with legacy in mind.

As Mary put it, "Now we have all these boys growing up with Larry's artistic work. And in terms of their development, they have the values that I learned from my parents, the Brown stamp. So it's the combination of Larry's life and my life; it's that whole combination. Here we have these boys growing up in public housing and poverty in the District. It's the values that I learned from my parents; that's the foundation of everything we do for the boys."

A FINAL THOUGHT ABOUT LIFE PIECES TO MASTERPIECES

FOUR MONTHS AFTER my initial meeting with the boys and young men of Life Pieces, I called Mary for an update.

In 2008, after ten-plus years renting space in a building that is probably condemnable, Life Pieces moved to a beautiful space in an old school, which became available when D.C. Public Schools decided to close twenty-three school buildings. The occupancy fee is far more reasonable, and the school is located in the same part of D.C.'s Northeast section of town, which has had a history of trouble but is now going through some redevelopment.

Seneca, the art student, has been selected by the ARCH to travel to Ireland. He will be talking about the Life Pieces program and how it can help with the Irish youth and their issues related to their turf wars. As Mary put it, "Over there, they have a history of struggles between the Protestants and Catholics. Over here, the kids might get into a fight because they live in different neighborhoods and have different allegiances. Life Pieces can help."

"And the other fellows?" I asked. We covered each one's situation and then I asked, "How's Terry, the one with the Coke-bottle glasses? That's a bit unusual to see those glasses on someone so young."

Mary said, "Actually, Terry isn't doing too well. I think he is going blind. His eyes are just getting worse and worse, and we haven't been able to get him in to see a doctor. He doesn't have any insurance. I took him to one clinic but the questions were endless, and he didn't have all the answers."

"Has he always had bad eyesight? What about his parents?"

"He doesn't have a father, and his mother isn't really able to help him," she said. "When he was three, there was a blunt force trauma to his head, and since then his eyes have had issues. For a while, he was removed from his home to protect him. But eventually, they returned him to his mother. Lately, his eyesight has just been getting worse. He's been feeling low about it, then having a hard time with his studies because he couldn't see. So he dropped out of college. He's having a hard time."

That night, I e-mailed a friend who is a surgeon at Children's Hospital to see if he knew of a good eye doctor there, and he e-mailed the chairman of ophthalmology at Children's. Because Terry is eighteen, Children's had no choice but to refer him elsewhere. The chairman called the situation "urgent" and told me to act quickly because it could involve Terry's retina. He e-mailed me a few local possibilities. One place he suggested was the Eye Clinic at the Washington Hospital Center (or WHC). Amazingly,

WHC's chairman of ophthalmology answered his own phone when I called the department the next day, and he immediately referred the case to a specific eye doctor at WHC's Eye Clinic. Upon hearing about Terry's situation, that doctor, in turn, immediately scheduled an appointment for him. There would also be a retina specialist on hand to examine Terry. It was an astounding concerted effort, and the whole referral process took less than four days. When Mary pulled Terry aside to tell him that he would have an eye doctor's appointment in a couple of days, he was grateful and then moved. Suddenly, he had hope. He looked up and asked her, "Why? How?" Mary said that he was moved that people in the community, who don't even know him, would reach out and help him.

The morning of the 8 a.m. appointment, Mary drove Terry to the Washington Hospital Center's Eye Clinic and sat with him through every part of the examination. She recalled that he could not stop smiling. Later that day, Terry called to thank me personally. Just hearing that he was smiling again was enough.

Within a couple of weeks, Terry had follow-up examinations, drops for his eyes, and contact lenses. Now, he is meeting with a college counselor about returning to school as soon as possible.

In the spring of 2008, Donnell Kie and two others with Life Pieces To Masterpieces were notified that they won a D.C. Achievers Scholarship from the Bill and Melinda Gates Foundation, which means that each student will receive a $50,000 college scholarship.

In mid-2008, after eleven years with Life Pieces, Ben Johnson left the nonprofit to start a business with his brothers. He is still a mentor to the boys and in constant touch with Mary. In late 2008, the board of directors voted to name Ben as one of the co-founders of Life Pieces. As Mary said, "He gave so much to Life Pieces. Ben is my heart. Naming him as a co-founder was a recommendation from the older boys who grew up with us."

In early 2009, Mary Brown received an Exponent Award for Nonprofit Excellence from the Eugene and Agnes E. Meyer Foundation, which recognizes strong and effective nonprofit leaders and provides $100,000 for leadership development and management training.

Now in its fourteenth year in 2009, Life Pieces To Masterpieces is stronger than ever and has been able to maintain the number of participants despite the economic downturn.

Contact information for Life Pieces To Masterpieces:

Mary Brown
Co-Founder/Executive Director
Life Pieces To Masterpieces
    at Merritt Middle School
5002 Hayes Street, NE
Washington, D.C. 20019
Phone: 202-399-7703
Web site: www.lifepieces.org

If you like Life Pieces To Masterpieces, you might be interested in these organizations:

1) Camp For All
   Houston, Texas
   Web site: www.campforall.org
   Phone: 713-686-5666

2) City Year
   Boston, Massachusetts
   Web site: www.cityyear.org
   Phone: 617-927-2500

3) The Dance Institute of Washington
   Washington, D.C.
   Web site: www.danceinstitute.org
   Phone: 202-371-9656

4) The Hobart Shakespeareans
   Los Angeles, California
   Web site:
   www.hobartshakespeareans.org
   Phone: 213-200-4700

5) Sitar Arts Center
   Washington, D.C.
   Web site: www.sitarartscenter.org
   Phone: 202-797-2145

QUEEN STREET CLINIC

THE STORY OF the Queen Street Clinic is different because it is not
a nonprofit. For that reason alone, I was hesitant to choose it.
But its mission is noble and effective. If the Queen Street Clinic
exemplifies a different winning strategy or business model, then why not
select it? Thinking differently about ways to be of help is a big part of this
book. At its core, the Queen Street Clinic epitomizes how a business can
help resolve a social need. It's social entrepreneurship without the nonprofit
status. M.B.A. students and business leaders, who crave to make a difference
while making a living, might relate to this story, for business can be good
and do good. Business and community: a different kind of goal. Here is the
Queen Street Clinic's story.

The City of Alexandria is a small and fairly wealthy suburban enclave
just a few minutes south of Washington, D.C. With roots dating back
to the 1700s, buildings in Old Town Alexandria commonly have an historic
landmark insignia near the doorway. The sidewalks are not concrete but
rather filled with bricks. A few of the cobblestone streets in Old Town have
survived. Architecturally, the houses in the Old Town part of the city are
a magnificent wonder. George Washington lived down the road in Mount
Vernon and often ate and drank in Old Town's taverns. Robert E. Lee was
born and reared in Old Town. Washington and Lee's homes are preserved
along with hundreds of others.

For all its wealth and historic charm, Alexandria is like any other community and has its share of those in need. In 2007, about 8 percent lived below the poverty line. With about 140,000 residents, the City of Alexandria is incredibly compassionate and reaches out to the most vulnerable with a wide spectrum of caring programs. However, similar to the rest of the nation, one pressing need has been health care for those living paycheck to paycheck, those living on the margins, and those who work but have no health coverage. Though Alexandria has a few health clinics, there is still need.

As a nurse practitioner, Anne Parish saw the need and decided she wanted to help by starting a clinic. But unlike most who want to make a difference, she wanted to try it not as a nonprofit but as a business. In August of 2001, Anne Parish became a social entrepreneur who created a health care option for those with few or no options.

Committed to serving the medically uninsured, the Queen Street Clinic is situated on the corner of a busy intersection in Old Town. As the clinic's name implies, one of those cross streets is Queen Street. (Some of Old Town's primary streets are named for royalty: King, Queen, Prince, Princess, Duke, etc.) Driving by in traffic, you might miss the clinic with its renovated look. The front façade boasts big windows and the wood frame is painted bright white. With an old-fashioned sign hanging above the door, the clinic has a welcoming feeling. The interior is inviting, open, and clean with big black-and-white tiles on the floor. Antique Windsor chairs and various antiques are in the waiting room and throughout the clinic. Pretty yellow daffodils are on the check-in counter. A glass-front cabinet displays medical equipment from the 1700s and 1800s.

And then there is Anne, the visionary behind the clinic. At age fifty-three, Anne Boston Parish works on average a twelve-hour day and cares deeply about her patients. Because it's her clinic, she can do a thorough examination and ensure excellent quality care at reasonable rates.

The one thing about Anne is that she has guts. Basically, she had a vision for what the clinic could be. That is, create a place where people with no health insurance can go and get quality care. She thought about making it a nonprofit, but then decided that for her purposes, it could be more efficient to try it as a small business that only charged $45 per visit and sometimes not even that. (In 2007, she raised the standard charge to $60 per visit.)

When asked about why she would start her own clinic, Anne said without hesitating, "Because I saw the need to provide a medical home for people to prevent long-term debilitating disease. I saw the pattern of symptoms in patients that appeared over and over again, that had been neglected earlier in their life span. Early intervention would stem the tide of chronic, debilitating diseases like diabetes, cardiovascular disease, and cancer. I saw the need to prevent long-term debilitating disease by offering a medical home that patients could come into prior to developing diabetes, etc. I could teach them good lifestyle changes so that they didn't end up with losing their sight or limb because of diabetes, or having a stroke because of having high cholesterol and not taking care of it. It's like giving them the tools. Another example is doing annual pap smears. It's easy to treat if caught early, but if it's metastasized, it's more difficult to treat."

She recalled, "I was working at a skilled facility, covering for physicians, doing physicals. People would come in with long-term problems, and I was only supposed to address what they were there for. I just said, 'It doesn't make any sense. If I'm going to do this, I'm going to do it right.'"

Though she would love to have another nurse practitioner or student join her, that has not happened yet. Maybe someday. For now, she is handling a load of seventy to eighty patients per week, and it is all consuming. She hasn't had a real vacation in years, not that she is complaining. She feels she is having an impact every day. But first back to how she got it started.

"The way the state of Virginia allows nurse practitioners to practice independently is with a supervising physician," she explained. "He and I stay in touch, so if I have a difficult patient or a medical question, then he is available. He came to me because of word of mouth. It was just by asking. He wasn't a friend. It's a business, a practice. I pay him; he supervises me. We have a practice agreement, and it comes out of the bylaws of the Board of Medicine and Nursing. It formalizes our relationship.

"He comes in monthly. I choose the most medically difficult patients I've seen, and we sit down and go over the charts. What the patient presented, what I did and the outcomes. My malpractice insurance isn't bad. I've never had any litigation against me. Sometimes, I have had to respond to a complaint and I respond by writing the Board of Medicine."

Like the clinic itself, Anne had a vision for the building, which has a lot of history to it, and you can feel its story call out to you. Proudly showing me around all the examination rooms and bathrooms and storage closets, Anne told the story with total wonder, "Built in the 1940s, it was the Queen Street Market and the family lived upstairs. Then through the years, they converted the upper level into a beauty shop. And downstairs, there was a temporary agency for day workers. It was vacant for probably three years. It fascinated me. It was real cute. So I walked by it all the time. I've heard from different people in the neighborhood that it used to be a brothel, but the whole area was not the most desirable neighborhood to live in. The area had many houses of ill repute. During the Nixon era, there was a resurgence of history and restoration. Some people are visionaries with buildings. I wanted a clinic that people could access by walking or by bus or by Metro. So this was a perfect location. I started the clinic to bring back a sense of community medicine, not to have people get in their cars. And many don't have cars."

So in 1999, against all odds, she bought the old building.

"After I bought it, I heard from a police officer that the building across the street, that housed a grocery store, was used as a gambling hall at night! So apparently, a stolen car could often end up in the back in the '50s and '60s. This was a seedy part of town. It wasn't until they started doing some renovation near the water that they started renovating other areas. People were too afraid to live in any of these homes. On the other hand, many of my patients lived around the corner here, and the house went from generation to generation. It was an impoverished area until fairly recently. One friend [in the neighborhood] had a house that had a tunnel that ran underground to the river to help the slaves escape! I don't know if that's true, but that's what I was told.

"I bought the building from a guy who at the last second, right before settlement, upped the price. I had to take a second mortgage out on my home to buy the building for the clinic. A local bank agreed to help me with the mortgage," she said with relief. "I had a business plan that I presented to the bank that detailed everything."

She gathered tradespersons who supported her with the clinic. Her idea worked. Others saw the need and stepped up to participate in the experiment. She inspired her team and said simply, "I'm trying to build a building for the medically uninsured, and I had three or four large companies help with reduced rates for electrical and plumbing and renovation.

"I always thought, build it and they will come. So I bought a building, and I have a note that I pay every month, and my first goal when I bought the building was to pay off the second mortgage on my home. I knew I was employable. I could get a job anywhere, but I wanted to [open the clinic and] have some stability financially in my personal life because if I lost my home—" her voice trailed off. Then she added, "Here I am, divorced. I'm on my own."

So the stakes have been high for Anne. But she took a chance to help others and slowly built up the little clinic. It was like the little engine that could. She hung out her shingle and people came knocking. Five years later, she sees between seventy and eighty patients a week, sometimes one hundred—all on her own. For a long time, she had a front-office person handling phones, scheduling and billing, but that assistant left for another job. Anne explained that at times it's not easy being the front person, because most of the patients are easy but one in ten will give you a hard time about the fee or about what tests they want or about wanting to see the doctor when there is no doctor. So it can get the best of you. But in the end, Anne tries to stay focused on the vast majority of patients who make it worthwhile.

"I went to the bank this morning," Anne said with a smile. "And a woman from across the way yelled, 'Hey, there's my doctor!' She came over to me and said, 'God, I've felt great since our visit.' That made me feel like it's all worth it."

There are numerous stories of patients who have made it all worthwhile. Inside the cabinet with the antique medical equipment is a small photo of a handsome, young man who lived into his late forties. He was one of Anne's first patients, a fellow who died of cirrhosis of the liver. She treated him for a few years, and said that he was in hospice home care the last two days of his life. After he died, Anne said that the family told her, "You've given him his dignity. He died with his dignity."

The Queen Street Clinic provides medical care while maintaining a person's dignity.

I still needed to see the clinic during office hours. One day in 2006, at the last second, I called Anne to see if I could come by in an hour to take some photographs. Everything I had learned about the clinic sounded good, but I wanted to see it in action. Like other clinics, there are scheduled appointments. And then there are people who just walk in and need to see a medical provider. So every day has busy times, lulls, and surprises. Every day is an unknown canvas.

Until I saw it for myself, the Queen Street Clinic was a fine story but still not outstanding. But then, while I was there for an hour, a sixty-year-old man named James Earl Parker walked in.

James had an old baseball cap on, and his face was cheerful with an easy smile. But I could tell he had been through something. When he walked into the clinic, Anne's face lit up as she jumped out of her seat and gave him a big hug. Anne said with her arm around his shoulder, "This is James Parker. He has been cancer-free for about five years now!" James smiled at Anne and looked at me. I thought they were both going to have tears in their eyes as Anne told of James' colon and prostate cancer and surgeries.

Anne had another patient come in, so James sat down to wait and I sat with him. His hands looked far older than mine, hands of a working life. If you walked by James on the street, you wouldn't know that this African American male had so many health issues to overcome. He is that brave, even stoic. His face was open, and he spoke with a slight and sweet sound of a country upbringing. Originally from North Carolina, he said he had come to Alexandria for work in construction. He had a refreshing way of speaking—soft and direct, no shields or screens.

"Can I ask you what happened to you? Would that be OK?"

"When I got sick," he began, "I was living in Alexandria. I was a construction worker. And I lost so much weight. In ten weeks, I lost forty-seven pounds. I was working every day and I couldn't see it. And people at work were concerned. And that's when I came to see Anne. A person I was riding around with, he recommended I come to see her because she is a blessing. Let me tell you. You didn't know who you're going to turn to. And she's a blessing.

"And I came to her, and she conferred with me through everything. She ran a bunch of tests and she diagnosed me with the possibility I might have cancer. After she did the tests, she sent me to different doctors. She sent me to a doctor for the colon cancer [who did the surgery]. I paid him something but it was basically free. When I came to Anne, all the work she did was basically free. I had $43 in my pocket, and it's $45 for a visit."

"So you clearly didn't have insurance through your construction work or on your own," I said to him.

"I worked but people don't take out insurance on you anymore. You gotta take it out on your own. And it's so expensive. You can't hardly afford it. And as you get older, it gets more expensive. Even on your job."

We sat there for a bit in silence. He was being so open with me, a complete stranger. Anne was still examining her patient, someone who came in with a bad ankle.

"You look good," I finally said, trying to be encouraging.

"I feel good," he said and nodded. "Gotta keep the faith. 'Cause a lot of things happen. It runs from generation to generation. It might stop a generation. A lot of diseases in [my] family. But it might not affect the grandchildren. My family history had it, but they didn't call it colon cancer. They called it 'ruptness.' My father died from it, and I lost two uncles from it. The doctors told me to take this operation, or you'll be gone in one month."

I had never heard of 'ruptness.' James said that that's what they called it in the old days. He said that it was called that because it's kind of like you're erupting, you're straining. And that straining is one of the telltale signs of colon cancer. Today, colon cancer is one of the most preventable and treatable types of cancer if it is caught early with a colonoscopy. Colorectal cancer, which includes both colon and rectal cancer, was the third most diagnosed type of cancer in men and women in the United States in 2008. Because it is not always caught early, colorectal cancer is the second leading cause of cancer-related deaths in the nation when statistics for both men and women are combined.

James' case was no different, except he had Anne working on his case. "When I took my first operation, if I had come in a year or so earlier, I wouldn't have had to have the operation. But I learned how to deal with it," he said looking down at this contraption under his T-shirt that removes all his "waste." He irrigates that contraption about three times a day. James added, "Anne started me in the right direction, 'cause I didn't know who to turn to. I don't like to be a burden on nobody. And then some caretakers came to the house. Now that I'm in the system."

Today, he is on 100 percent disability, but James Earl Parker was not always in the system. Anne took care of that, too. When James had tried, he had gotten the run around, and that wasted precious time—time that could have helped with earlier detection and treatment of the cancer. After multiple applications, James finally obtained medical disability. Anne says that in her experience that it usually takes about three attempts to get it.

James said softly, his strong eyes suddenly filling with tears, "I signed up one time for unemployment out of forty-eight years of working. And they refused me two times for disability. I applied for help with Social Services. I went to the hospital, and the caseworker told me that the help wasn't meant for me. So I moved from here in Alexandria to Fairfax County and got medical care there and at the University of Virginia [medical system] in Charlottesville. Now I live down in Chesapeake, Virginia. I came up here today for a funeral. Whenever I can, I come up here to see Anne at the clinic."

No one would see James as a patient. Like many workers, he didn't have health insurance, and many doctors wouldn't see him with his symptoms. Anne later explained, "With his declining health—weight loss and other physical complaints—it was difficult to find a doctor who would evaluate him for weight loss and bloody stools. Not only was James considered a challenge medically, the doctors would have had a hard time getting reimbursement." But James was losing weight fast. Luckily, he had heard about Anne from one of his co-workers.

Now finished with her patient, Anne zoomed to the basement and brought back a grocery bag overflowing with supplies. Even though James is on disability, he is not eligible for certain social services, including free medical supplies.

Going through the bag of supplies, Anne told James, "I've been saving these for when you came back by. These are top of the line and won't leak."

"Thank you, Anne."

Turning to me, she added, "A lot of his supplies aren't covered."

As she and James went over the supplies, he was clearly grateful and didn't have to say a thing. His face cheered up. Anne explained, "His colon and prostate cancer had spread to his bladder. They gave him about a 20 percent chance of survival. After all the surgeries and treatments, and five years later, he is going strong. My dad always asks me about James. James was one of the first patients that was touch and go."

James smiled, "My Mama liked her so much. She says to me, 'Whatever you do, you always go by the clinic and say hi to Anne.'"

With an arm around James, Anne added, "He's got such a bright attitude."

James just said, "Gotta keep the faith." As if praying for a second, he paused and then repeated, "Gotta keep the faith. She was a blessing. Her help made me keep my faith. You have to have a real strong family. I have a big family. My brothers and my cousins are just like brothers."

I took some photos, listening as they caught up with each other. I felt blessed to meet James. I don't think I will ever forget what he said about working for forty-eight years and asking only once for unemployment and then getting turned down for disability at first. He had no safety net but had worked hard all his life. He had a family and friends but no health coverage.

While we were finishing up, a woman in her late forties named Theresa Diggs came in. Theresa works at Head Start and said, "I've known Anne since twenty years ago when Anne started as a nurse at Head Start in Alexandria. I've been coming here for a few years. At least one of my co-workers does come here. It's real good here."

Everyone who came in said that they had heard about the Queen Street Clinic through a friend or co-worker. Except for James, they all had jobs. But no health care. The clinic was their health care.

Anne knew almost every patient by first name. Sitting there and watching her talk with her patients demonstrated her deep care for each of them. It's her commitment to personal service and the dignity of each patient that sets the clinic apart.

One of the fun parts of Anne's work involves working with five or six school coaches and their athletes. "A few of the coaches send me their athletes. Their athletes need a sports physical, and their parents can't pay for it. The coaches pay out of their own pockets for the athletes to come to me," she said with a shrug. "One of the coaches said, 'Next May, maybe we'll have a fundraiser and have you come in and work with the nurses and do a bunch of sports physicals for the kids while at school.' These coaches want so bad for the kids to stay on the teams. They know that by playing sports, the kids are surrounded by other kids who are taking care of their bodies, learning collaboration, team spirit, and discipline. They're less likely to stray and get into trouble. They couldn't afford the sports physical, and the coaches want the kids on their teams, so they pay."

Some young people are not so lucky. Anne explained, "We're seeing a whole generation of HPV, or human papillomavirus, which is a major cofactor in the development of cervical cancer. Pap smears test for it, and in some cases HPV does resolve; however, there are cases that demonstrate, years later, HPV can resurface with dysplasia and needs further evaluation by a specialist. It is another example of the importance of early detection and the need for annual screening for those who are sexually active and have multiple partners."

In addition to working within the community, one important aspect of the Queen Street Clinic is that it keeps the high cost of emergency room visits down. The rising cost of emergency rooms in cities throughout the country is a great concern to city managers and mayors everywhere.

Anne explained, "At the ER, it's not a $45 fee. And I have a pricing agreement for a chest X-ray for $40, a mammogram for $40—all discounted rates that help keep down the price of the ER overhead. My role is not to take care of what surgeons spend years learning to do. My role is to identify the problem, handle it if I can, and if necessary, send the patient to the specialist for treatment."

Sometimes people don't understand the Queen Street Clinic and they question Anne's rates. Anne shrugged and said simply, "I'm a small business. I had a mother whose child had fallen and scraped her knees and hurt her shoulder. The child wasn't wearing protective gear and the mother wanted her daughter to get an X-ray for her knees. I said for the mother to bring her in. After the examination, I said that the child doesn't need an X-ray, but she needs antibiotics and a tetanus shot. Her knees and shoulder were infected. They hadn't even cleaned out the wounds. And the mother moaned about the tetanus shot and paying for it. I charged her the $45 for the visit and a charge for the tetanus shot. The lady said, 'You mean you're not free?' I told her this is not a free clinic."

Anne elaborated, "The emergency rooms are no longer free, especially if you have some income. For someone who has an unresolved cough or something that is not acute, they should go to a family practice. But if they go to the ER because someone is wheezing or is having heart issues or something life-threatening, now they have a huge emergency room bill. If they are employed, the hospital will go to the employer and have their wages garnished. If you can document that the patient is critical, we can expedite the process for getting them into the system. There are clear guidelines: income, residency, citizenship, disabilities, etc."

Anne knows how to stand up for herself. As Anne put it, she grew up as a Navy Junior; her father was a lawyer in the U.S. Navy. His job took Anne all over the world until she moved to Alexandria in 1983. She recalled, "I was a nurse for fifteen years while being a full-time mom for my two kids. Every time, I added a different degree, I was able to utilize my education. First with an associate's degree in nursing. Then, when the kids were young, I got a bachelor's degree in nursing from Marymount University. Later, I got my master's degree in nursing administration. Later, I got a post-master's certificate to be a family nurse practitioner in 1995."

And that gave Anne the ability and privilege to be a clinician and fulfill her dream.

With a gleam in her eye, Anne said simply, "What I realized is that my first love is medicine."

But she wanted to love medicine and help others, without the confines of a nonprofit.

"I don't want to be under the auspices of a board. They either wanted me to be a nurse practitioner or a manager, not at the helm. And the board wasn't going to write the grants. I was going to have to do it, and I did. But I realized I wanted a small business and to really make a difference. This way the clinic allows me to do my work and have a breather. Last night I had to stay late to pay bills and transfer the information into my Quickbooks for the checks that were written to support the operational budget of the clinic. I pay myself when I have to pay my bills, but the money generated goes back into the business. I fill out forms all the time to get the patients into the public health system."

Anne Boston Parish had a vision for how things should be done and she just went out and did it. Her first love is medicine. Her patients benefit from her dedication and service. The whole community benefits.

UPDATE ABOUT THE QUEEN STREET CLINIC

BY SHEER CHANCE, I ran into James Earl Parker in Old Town Alexandria in the summer of 2007. At sixty-two, he looked even healthier and was enjoying a walk on a beautiful day. With a father's pride, James told me about his three sons who are grown and, as he put it, have never given him a day of trouble. Two of his sons, ages thirty-eight and forty, are in the military and have each had two rotations in the Iraq war.

I told him that he looked good. With a big smile and brimming with gratitude, James said, "I feel great. If it hadn't been for Anne, I don't know which way I woulda went, 'cause she pointed me from one place to another, and she stuck with me through it all. She's helped a lot of people. I'm going to go to the clinic tomorrow just to say hi to her while I'm in town."

The Queen Street Clinic celebrated its seventh anniversary in 2008 and continues to thrive in Alexandria. In the last few years, a nonprofit health care clinic opened its doors a few miles away in another part of Alexandria. There are plenty of uninsured and under-insured patients who need health care. To date, Anne has never turned away a patient and has always managed to squeeze a patient into the same day's schedule even if she is swamped.

In early 2009, due to the economic downturn, Anne said that she had noticed that many people were putting off their preventative care until there was a health crisis.

Contact information for the Queen Street Clinic:

Anne Boston Parish
Founder/Owner
Queen Street Clinic
1000 Queen Street
Alexandria, Virginia 22314
Phone: 703-299-9701
Web site: www.queenstreetclinic.com

If you like the Queen Street Clinic, you might be interested in this organization:

1) Los Barrios Unidos Community Clinic
   Dallas, Texas
   Web site: www.losbarriosunidos.org
   Phone: 214-571-6132

THE READING CONNECTION

A S A SMALL child, my all-time favorite books included *Goodnight Moon, Where the Wild Things Are, There is a Nightmare in my Closet*, and of course the Beatrix Potter books about Peter Rabbit. I also adored a tiny book called *Pierre* by Maurice Sendak. In the book, the little boy constantly replies, "'I don't care,' said Pierre." Giggling every time my mom read that aloud, I romped around our house imitating that little boy's famous line. Of course, at the end of the story, Pierre learned to care. I was blessed with shelves of books and with parents who read with me every night. I did not realize then how that time with my parents was special. It is only as an adult that I sense the impact, that I cherish the memories, and that I know how blessed I was and am.

All children need to learn to enjoy reading *before* school starts. But that begins at home with the parents. "At home" is something many of us take for granted but not so for parents who are struggling. And reading to a child takes time, patience, and the ability to read. It also takes money to buy books. And though books are free at a local library, a library is not always accessible. Transportation is not a given. Time is not a given either when you're struggling. The Reading Connection is a literacy outreach program for children in housing crisis—helping those children get the bug and the buzz about reading at an early age. This is their story. And unlike little Pierre at the beginning of the Sendak book, The Reading Connection is all about caring.

As their mission states, "The Reading Connection is a nonprofit organization dedicated to bringing books and a lifelong love of reading to children in housing crisis."

The Reading Connection began in 1989 in Arlington, Virginia, a suburb a few minutes south of Washington. Judy Hijikata, the nonprofit's program director, explained, "It all got started by Beth Reese, a longtime Arlington resident who was raising her children and was on leave from teaching at an elementary school. She was probably in her early thirties. She heard that some children were living in shelters in the neighborhood and had a different set of needs. She followed up; and as a result, she started The Reading Connection. She and a couple of other teachers started going to the shelters and reading with the kids."

"The children had left their homes," Judy continued. "Once they were living in the shelter, they didn't come to school with their school supplies and backpacks, as kids usually do. They would have left their homes with very little, and sometimes in a rush. School supplies and children's books can easily get lost in the tumult. Families in shelters have a very structured existence. They are busy all day looking for work or doing job training and financial and other counseling. They have to figure out where their next home will be. They just don't have time to be reading to their kids because they're worried about food, shelter, and medicine. There are also no books." Judy figured, "For a low-income family, typically there just aren't any children's books in a home. It's not a priority or if it is, there is nothing the parent can do about it."

Though Beth went back to teaching in the Arlington public schools in the 1990s, she has stayed involved with The Reading Connection. Judy said, "Beth's always supportive and says how rewarding it is for her to see how The Reading Connection has developed with all these programs and all these volunteers."

Judy recalled, "I first found out about The Reading Connection eight or nine years ago when I was working in a bookstore, and Beth called for some donated books. That was my first connection to Beth. From an outsider's point of view, it was such a wonderful organization. So I knew the organization from the outside long before I joined the staff in 2003."

The Reading Connection's staff has three full-time people and one part-timer, plus approximately 200 volunteers. In 2005, the annual budget was $335,000; about $90,000 of that budget was in in-kind contributions. The nonprofit stretches every dollar. In 2006 alone, The Reading Connection gave 7,600 new books to children in housing crisis, and more than 300 parents participated in The Reading Connection's parent workshops.

Getting parents to participate assumes that the parents are able to read, and that is not always the case. According to the *Washington Post* on March 19, 2007, the State of Adult Literacy Report, which was released in March 2007, found that "nearly 36 percent, or 170,000 of the District residents are functionally illiterate, compared with 21 percent nationally." Illiteracy is directly tied to one's employability and earning power and therefore has a direct impact on the children. The poorest neighborhoods in D.C. are in Wards 7 and 8, which are in the city's Southeast quadrant and include Anacostia. Those same wards also have among the District's highest illiteracy rates. Whether in Washington or elsewhere, if the parents are illiterate, the volunteers of organizations like The Reading Connection are often the only connection these children have to books and reading outside of school.

Because there are approximately 14,000 homeless in the Washington region, The Reading Connection reaches out to kids beyond Arlington, helping around 2,000 kids per year learn the love of reading throughout the area—from Alexandria and Fairfax County to the District. Homelessness and housing crises are not only inner-city issues in Washington, but are also in the wealthy suburbs of Northern Virginia. In fact, most of The Reading Connection's work is focused on children in Northern Virginia, which demonstrates how poverty is both urban and suburban.

The Reading Connection has two programs. One is the Shelter Read-Aloud Program. Judy elaborated in the fall of 2005: "Two hundred volunteers go to thirteen shelters in the D.C. metro area. Ten out of the thirteen shelters are in Northern Virginia; the other three are in D.C. The thirteen shelters are of various sizes—from tiny to large. They work to directly address the literacy needs that are missing from these children's lives—children's books, time reading with a caring adult, and school and art supplies. We give each child who comes to a read-aloud session a brand new book, because research shows that book ownership is a powerful incentive for helping a child become a reader. For at least that one hour a week with The Reading Connection volunteers, the children have a language-rich experience—books read, conversations held, jokes told, poems recited. It's great fun, and all that language is a wonderful educational benefit. And finally, we give the children new notebooks, crayons, gluesticks, etc., along with books, in Welcome Bags, handmade cloth bags that are theirs to keep and to take with them when they leave the shelter for other housing. For a kid who doesn't have much, this is huge."

Building with Books is The Reading Connection's second program, and its monthly Book Club is a big part of it. Children at the shelters or other partner agencies can order a book per month. It's a bit similar to Netflix, only it's for children and books! And it's free for the kids. It's like getting a gift every month.

The Reading Connection's Book Club came about because founder Beth Reese wanted to continue serving the families after they moved out of the shelters. So she and longtime supporter/first part-time program director/volunteer Dru Kevit came up with the Book Club idea. And then The Reading Connection team made the idea happen for the kids.

Eileen Hanning, their education specialist who has been with The Reading Connection for about ten years, further developed the idea for the Book Club and its Building with Books program. Judy explained, "While Eileen was working on her master's degree in education, she designed a way to continue to give the kids books after they left the shelter. It's a good thing to move from the shelter, but for the kids, it meant losing the books every week. So Eileen hammered out the idea for the Book Club, in which the kids order a book from a list that The Reading Connection gives them. They turn in their wish list, and then The Reading Connection mails the books to the kids. Again, this is a population that doesn't have books. So without this program, there probably would be no kids' books in their homes.

"At ALIVE! House, which is a long-term shelter for families staying about nine to twelve months in the City of Alexandria, there was a period in 2004 when our volunteers helped two or three girls for a number of months. The girls were around nine to twelve years of age. And that was one of those periods when they really saw change. One little girl went from being very timid about books and very insecure about being able to read, much less read aloud to our volunteers. As the volunteers saw the little girl over a period of months, the little girl really blossomed socially, and her reading improved so much in terms of confidence and reading level. She was able to read more difficult things; her whole demeanor changed as she had this positive exposure to books. She moved from ALIVE! House and last we heard, she was in Maryland."

As that last anecdote illustrates, a great deal hinges on the volunteers—their caring, patience, and commitment to the children. Clearly, a significant part of The Reading Connection's success derives from their many volunteers.

Judy loves the volunteers and said, "Many of our volunteers have been with us for six or eight years. Some start out with a perspective such as, 'When I started doing this, I thought I was doing it for the kids.' They think it's something they should be doing. But the kids give so much back to the volunteers. The volunteers begin saying, 'I can't imagine that I've given as much to the kids as they have given to me.' People have fun with this. The kids are sweet, funny, and have a lot of energy. People also often say that it's such a bright spot in their week."

Also in the Building with Books program, The Reading Connection trains parents and social workers in the importance of early reading for early language acquisition and early language skills. "It's saying to parents that it's tremendously important for you to sit down and read with your child," Judy emphasized. "If your child throws the book on the floor, that's fine. Just try it again, and one time, you'll make it through and you'll both have had fun. We also show them that children need to learn the simple things: how to hold a book, how to turn a page, who is an author, an illustrator—all things we take for granted. If the children already know how to sit and look at a book, how it works, then that is helpful in school. For the really little kids, there is an element that it is a good thing to hold your kid over a long period of time and be together. Books should be a part of their everyday life. That is something that has to be taught."

The Reading Connection's success with its Shelter Read-Aloud Program continues to grow. In the past year, The Reading Connection has opened two new read-aloud programs and increased families served in the Building with Books program by 25 percent.

"There is research that shows that the process of being read aloud to is the thing that makes kids able to cope in school," Judy continued. "We don't have the staff or the funds to do long-term evaluation of any of these kids over time. And this population has a lot of transition. So we have never done any long-term study. But we have the Book Club. And it asks for feedback from the parents, and we have parents giving us written feedback, saying how much a child enjoyed a book."

With its tiny staff, The Reading Connection does an excellent job of engaging the community in its efforts. It often links up with corporate giving programs as well as other nonprofits that are providing complimentary services. For example, in 2005, Boeing employees had an August Backpack drive to benefit The Reading Connection, and they collected school supplies and sixty-five new backpacks. In early September, volunteers distributed the supplies and backpacks to children who participate in The Reading Connection's Read-Aloud programs.

There is an ongoing book drive at Taylor Elementary School in Arlington. It started in 2003 with one bag in the lobby of the school. Today, on a quarterly basis, students contribute new books to the children served by The Reading Connection. The students also contribute some of their favorite books, thereby learning what it means to give something you love.

A sixth grade class at H.B. Woodlawn, a secondary program in Arlington, also got involved with The Reading Connection's cause. A sixth grade English teacher named Catherine Frum challenged her students to write about a cause of interest to them. Two students, Makshya Tolbert and Haley Sanner, organized a book drive and a bake sale for The Reading Connection. The students collected more than three hundred books in about two weeks.

A primary part of the job of The Reading Connection's executive director Sarah Koch is to fundraise and write grants. But Sarah Koch also counts herself among those who volunteer time with the children—time that she has come to cherish.

Sarah related a personal story by saying, "I started reading at House of Ruth to see what impact we have. I was one of the first readers when we launched our program at House of Ruth, a long-term transitional housing program for battered women and their children in Washington. So the first night we went in and met the kids, and we met a group of three sisters, who were between the ages of four and eight. They didn't know how books work. They didn't want to sit down in our laps and take out a book. They didn't know that reading would be something pleasurable for them. So I remember going home that night and thinking this is kind of a lost cause. They had such an extreme lack of interest. And you can tell they've never been read to. But we kept going back, month after month, and by Christmas, I remember thinking I couldn't believe these were the same sisters. The three girls were showing an interest in books, picking out what they wanted to read, excited about reading. They now have their favorite books. They're excited about the books. Now Read-Aloud time is something they get excited about. They will sit down in your lap and read for forty-five minutes. This is a huge thing to have that attention span. They just want to read the entire hour!

"This is just one anecdote about what we're about. And now every time I go and read, I can't believe they're the same girls I met a year ago who couldn't even go and pick out a book. I can really see the impact that the Shelter Read-Aloud Program has had. And one of the social workers at House of Ruth said that some of the moms are going to the reading corners now and choosing books and reading with their children. The social worker said she had never seen the moms go and read with their children before.

"So for me, our mission is very simple," Sarah concluded. "I love to read. And I think back to all the memories I have from my childhood that revolved around books. And we're giving them this gift. I don't think many would argue with us about the value and the power of reading in a child's life."

Volunteers Loren Zander and Ann Mabe have also had the thrill of seeing how the reading program helps. During a school night, even though Loren had taught sixth grade social studies all day at an Arlington middle school, she savored working with the children at the shelter. She has been volunteering with Reading Connection since 1999. Ann, a lawyer with the government, has been a volunteer for three years straight.

And there they were, waiting for their young charges to arrive at ALIVE! House, which, as Judy mentioned, is a house in the heart of Old Town Alexandria. But this house was a shelter, too, and it didn't look like any shelter I had ever seen. This shelter was clean and homey and quiet, not to mention located in the historic part of Old Town. Flowers in window boxes sat out front, and pumpkins for Halloween adorned the stoop. It was a place the families had come to call home, at least temporarily or probably nine months or so. One family was a mother with two young boys and a baby.

As scheduled, at 7:30 P.M., that mother's two young boys arrived with their book bags. This place has been their home for many months now, and they headed right upstairs to a room with a small dining table, a television, a couch, a washer and dryer, and a closet full of school supplies and books. The boys, one eight and the other ten, sat at the table, looking a bit bedraggled from a long day.

A girl who is in middle school joined them at the table, too. Mature for a seventh or eighth grader, she lives at the shelter and often helps Loren and Ann with the boys, but she and her mom will be moving out of the shelter soon. That's what her mom has said. She knew all the Harry Potter books and discussed which ones were her favorites and why. All three youngsters got along well with each other—helping and sharing with one another with total ease. The older of the two brothers had a distinct gift for drawing and said his favorite subject was math. The younger of the two boys was more rambunctious and said he was sore from a bicycle accident the previous day. All three had beautiful smiles.

Loren brought books about Native Americans. Once she started reading, everyone settled down and listened to the story, one of which was called *Frog Girl*. The older of the two brothers read a couple of pages aloud.

Loren spoke about the Native Americans' beautiful heritage, beliefs, and respect for nature. Then she and Ann worked with the boys and the young girl on a crafts project that related to the books they read. Soon, they all enjoyed a homemade snack of gingerbread that the resident manager of ALIVE! House had made for them. Each of the kids then chose a book to take back to their rooms. The book was theirs to keep. Before we left, the younger brother went on his own without someone asking and got a wet rag to wipe off the table.

As we left, Ann whispered proudly, "They are doing so much better."

Loren added, "When we first came, they couldn't sit still and focus on the book. They wanted to know when it would be over. Now they listen to the story and read along! They were way behind when we began, but they are now catching up. Not quite there yet, but on their way. We can really see a difference." Loren and Ann's faces said it all. Though tired from a long day, they were now energized.

And it all started with Beth Reese, a young mother with two small children at the time. An elementary schoolteacher in Arlington, Beth had left teaching to raise her children in the late 1980s, but she saw a need and decided to do something about it. Genuine warmth and commitment come through in Beth's gentle voice and choice of words.

As she put it, "I was involved in a reading educators organization. I was on the board of that group, and was put in charge of the social action committee. It was 1988 or 1989; homelessness was on the front page a lot. And yet, here we were in the suburbs. I don't think anyone thought it applied to our life here in the suburbs. But there were schoolteachers that I knew in the suburbs who had students who were homeless. It was not just an urban issue. It was at that point that it was shocking to me. But it was something we could do something about. Doorways for Women and Families [formerly called The Arlington Community Temporary Shelter] was our first shelter that we helped. Finding these shelters tucked in nearby neighborhoods was eye-opening," she admitted.

"The main purpose of The Reading Connection at the beginning was simple," Beth recalled in 2005. "The act of being held and read to by an adult that cares about you is one of the most powerful and longest lasting and positive experiences that a child can have. Because in that experience, everything a child is longing for is provided: closeness, being valued, being the center of attention, tenderness, adventure, and imagination—all of the places your mind goes.

"It seemed like an important thing to do. It is about loving children in a way they can understand and in a way that can last a lifetime. And now The Reading Connection is providing parents with the tools to do this with their kids, regardless of their financial or housing status.

"Making a tangible difference in an area of suffering that you see is such a gift. I was a teacher who found a way to be of help that was important to me. There is a double awe when you get involved in this kind of service. One is [you're] actually making a difference yourself, and the other is the awe of helping others find out what they're capable of. Being with volunteers when they find out what they're capable of—how much they can make a difference—is so exciting. Not just the good work of your own actions, but being part of helping other people do the same thing. I'm grateful to be part of that.

"Anyone who has volunteered knows that sense of being part of a larger force that is able to relieve suffering. And when you start something or manage one of those groups, you feel the tremendous honor and awe of helping people discover the power inside themselves. You get positive feedback about your value that you may not get in your everyday life. You walk in with a bag of books, see the impact, and you're hooked. I think we are all longing to make our corner of the world a little better."

Now in her late forties, Beth sees how her life has had a meaningful trajectory. "In the late 1980s, I was getting my master's degree in reading education and having my third child," she remembered. "And then I launched The Reading Connection. Then in the '90s, I went back to teaching and launched the Discovery Schoolyard Program, which is teaching in the schoolyard. Now I've retired from teaching to write. The Reading Connection started with ten teacher volunteers and a bag of books in a small shelter, which had about six kids. And look what happened! It's that connection from doing good together. It's so simple and doable. And now The Reading Connection serves over 2,000 kids a year."

A bit philosophical about making a difference, Beth emphasized, "It's more about connection than it is about a great result. On the flip side of that, you don't have to know exactly where it is all going. People are concerned about the result. If you follow a simple, sound mission, use it as your compass, you know the effort is true. Mother Teresa taught us that it's one person at a time. When asked how did you ever dream up serving all these people in Calcutta, she said, 'I didn't. I just served the child in front of me...and then the next.'

"In the same vein, that connection happens when you're working with volunteers or if you're a volunteer leader. That is another form of connecting.

We have phenomenal power. Often, our true power is all this power we don't use. You volunteer, and you join with some other volunteers, and there's this synergy going on. There's real magic you feel when you're leading volunteers. You are connecting to a much bigger pool of energy than you could ever tap on your own.

"I gave my blossoming twenty-one-year-old daughter a card recently because she is trying to decide what to do with her life. The card had a quote by Marta Kagan that said, 'Listen to your heart above all other voices.' I gave her the card because I want her to trust her own heart and intuition. It always leads in the right direction."

Beth Reese is still awestruck by the courage of others around her, not realizing that it was originally her own vision of a better way that inspired it all. Looking back, she is simply grateful for the chance to do something for others.

"There are many stories, but one story that stays with me," she began softly. "One of the Doorways' shelters is for families that are temporarily homeless. I was there one Saturday, working on our reading library. A man, one of the fathers, was working on the porch, painting or fixing a pillar or floorboard, which might have surprised people who incorrectly assume things about the homeless. How wrong we are about who a homeless person is—the stereotype of people who are down and out. And he was there with his wife and kids. He was using his Saturday while staying at the shelter to help fix up the porch. On his own, doing it. No one asked him to work on the porch. He saw something that needed to be fixed and got to work on it.

"He took my hand and said, 'Thank you for treating us like real people. This is the last place that I ever expected to find myself, and yet here I am with my two children and my wife. It's easy for people to look right past you and assume you're different than them. By coming in and reading to our kids, you're giving us books to read as a family. You're giving us our dignity.'

Beth paused and added, "Here is a guy because of a lost job and some illness, he is there at the shelter. We treated them as a family, as the family that they were, and the father that he is, a father who was trying to get back on his feet. People make assumptions about adults and their children and the homeless. And that it's his fault or that he didn't care enough. People might assume that he and his wife didn't care about his kids, but that wasn't the case. I was in awe of him, and he was thanking me for going out of my way when we treated him the way he or anyone deserves to be treated. That is just a natural part of The Reading Connection's mission.

"This guy could have been dying inside," Beth felt. "He's humiliated but he's keeping it together, surviving and still standing. He's finding time to read to his kids. I don't know if I could have been that strong."

In the early winter, The Reading Connection held its annual fundraiser at the headquarters for the National Education Association. They called the soiree, "Of Wine and Words," and raised funds for their reading and book programs. Ann Mabe, one of The Reading Connection's volunteers I met at the shelter, helped check people in at the front door. She and I chatted briefly about the children they tutored at the shelter, and she told me that all three youngsters, the two brothers and the teen, moved away with their families. She didn't know where they went, but she and the other Reading Connection volunteer, Loren Zander, had a chance to go to the shelter and say goodbye. Ann shrugged slightly, as if fighting back emotion. Volunteers get attached to the kids they tutor. At least, Ann and Loren had a chance to say goodbye to the children. Then Ann said that she believed the families had moved to a more stable living situation. If the children and their mothers stay in touch with The Reading Connection by mail, then the children can continue to receive free books through the Book Club.

At the fundraiser, Steve Roberts—the renowned journalist and syndicated columnist—was the keynote speaker. Inspiring the crowd, Mr. Roberts said, "There's nothing more wonderful than being read to. This is a priceless gift you're giving the children, showing them they're precious, that you care."

Update about The Reading Connection

Sarah Koch moved to another region shortly after this story was written. The new executive director is Courtney Kissell. Though Judy Hijikata still works with the programs, she became the Communications Director.

In 2005-2006, the Catalogue for Philanthropy selected The Reading Connection as one of the best small charities in the Washington, D.C., region.

By early 2009, The Reading Connection was giving about 9,500 books per year to children in housing crisis and still sharing the joy of reading with about 2,000 children per year with an army of volunteers.

Contact information for The Reading Connection:

Courtney Kissell
Executive Director
The Reading Connection, Inc.
2009 North 14th Street, Suite 307
Arlington, Virginia 22201
Phone: 703-528-8317
Web site: www.thereadingconnection.org

If you like The Reading Connection, you might be interested in these organizations:

1) First Book
   Washington, D.C.
   Web site: www.firstbook.org
   Phone: 202-393-1222

2) House of Ruth
   Washington, D.C.
   Web site: www.houseofruth.org
   Phone: 202-667-7001

3) Reach Out and Read
   National headquarters in Boston, Massachusetts
   Web site: www.reachoutandread.org
   Phone: 617-455-0600

4) Recording for the Blind & Dyslexic
   of Metropolitan Washington
   (Part of a national organization)
   Washington, D.C.
   Web site: www.rfbd.org/dc
   Phone: 202-244-8990

5) Room to Read
   International headquarters in San Francisco, California
   Web site: www.roomtoread.org
   Phone: 415-561-3331

C.H.O.I.C.E.

As *THE GREAT GATSBY* begins, the narrator reminds himself what his father advised him as he set off into the world: "Whenever you feel like criticizing any one, just remember that all the people in this world haven't had the advantages that you've had."

You can never tell about people—what they've seen or gone through, how they've handled adversity, if they've had adversity at all. Adversity isn't only financial. It could be a harsh or detached parent, a learning disability, or an ill sibling. Things are not always as they appear. Some appear to have it all together, but they don't. Some look as if they won't amount to much, but they do. Some, probably not enough, are just themselves, open about their hard knocks, and leading an honorable life. The latter is the case of Aretha Lyles. She hasn't had all the advantages that a lot of people have had in life, but she is committed to helping steer other young people away from trouble. Unlike the other visionaries in this book, Aretha saw need in the community through her own experiences and decided to do something about it. She was a visionary not because of a need she witnessed on the streets; she became a visionary because of need she witnessed within herself and her own family. For many years, Aretha Lyles could hardly help herself or her children, but once she was self-sustaining, she had a vision for a better way to help others. This is her story.

Aretha Lyles grew up in Spartansburg, South Carolina. By the time she made it to D.C., she was twenty-four and raising her three little children alone. Without a high school diploma, she was trying to keep it together, working odd jobs and doing her best to raise her young family. Sounds bleak, and it was. That was 1990. By 2005, at age thirty-nine, Aretha had been working full-time for a number of years, had three grown children, and was the founder/executive director of a nonprofit committed to helping others help themselves. So technically, she had two full-time jobs. Only one was paid.

Through the years, Aretha watched and worried as her own son struggled with truancy and suspensions. Kids who are suspended from school suddenly have nothing to do but get bored and possibly get into more trouble. Without guidance and structure, suspended kids don't learn to channel their anger, and they get behind in their schoolwork, which can cause more frustration. Aretha knew that her son had nothing positive to do, wasn't learning a lesson from the suspension, and was falling behind academically. It was a death spiral of trouble. Finally, when her son turned around and began to do better, Aretha saw a need for troubled children and developed a better way. She launched a nonprofit called C.H.O.I.C.E., which stands for Children Having Opportunities in Changing Environments.

By late 2005, when I first met Aretha, C.H.O.I.C.E. had two years under its belt but didn't have a huge budget. In fact, it was only around $100,000. Aretha's printed materials weren't slick. But what C.H.O.I.C.E. lacked in budget and materials, it made up for in heart and impact. Working with children in Barry Farm, one of D.C.'s most troubled neighborhoods, C.H.O.I.C.E.'s success rate was stellar. Out of the forty kids who were in C.H.O.I.C.E.'s programs, only four had gotten into trouble again. Amazingly, C.H.O.I.C.E., at that point, was the only program of its kind in D.C., a baffling point. With all the troubled youth in the inner-city neighborhoods of Washington, D.C., no one else had this idea for a program that helped kids who were suspended from school.

C.H.O.I.C.E.'s main program is the Alternative Daytime Academic Program, which reaches youth who encounter suspension, truancy, and/or dropout situations. Their target population is youth between the ages of seven and eighteen in Washington's public schools. The average age is fifteen, and most of their participants live in Ward 8, a section of D.C. near the waterfront that is economically poor and in recent decades riddled with drugs and crime. A youth helped by C.H.O.I.C.E. has a typical suspension that can last from three to twenty days. Anything longer than that, C.H.O.I.C.E. doesn't work with the youth. C.H.O.I.C.E. has two sites in Barry Farm and one site for court-related use in D.C. Superior Court, which is called the C.H.O.I.C.E. WRAP Program. (WRAP stands for Working Rapidly for Alternative Placement.) The two sites in Barry Farm can accommodate up to forty participants total. On average, C.H.O.I.C.E. helps about twenty participants at each site each week.

The program is straightforward. The staff conducts an initial assessment for each participant. They look at behavior and academics and then share their assessment with the youth and parent and then make referrals, as needed, to other organizations. According to their materials, "This is a critical part of the program because we are looking for underlying issues that could be affecting the youth's learning abilities, including hearing, seeing, home issues, and self-issues."

All participants receive help with anger management, crime intervention, and life skills. They also go on a field trip related to the reason for their suspension in order to educate them on the consequences of their actions. The staff then obtains school assignments from the youth's teachers for the suspended days. The youth receives assistance with the schoolwork so they won't fall behind. And the youth is matched with a recreational or extra-curricular activity. C.H.O.I.C.E. insists that "parents must participate in creating a realistic plan for their child."

C.H.O.I.C.E. follows up and tracks their youth after the suspension is over. The staff creates an academic plan for the youth and continues to track them throughout the school year in order to decrease any other suspensions. For youth involved in the court system, C.H.O.I.C.E. helps find appropriate educational settings on an individual basis.

Aretha came up with the name for her program a decade earlier while she was living with her three small children in a small D.C. shelter for young, single mothers. She recalled, "Rita Bright was one of the community people who always tried to make things happen for single moms and youth in the community. Rita was actually part of Community of Hope, which was a shelter on Fourteenth and Belmont Streets. She asked the shelter to give her two apartments to let single moms move into while they went back to school and got their GEDs, high school diplomas, and job training. And that would allow them to gain some stability to move out and provide for their families. It was a big apartment building that had become a shelter, and she arranged for two apartments. I was one of those families. Today, Community of Hope is no longer in existence.

"Rita inspired me to grow and develop. Every day that I was there, I said, 'I'm going to have a program like Rita has and help someone.' In fact, I'm still in touch with her, and she's a very important mentor in my life. She helps me make decisions even still now. I can call her for anything."

So there Aretha was in her early twenties and living with her three children in one of Rita's apartments in the shelter, and she came up with C.H.O.I.C.E. Aretha remembered, "One day I was laying across my bed, and I wrote the word, choice, on a piece of paper. And I thought, 'Now this is an important word,' because the choices I have made affected my children and my life. What I did was play with the letters in the word, choice.

"My children are first in my life. 'C' for children. If I don't make better choices, they're not going to have good opportunities. 'O' for opportunities. If I don't make better choices, look at the environment I have my children in. 'E' for environment. So that's kind of how I came up with the acronym for it. And on that day, I ran outside to Rita and told her about the idea I had and the word I had come up with, and I told her, 'This is going to be the name of my program one day!' C.H.O.I.C.E. has been in my head from that summer of 1993. Every day, I would chart what was going on in my life, all the trials and tribulations we were going through, and I would think about C.H.O.I.C.E. until I founded it in September 2003."

Almost a decade to the day later, Aretha's dream of creating C.H.O.I.C.E. came true. But during that decade, she couldn't have planned or imagined that it would be influenced by one of her children and her answered prayers.

Candid about her life choices, she explained, "I met the father of my children when I was fourteen. By the time I was eighteen, my boyfriend and I had two daughters, and we got married before our third child, a son, was born. I was divorced by the time I was twenty-one. He had become incarcerated, and I moved away from Spartansburg and came to D.C. At that time, my oldest daughter was seven and my son was three. And my son missed his father terribly."

Staying in one of Rita Bright's apartments at the shelter, Aretha got her life together. She said, "I got my GED, and then I went to school and got certified as a nurse assistant. From there, I went back to school and got certified as an emergency medical technician. And that led to my employment with EMS. I love my job. I have delivered three babies since I've been here. I've seen inside the body, from the gut to the brain. I have performed CPR numerous times," she added proudly.

"What led me to launch C.H.O.I.C.E. was really my son," she said and paused. "His problems started when he was about five. This was the effect of seeing his father getting locked up when he was three. By five, he was very angry. He was rebellious in school. I could even say he didn't have a very happy childhood. He was the type of little boy who wanted his father to be a part of his life. They all do, even little girls. But my son took it extra hard. As years passed, by the time he was nine, he was already formally introduced to the streets of D.C. He was introduced to drugs and a life of crime. By the time he was fourteen, his lifestyle landed *all of us* in the hands of the law. When you have one child introduced to the system, all of you are in the system. Even though my daughters weren't in trouble or in the system, they were affected by it. We all were.

"When his father got out of jail, I allowed my son at age twelve to go to South Carolina to live with his father. And there, he saw what his life was like with his father. And that's when he began to grow and he came home to me changed. He respects his father, but he understands this is not going to happen, that having a life together with his father is not going to happen. From fourteen until sixteen, he continued to go through different episodes until at sixteen, he realized he wasn't going to have his life with his father. And he began to move in a positive direction.

"Once he came back, there was some additional troubles, but he ended up going to Bowling Brooks Prep School, an all-boys prep school that the court sent him to. There he obtained his GED and a Maryland high school diploma. And from there, he went to the University of Maryland, Eastern Shore College. He's a business major. And my daughters are in college, too. One is studying mortuary science and the other is in marketing."

Out of Aretha's heartache, C.H.O.I.C.E. was created in 2003—a couple of years after her son started getting his life back on track. It was all connected. Aretha remembers worrying as her son kept getting suspended and into all kinds of trouble, always wondering if someone would call with horrible news.

"Never knew if he would be the next body I would pick up off the sidewalk. Always used to say that," Aretha added, her voice becoming shaky. But keeping him out of trouble didn't help matters for long. He kept acting out, running with a rough crowd on D.C. streets. Because of her work as a paramedic, the police knew her and tried to be of help, picking up her son and bringing him to her now and then.

Ultimately, she believes it's up to the parents to get resources.

"Frankly, I couldn't get any help for him until he got into trouble. No way for the government to assist me until he actually committed a crime and was in the system. The more I asked for help, for a program for youth, the more I realized I wasn't getting anywhere. He actually ended up getting charged for a stolen vehicle."

No matter how hard she tried, the system didn't really help her son get better. Overwhelmed, the system wasn't built to deal with the underlying problems; it was built just to deal with the aftermath. Nationally, about 2.5 million youth end up in the juvenile justice system. Aretha understood the underlying problems and created C.H.O.I.C.E. and its Alternative Daytime Academic Program. As mentioned, only four out of forty who have gone through C.H.O.I.C.E. have gotten suspended again. Ask anyone who has worked in the system, and they will tell you that that turnaround is magnificent.

Sometimes it takes a mother's love to create a program that cuts through all the mess and gets to the heart of the matter—developing a program that reaches unreachable parents and unreachable youth.

"Education starts in the womb," Aretha believes. "The baby is learning its own emotion, when it's hungry, how to move, kick, survive. That's their environment. And if you just lock him up in jails, then they're going to adjust to that environment and survive. But they'll be angry. They're already angry for what they're missing at home and in life, and then they act out and get into trouble. And the system throws them in jail and makes them angrier when the answer is love, guidance, education, attention, leadership, and hope.

"These kids can do it; they just need a person in their corner. If I could be in every youth's corner and find out their interests and what they want to be when they grow up, I would get them on that career path and push them and make sure they would be successful in life."

Aretha has worked full-time as a paramedic with D.C. Fire/Emergency Medical Services (or EMS) in Southeast Washington since 1999. Actually, she works the night shift for EMS. That is no small feat in D.C. with all the gunshot victims and violent crime. She also works full-time for C.H.O.I.C.E. during the day. The woman hardly sleeps. She explained that she goes on the night shift and prays that it's a slow night so she can catch some sleep. Otherwise, she just catches a few hours of sleep after her shift and before the job with C.H.O.I.C.E., so that means a few hours of sleep from 5:00 A.M. to 8:00 A.M. The fact is that she doesn't want to quit her hard-earned job with EMS. She loves her job. But she also loves C.H.O.I.C.E. So EMS adjusted her schedule to work nights, and that way she can work at C.H.O.I.C.E. by day.

When we first spoke, I had to ask, half-jokingly, "Forgive me, Aretha, but how do you get stuff done like housework?"

"Well, I'm never there to mess things up. I clean and mop and dust during a day off, but there's never any mess. I'm hardly there." And we laughed.

A woman with a steel core and a heart of gold, Aretha is also a true believer who is soft-spoken and calm. She believes fervently in what she is doing. Her supporters and a handful of volunteers share her view that it's a slippery slope from a suspension to being in some kind of trouble with the law. C.H.O.I.C.E. is there to stop and even turn around that slippery slope, to bring hope back, to work with the kids and the parents.

Aretha's personal story relates more to the foundation of C.H.O.I.C.E. than almost any other visionary in this book. She isn't helping a thousand kids per year, but people in Northwest D.C. and throughout the city are calling and begging her to duplicate her program there. But she can grow only as she has funds. Her program is perfect for replication, and the dividends of her program pay for itself by helping kids get back on track and graduate from high school.

Barry Farm is known for being one of the roughest sections of the Southeast quadrant, which is the most crime-ridden part of Washington. Some in law enforcement have dubbed it the number one hot spot area in Washington when it comes to crime, violence, and drugs. Yet, it's only about a five-minute drive from Capitol Hill. Because I had worked with teens in the adjacent Anacostia neighborhood during the crack wars, I wasn't particularly nervous about the blight by the roadside, the liquor stores on every corner, and the numerous people standing around with seemingly nothing to do. I had seen this many times before. It still saddened me, but didn't faze me. What troubled me was that Anacostia also had a great deal of beauty, stunning views of the river, historic buildings, and caring people, but only the blood in the streets seemed to make the news.

The afternoon I was there to photograph Aretha and her colleague, Crystal Hall, the truth is that for some reason being there did faze me, for not much had changed. I realized that I had forgotten how things were in Southeast, how the roads are full of potholes and trash, how the streets are not going to win a beauty contest. I thought about the parents I had gotten to know in Anacostia years earlier, how we all wanted the same things: whatever is best for the children. Like me, they wanted good schools and safe streets. But that's far from what they got.

The Section 8 housing in Barry Farm was what you might expect: cookie-cutter, low-rise buildings that looked old and run-down. Everything seemed gray. A couple of doorways had a festive red and green decoration for the upcoming Christmas holiday. The community pool was locked up and almost emptied of water for the winter. A motorcycle helmet, an old bike, and a ton of garbage filled the cavernous pool.

Though I easily found Barry Farm, the exact location of Aretha's headquarters was less than clear. I drove through the streets, trying to make sense of my directions. Christmas music was on every radio station, and once in a while, a disc jockey came on and reminded listeners about our troops in Iraq and Afghanistan, or about the people who moved to our region after losing everything when Katrina hit the Gulf states. For most Americans, the economy was going well in 2005. But it was tough for many, like the troops and their families, the victims of the hurricane, and the families of Barry Farm.

I parked my car near the pool's fence among the Barry Farm buildings and sat there and listened, watching for a few minutes. It was a bitterly cold day, and I hesitated to get out of my warm car. The playground was empty, except for one little boy on the jungle gym. Nearby, an elderly African American woman braced herself against the wind and patiently helped a teenager with special needs out of an old van. I grabbed my camera gear out of the car and as I walked by, I said hello to her and the teen. The elderly woman said something about my parking the car where there were no lines on the concrete to park. She suggested I move my car closer to the fence in order to avoid a ticket. I trudged back and moved my car and then chatted with her briefly, noticing her kind face as she spoke. I wondered what kind of life she had had, what she had seen and wished for in her years in Washington. She seemed instinctively protective of me and pointed me in the right direction.

At the community center, I couldn't find C.H.O.I.C.E.'s office space. A little girl with pigtails showed me where to go. A few children played nearby; some roamed about looking around for something fun to do.

Crystal Hall, who runs the administrative side of C.H.O.I.C.E.'s Barry Farm facility, welcomed me and explained her work, "We offer tutoring, anger management, crime intervention, and spiritual counseling to the kids. And the parents must attend a four-hour session once a week. Just to monitor things, we sit down with the parent or parents and go over stresses that may be caused at home, or any other services that they may need, whether it be financial or clothing. We also help parents obtain their high school diploma or GED, and we have a job bank. At Barry Farm, we have a very high success rate. I would say around 90 percent."

It's curious why some kids get into trouble while others stay on track. From Crystal's point of view, so much about the kids reflects what is going on at home or in the parent's life. She observed, "These are a lot of single parents who are really just struggling to keep their heads above water. A lot of them don't have their high school diploma, or they may have their diploma but just lack job training. There're a lot of hard-working parents, but just lack resources in my opinion. At C.H.O.I.C.E., we try to provide resources that they are lacking. Once the kids are doing better, they come back and volunteer in the reading program at C.H.O.I.C.E. I just think that kids need a chance, an outlet outside their everyday, normal environment."

The parent of a thirteen-year-old daughter, Crystal believes that it comes down to the parents. Focused on her child's well-being, she believes, "It's *all* about the parent. After dinner, instead of letting the TV raise your child or sending them outside to get them out of your face, you need to set aside at least an hour out of your day to devote to them. That's what I do. After my daughter gets home, she usually has a snack and then we go over homework. After homework, she eats dinner, and then it's an hour of just me and her—talking about her day and her friends, what happened at school, what's on her mind. Then she reads a book she got from the school library. She takes her bath, and she's in bed no later than 9:30. If I didn't keep her routine regular, she would be bouncing off of the walls. She cannot go anywhere I cannot see her. I can see the front porch, but I can't see around the corner, so she can't go there unless I know the adult there.

"We may be tired or whatever, but we have to make time for our children no matter how tired we are, or if we don't want to be bothered. It's a must that we make time for our children. As a parent you have to push yourself. You have to do it for your child."

Right away, I could see why Crystal was perfect for her job.

There are influences outside the parent's control, such as friends. "With regard to friends, my motto is: 'Explain to your friends my rules so they won't be shocked, disappointed, or surprised. Then they can come over and we can have a good time,'" Crystal said and then laughed a bit. "Her friends gravitate towards me, too. They see that I pay her lots and lots of attention. We always have a houseful. Every day at my house, dinner is at six."

Crystal loves her job with C.H.O.I.C.E. and said, "I get to see the people we are helping...to see their success when they get their GED, or a job, or when a child is not in trouble anymore."

Like Aretha, Tammy Winslow, the assistant director for C.H.O.I.C.E., works a second job. Tammy works as a radiology tech at area hospitals. Now in her late thirties and philosophical about the vast array of problems they see in the inner city, Tammy said, "The community needs to be united, as opposed to being divided. We have a lot of parents who don't know how to be involved. They need to speak up for city services, for education. Be an active voice in your life, I say to them. They're so intimidated. They say, 'Well, I don't want to go to the school for my child. They talk to me like dirt. They know I live in a low-income complex.' We at C.H.O.I.C.E. can build up the self-esteem so they can express how they feel.

"When we don't see a kid for a while, Aretha and I go to their door and knock. Sometimes the parents will have us in and sometimes they won't. We have kids living in government housing—with no lights, no water, no heat, and no food. It's not the government's fault they don't have those things. The parents either misuse the money they get or they don't have any. No wonder some of these kids are so miserable and frustrated and mad.

"We have a five-year-old kid [in C.H.O.I.C.E.]. She hates herself and she keeps telling us that she wished she were dead. She wants to kill herself. She's the prettiest little girl, and she's very intelligent. But she hates her life. And she's five! She wants love from her mother, but her mother won't provide the nurturing the child needs. The child gets clothes but the child is looking for affection. She'll come here and say, 'Ms. Winslow, my mother don't want me around. What did I do? She don't ever want to hug me, or be bothered with me.' They're already in a counseling program for families in need."

Tammy knows that the kids love C.H.O.I.C.E. and said, "After the tutoring, the kids say, 'I don't want to go home.' At C.H.O.I.C.E., they're going to get a hot meal, tutoring, anything they need if we're able to assist, or we'll talk to them about life skills or just listen.

"We ask the parents, 'How can we assist you?' If a working mom is struggling and needs a little grocery money, Aretha or I will go to the store and get groceries. We try to assist. Sometimes it's been $60 of food. We can't do it all, but we try to do what we can," Tammy reiterated.

One early evening, Aretha and I had a brief chance to talk on the phone about C.H.O.I.C.E. again. She was at her EMS job. In the background, I could hear her sergeant talking with other paramedics. Colleagues asked her things now and then. Somehow, she was able to juggle it all and focus on our conversation.

Winter and freezing temperatures are settling in now, and the nation is bracing for what will be record-high prices for heating our homes in the coming months. In addition to concern over heating their homes, low-income families worry about the basics for their children's warmth. So Aretha created a program called the Winter Care Package.

"I wrote a proposal to the Far Southeast Strengthening Family Collaborative, and they gave me some funding for this program for families in Barry Farm," she explained. "A family can apply, and the application is user-friendly. We just put out flyers this week, and we've been inundated with phone calls. The Winter Care Package includes the following for a child: a winter coat, a pair of boots, hat, gloves, scarf, one blanket, a pair of thermal underwear, a thermometer, a bottle of Motrin, a bottle of Tylenol, a $10 fare card for the Metro to enable them to take their child to the doctor, and an information packet on colds and flu. They gave us enough money for ten families with two kids per family. So we're helping twenty kids. This week is the signing-up process, and *every day*, we have eight or ten families signing up. So with more money, we could help more families."

The overwhelming response demonstrates the growing need. But obviously, all the families will not be served when her program is budgeted for only ten families with two kids each. But Aretha and C.H.O.I.C.E. do what they can. In the end, they gave the Winter Care Packages to ten families in Barry Farm. They had forty other families on the list, but C.H.O.I.C.E. didn't have the budget to accommodate them. Crystal said, "The families that received their packages were so grateful. It was wonderful to see their faces! Some said they were going to wrap some of the items for their kids for Christmas next week. For some, these were the only things these kids were going to get for Christmas."

A year later, at the end of 2006, Aretha summarized their progress: "Since we started in 2003, each year we have helped about seventy-five kids and their families. I would say about fifty of the seventy-five are still involved with C.H.O.I.C.E. and doing OK. The other twenty-five might be doing OK, might have moved away, or might be having problems. Not sure. In Barry Farm, C.H.O.I.C.E. has a 90 percent success rate. In 2005, four out of the forty got into trouble again. Same was true in 2006.

"In 2006, we started to help the parents. With our help, one got her high school diploma; three obtained their GED; and one parent is now a certified nurse assistant. One is now a dental assistant. It all started with the kids. We asked the parents, 'How can we assist you?' And that's how we got involved with their needs. By helping the parents, clearly we are helping the kids see a better way."

Today, Aretha feels, "If I had it to do over again, I would have gotten educated first. I would have waited before having children and gotten a better understanding of economics and credit. I love my children, of course, but if I had had all that understanding, I could have given them a better life.

"I always used to say, 'I thank God for my life of ugly trials and tribulations, because now I can give the beauty of it to a family and give them a smile.'

"My dream is to expand C.H.O.I.C.E., not only in D.C. but nationwide.

And my dream is to start a children's clothing line using the C.H.O.I.C.E. logo. I'm in the process of working on that. It's called C.H.O.I.C.E. Children's Clothing."

And with that new dream of growing her vision set forth so long ago, Aretha went back to her work as a paramedic on the streets of D.C.

UPDATE ABOUT C.H.O.I.C.E.

D.C.'s TRUANCY RATE in 2008 was 19 percent. As of late 2008, C.H.O.I.C.E. continued to have a 90 percent success rate, and now the nonprofit has partnerships with other organizations. News of their success rate has spread. Local probation officers in Northern Virginia have asked C.H.O.I.C.E. to work with them as they help those coming out of the prison system. In addition, the D.C. government gave a grant to C.H.O.I.C.E.

Aretha said proudly, "We've been in service for five years! We had our first graduation in June. We had kids and parents that graduated. So we're graduating families! We had five complete families that graduated. A total of sixty youth. We work with the kids and then the parents get involved. We have parents who went back and got their high school diploma or GED or went through vocational training and got employed."

As need has grown, C.H.O.I.C.E.'s services have grown. Their annual budget in 2008 was still $100,000. Focused on sixty youth and their families each year, the four main programs have been formally named and still include the Alternative Daytime Academic Short-Term Suspension Program, the After-School Program, the WRAP Program, and the ACE Program for Continuing Education.

In addition to receiving referrals from the D.C. Public Schools, more calls are coming in from parents as well as school districts around the region, including Prince George's County in Maryland. Aretha said that they are doing case management, partnering with case managers and social workers in order to ensure that their families are getting wraparound services. Aretha's team is committed to working with the families to build them back up and help them create a better foundation for self-sufficiency and financial stability. Urgent calls for replication have come in from Atlanta, Memphis, and Milwaukee, but for now, Aretha is staying focused on the Washington region. She may train others in the future.

One hitch in the near future will be C.H.O.I.C.E.'s location. When Barry Farm is demolished in the coming years, everyone living there will have to move, and Aretha will be forced to relocate the nonprofit's headquarters to another D.C. neighborhood in Southeast. Community leaders keep wondering where all these families will find affordable housing, much less find housing that is that close to the city with its mass transit and job opportunities.

An asset to the team, Crystal Hall went to work elsewhere. Tammy Winslow is now the nonprofit's educational coordinator.

Aretha's three children are doing well. Her two daughters have graduated from college and are working. Her older daughter is helping Aretha run the nonprofit's programs. Her son is expected to graduate from college in May 2009.

Contact information for C.H.O.I.C.E.:

Aretha Lyles
Founder/Executive Director
C.H.O.I.C.E., Inc.
1230-D Sumner Road, SE
Washington, D.C. 20020
C.H.O.I.C.E. Office Phone: 202-321-1420
D.C. Superior Court Phone: 202-879-1904
Web site: www.choice4kids.org

If you like C.H.O.I.C.E., you might be interested in these organizations:

1) Huckleberry House
   (Part of Huckleberry Youth Programs)
   San Francisco, California
   Web site: www.huckleberryyouth.org
   Phone: 415-668-2622

2) Living Classrooms Foundation
   Baltimore, Maryland
   Web site: www.livingclassrooms.org
   Phone: 410-685-0295

3) The Safer Foundation
   Chicago, Illinois
   Web site: www.saferfoundation.org
   Phone: 312-922-2200

SISTERMENTORS

S OMETIMES, A LIFE is influenced by the closest of relatives, and
sometimes a life is influenced by the circumstances in which a child
is born. In the case of Dr. Shireen Lewis, it was a combination of
both. Encouraged by her family and homeland of Trinidad, Shireen's focus
on education started as a child and she has achieved much. Now, she has
channeled that focus into a way to help women and girls achieve their
dreams. Her creation, SisterMentors, is already having success.

SisterMentors is a program of EduSeed, a nonprofit in Washington,
D.C., which promotes "education among traditionally disadvantaged
groups such as women and people of color. SisterMentors helps women of
color to complete their dissertation and get the doctorate. While they are in
the program, the women, in turn, are obligated to give back by mentoring
girls of color in middle and high school—encouraging them to go to college.
EduSeed believes that real social change and economic advancement begin
with promoting the value of education in disadvantaged communities."
As of 2005, twenty-five women of color had earned their Ph.D. with the
support of SisterMentors, and the program has mentored more than fifty-
five girls of color.

When people make far-reaching decisions in their lives, they often base
those decisions upon their core beliefs and circumstances. There is also a
measure of fortitude involved. Shireen Lewis has fortitude in the marrow
of her bones and created a way to share that drive. Nothing happens in a
vacuum. And SisterMentors did not happen out of thin air. This is a story

about achievement against the odds and the story of a little program that does a lot of good.

In Shireen's youth, her maternal grandmother, Beatrice Davis, was a life force. Shireen recalled with a loving chuckle that Granny, as she was known, liked to say, "Don't talk about it. Just get it done." Shireen added softly, "I had a lot of great respect, love, and admiration for her. And for me, she is very much present in my life." And she paused for a moment, as if remembering her in her heart.

The acorn doesn't fall far from the tree. Shireen says those exact words to the women and girls in SisterMentors. In fact, she said it to *me* with regard to writing this book! At the end of our inspiring interview, I told Shireen that in a few days I should have a draft of the essay. Like her beloved Granny, Shireen responded without pausing, "That's good. Set goals. Now don't talk about it. Just get it done." Shireen's energy is contagious; she is a force.

When you meet Shireen, there is no way to describe her except to say total integrity with a bundle of positive energy. In her mid-forties, her face is strikingly open, reflecting her bountiful heart within. She is tall and thin but strong in voice and spirit. Originally from Trinidad, a small island of about 1.3 million people, Shireen speaks with a slight British accent. Polished, she is also at ease in the way she can speak with anyone. Though from humble beginnings, Shireen has accomplished a great deal. She attended Douglass College at Rutgers University, the last remaining all-women's college at a public university in the nation. At Douglass, she received a bachelor's in Spanish and French, then earned a law degree at the University of Virginia, and practiced corporate law in New York City. In 1998, she received her Ph.D. from Duke University and taught at several universities. Shireen's Ph.D. is in French literature, specializing in Francophone West African and Caribbean literature.

Granny would be proud. But Shireen's education is merely the launching pad for her life's work of helping others.

Shireen recalled how SisterMentors got planted in her mind, "I was working on my Ph.D. at Duke, but I was here in the Washington area. Once you're done with your coursework, you can be anywhere as long as you keep in touch with your dissertation advisor. That's why we at SisterMentors have women in the D.C. area who are getting their doctorates from all over the world, including the University of London and the University of Paris. So I realized I felt increasing alienation and isolation. Then I got up one morning and decided to do something about it. So that was my 'Aha' moment. I thought there must be other women of color in the D.C. area who are doing the same thing: working on their dissertation—alone. So I called the owner of SisterSpace and Books. It was a bookstore in D.C. owned by two African American women, and it carried books by and for African American women. I used to volunteer there. I called them up, and they said it was wonderful. 'Let's start!' They provided the space and we got going.

"I couldn't have gotten it done, at least not in that timing. Finishing the dissertation would have been *a lot more suffering* and taken *much* longer without the group. In the first set of women, all but one woman got her Ph.D., and the one who didn't had to abandon it because her mother got cancer and she went to be with her mother.

"So it was September 1997, the first night the first group of us got started, and the thing just kept going. And we quickly outgrew SisterSpace. At one point, there was a group of fifteen women and a second group of about eight to ten women meeting. The thing was that it was supposed to be three different groups, but people get really attached to each other, and the group of fifteen women didn't want to be split in two. And that's a big part of SisterMentors: connecting with each other through this sort of process."

It sounded like a "birthing" process, and Shireen laughed and agreed. I know. Getting this book completed has become a bit of a birthing process!

By 2000, EduSeed was created as a nonprofit for SisterMentors. The reason for creating the umbrella organization is that it is Shireen's hope to have other programs in addition to SisterMentors.

Shireen speaks about how connecting with each other is a key part of SisterMentors, and connecting and being a part of something larger than oneself is a key part of the stories chronicled in this book. Like Shireen, each visionary in the book has created an avenue for people to re-engage with one another, to thrive again in the community. Like SisterMentors, all the nonprofits connect us to what is important and everlasting in an increasingly alienating world. In other words, individually, we are strong, but together, we are that much stronger. SisterMentors exemplifies the meaning of strength in numbers.

After Shireen got her Ph.D., the other women in the group continued to meet, but the group started to come apart. Shireen recalled, "So the women called me and said, 'You started this; you really should come back and make sure this survives.' So that's what I did. But at that time, I had no idea that it would be what it is today!"

Today, in 2006, SisterMentors each year helps eighteen to twenty women who are working on their dissertation. Out of that number, about three get their doctorate each year. There is always an active waiting list as well. While the women are in SisterMentors, they give back to the community by mentoring girls of color in middle and high schools. The women and girls are African American, Latina, Asian American, and immigrants. By mentoring the girls, the women's goal is "to successfully encourage girls of color to stay in school, excel academically, and go on to college," as their materials state.

Shireen is the kind of person you can ask anything, and I had to ask her about her phrase, "women and girls of color." That phrase really threw me for a loop. After all, our nation switched away from saying *color* a long time ago. I was barely born when that word began to be considered incorrect. Yet, if someone must be categorized, then I wanted to make every effort to do so in accordance with their wishes. And Shireen had reasons for her specific choice of words.

"Women and girls of color is a phrase used in literary theory and feminist scholarship referring to women who are not white," she explained. "For example, I never use the word *minority* to refer to anybody who is not white. And women in SisterMentors have told me they prefer not to be called 'minority.'" Hence the phrase.

"Once every three weeks, there's a SisterMentors meeting for the women," Shireen continued. "We have those meetings January through December except for August. Then with the girls, we have a once-a-month mentoring session, an annual college visit during their spring break, and at least one workshop during the school year. We also have an etiquette session with a professional. Their annual college visit with the girls in the spring of 2005 was to the University of Virginia."

Their meetings are all held in a space that is donated by the D.C. law firm of Schiff Hardin. The law firm also provides the nonprofit with office space. The nonprofit's budget, as of 2006, was $177,000, of which about $62,000 was in-kind. With more funds, Shireen is certain that they could expand and help many more women and girls, including all the women from the waiting list.

In the beginning, Shireen facilitated all the meetings. But today, she encourages the women in the group to rotate as facilitator, thereby building up their own leadership and facilitator skills.

SisterMentors has a tradition of celebration for each woman as she earns her doctorate. All of the women in SisterMentors organize a celebration and buy gifts for the honoree. The girls are always invited, and many times they attend. Describing the gifts for the woman getting her Ph.D., Shireen said,

"The women buy her a Waterman fountain pen and a bouquet of roses. The Waterman pen's cover must be engravable because we engrave the woman's initials plus Ph.D. behind it. The reason we do the initials and not the full name is because the first woman in SisterMentors to earn her doctorate had a name that was too long, so we used initials. Since we wanted everyone to get the same thing, we kept the tradition."

A close friend of mine from college, Maria Moreno, provided some personal insights. Maria, who lives in the Midwest, worked diligently on her dissertation for many years and recently earned her doctorate. Writing her dissertation was a huge undertaking and accomplishment, especially because she and her husband had twins in the middle of writing it! Like Shireen, Maria is an immigrant; only Maria is from the Dominican Republic. When I mentioned SisterMentors to Maria, she immediately said, "What a fantastic idea! I wish I had had that here. It would have helped tremendously. You feel so alone while working on the dissertation."

Maria fought hard to finish. Of course, the All-But-Dissertation (or ABD) people are everywhere. Those I have met who are ABD have a certain look in their eyes when they discuss the dissertation that has languished.

"It happens to me all the time," Shireen agreed. "A black woman came up to me at an event and handed me her card and said, 'If I had had a group like yours, I would have finished. I went on and got an M.B.A. instead.' But she had real regret. I can't tell you how many women have come to me and said, 'I started a Ph.D. and never finished.'"

According to various studies, approximately 50 percent of all doctoral candidates drop out of their programs during the dissertation writing stage. The numbers are higher for women of color. To give a sense of the overwhelming odds against earning a Ph.D. for a woman of color, here are the statistics on those earning their doctorates in the United States, according to The National Science Foundation. In 2003, in the United States, a grand total of 28,044 individuals earned their doctorates. Of that total, about half, or 14,185, were women. Of the 14,185 women earning their doctorates, 10,696 were White/Non-Hispanic women. The following is the breakdown of the remaining 3,489 women: 1,143 were African American; 991 were Asian or Pacific Islander; 757 were Latina; 83 were Native American or Alaskan Native; and 515 were other or unknown.

Shireen believes that the breakdown demonstrates how women of color are under-represented. She said, "In general, there is a disproportionately small representation of women of color." Clearly, SisterMentors was created to help change that imbalance.

Admittedly, at first, I wondered how significant twenty-five doctorates were, given the impact that other nonprofit programs have on dozens or hundreds of people. But upon reflection, I needed to do a reality check of sorts, for there are not that many women working on a Ph.D. in the nation, and SisterMentors is focused only on women of color in the Washington region. On top of that, the women with their doctorates are going on to their careers in academia, research, or business and will help create a path for other women. If they teach, they will have women in their classes who will see what is possible. If the women also raise children, their children will see by example that their mother also worked hard on her education. Each doctorate for a woman of color is significant and worthy of special laud. That doctorate can set forth a ripple in that woman's world, wherever she goes. Therefore, in my mind, twenty-five doctorates out of the numbers mentioned above are significant. It makes me wonder how many more women of color would pursue and receive their doctorates in our nation if SisterMentors were there to support them through the process.

While considering whether or not to select SisterMentors and Shireen Lewis for the book, I also thought about *To Kill a Mockingbird* and how that story still resonates, how our nation has come so far in race relations and yet has work to do. Finally, I reminded myself that there are things that I take for granted, such as how a clerk in a store might treat me simply because I am white. Rayvon Hicks, a teenager from the inner city of D.C., explained it to me once.

I had first gotten to know Rayvon in 1994 when I had launched a non-profit called Lights, Camera, Action! (or LCA!), which was committed to helping inner-city youth realize their potential through film. Like Shireen, I have seen the magic of mentoring. LCA! used film as a vehicle to reach youth and encouraged the participants to believe in themselves. My program focused on youth in Anacostia, a D.C. neighborhood riddled at that time with a drug war, shootings, and daily tragedies. During the week we made our short film on location in Anacostia, there were seven shootings in that same vicinity. Despite untold hurdles, the LCA! students prevailed. Their high school's dropout rate was high; yet, seven out of eight of the LCA! participants, including Rayvon, went to college, and our short film, *Poppy*, won two awards and has aired dozens of times on local PBS stations.

Today, Rayvon is a strapping, young African American in his early thirties. While I was teaching him in his late teens, he told me in a matter-of-fact way what happens in the day-to-day. In 1994, he said that when he has gone into a store in Georgetown, for example, many eyes have suddenly preyed upon him. He can see it and feel it. He is well-dressed, and yet he is basically followed through the store and asked constantly if someone can be of help to him. They're not being solicitous; they're letting him know they're watching him. Rayvon paused and then added, "And I didn't do anything and wouldn't do anything. I just wanted to look at the sweaters and jeans like everybody else." His hurt feelings coupled with quiet rage sat in the air. He didn't have to say anything more. He knew I understood, and he knew it enraged me.

As a white person, I can only imagine the barriers, whether pronounced or not, that fly in the face of fairness. After years or a life of such treatment, what does that do to a soul? Does it make someone bitter or make that person determined to achieve more? For Rayvon, it meant the latter. Determined to do well, he graduated from Delaware State University. By 2006, he was managing his own successful office supply business, a growing wholesale enterprise. In late 2006, he called to tell me he was establishing an annual $1,000 college scholarship award at Anacostia Senior High School and at Delaware State. Rayvon is an example of a ripple effect.

As with all of the LCA! teenagers, another participant named Robby Preston could have gone either way when I met him; he could have become another statistic, a kid of the streets. But he decided to give LCA! a chance, and he made a tremendous difference with the writing and directing of our film. He told a reporter from Black Entertainment Television (or BET) that before LCA!, he was angry and didn't know why. He said that LCA! made him see that he could be part of the world and that anything is possible, and ultimately, that he has value. Today, Robby is a teacher and mentor at a school that helps troubled youth.

SisterMentors creates that same ripple effect. It is one way to help someone finish their education, thereby leveling the playing field and helping launch new voices in our nation. Try to think about where our nation would be without Toni Morrison's literature filled with memorable insights into the human condition. It is unthinkable. Or where would our nation be without Barbara Jordan's courage in the Congress in the 1970s? And now with President Obama's stunning election and hope for a better America, will our nation finally be able to let go of any vestiges of intolerance? Our nation needs more of these voices.

What Shireen Lewis is saying with SisterMentors and EduSeed is larger than a small nonprofit helping groups of women and girls. She is making a point that our nation would be far more enriched—intellectually and spiritually—with programs like SisterMentors and its umbrella organization,

EduSeed. The reality is that our nation is not quite color-blind, and the Ph.D. is a marker that announces, "I'm here. And I have expertise." A Ph.D. is earned the old-fashioned way, through hard work and study. With SisterMentors in tow, a Ph.D. is completed with a little more compassion for the doctoral candidate, especially someone who has already overcome so many obstacles. As written in their materials, SisterMentors "builds community among women and people of color by promoting collaboration and cooperation in the learning process…creating a community of scholars working to help each other achieve academic success."

At SisterMentors, the women read each other's work and give constructive feedback, get together in small groups to write, and share resources. Their mentoring of girls includes sharing with girls some of the challenges women of color encounter in pursuing their education and strategies they devise to successfully move forward.

There are many support groups—from investment clubs to grieving circles for those who have lost a loved one. We know that support groups work. SisterMentors takes that proven model and applies a version of it to women of color involved in intellectual pursuits.

Women from all over the country have contacted Shireen to see if they can join SisterMentors. But Shireen has had to answer, "Not if you're not in the Washington, D.C., area." Of course, she would love to replicate elsewhere. Funding would make that possible. But first, she is solely focused on the Washington area.

Besides Granny, there was more to the formation of Shireen Lewis, including her parents and their commitment to education. "It wasn't just my parents," Shireen explained. "You had this whole country [of Trinidad] being indoctrinated with, 'Send your kids to school so they can learn well. It was the neighbors, everybody. It was a big thing. The context was a newly emerging nation with a new prime minister, Eric Williams, who was highly educated himself with a Ph.D. in history from Oxford. He was a historian, and he knew the history of slavery, colonization, and oppression—not only in the Caribbean but in the rest of the world. So this was his consciousness, his mindset. He was not a bureaucrat. He was an intellectual, and he was inspiring. My parents adored this man."

There was something more that motivated Shireen and continues to drive her vision. "The inspiration for my work is derived from my experience attending the first school in my village in Trinidad," she began. "What that meant for me was a community of people who were there to support *me* and all these kids who had a school in their village for the first time.

And it was a brand new school with brand new teachers. The teachers were just out of teacher-training college. And they were all young and had lots of energy and were very passionate about the work they were doing. That experience has influenced a lot of how I look at who I am and a lot of how I look at education for children, because what happened there is a lot of mentoring and nurturing. And it just infused us with this desire to do extremely well in school. We wanted to please our teachers. They wanted us to do well, and we wanted to do well.

"Before Trinidad became independent [from Britain], Prime Minister Williams was very involved in the independence movement. He used to hold public lectures. There is a square called Woodford Square, and it was dubbed The University of Woodford Square because this is where Williams would give his lectures. And he would stand there and give lectures to hundreds of Trinidadians about the history of the Caribbean, about independence, about what it would mean to be truly independent from Britain. So this man endeared himself even before he became prime minister. And when he became prime minister, people really worshiped the ground he walked on. My father used to have a saying: 'Eric Williams has brains he hasn't even used yet.' He also wrote several history books and taught at Howard University before returning to Trinidad. Fairly young, Eric Williams died while in office."

Shireen explained that Prime Minister Williams pushed education and insisted that their nation invest in the nation's children. Her family's focus on education echoed Trinidad's. Shireen recollected, "My father would always say, 'If it's one thing people cannot take away from you, it's your education. They can strip you of everything else but not your education. Whatever you know, you know. But you have to go to school for it.' For us at that time, education was extremely, highly valued. That's a different philosophy than in America. My parents expected us to do well in school. There was nothing else for me to focus on. We're a little country. Unemployment was high. Even if we wanted to work, there were no jobs for kids. The jobs were for the adults."

Shireen and her siblings took the lesson about education to heart. She said, "My eldest sister went to Rutgers at the same time as I did. She got her Ph.D. when I went to law school and practiced law. Today, she is a clinical psychologist. My youngest sister is finishing a master's in jurisprudence and is planning to go to law school. Another sister works in management at United Parcel Service. My brother, the oldest of all of us, is what we call an A-class mason and does specialized work on houses."

As Prime Minister Williams and Trinidad had a tremendous impact on Shireen and her siblings, SisterMentors has had a tremendous impact on the women in the program. Shireen noted, "I'm seeing more and more people who join SisterMentors who have not worked on their dissertation for a while and that's not a good sign. But those women come in and they finish!" she said proudly. "One of the women, Shona Jackson, got her Ph.D. through SisterMentors, and she is now a tenure-track professor in English at Texas A&M."

A 2005 graduate of SisterMentors, Shona is an excellent spokesperson for its impact. She said about the program, "Through word of mouth, I found out about SisterMentors but could not join for a year. While on the waiting list, I achieved little work on the dissertation. Shortly after joining SisterMentors, however, I began to meet goals set for myself. One of the most valuable aspects of the group is the goal-setting, which helped me to see and approach my work in more manageable ways. I also had the amazing opportunity to mentor young girls of color and encourage them to continue seeking success through education. In SisterMentors, I was encouraged by a group of caring women and had the opportunity to encourage others as well. The lessons about perseverance that I learned from SisterMentors women stayed with me and carried me through. These lessons are what I take away from the group and hope to continue to share with other women."

Another 2005 graduate of SisterMentors was Koritha Mitchell, and she is now tenure-track at Ohio State University. Both Shona and Koritha got several offers. Shireen mentioned, "In this tight market, that's very impressive; their work was very good."

Then there is Genevieve Yirenkyi. Beaming with pride, Shireen said, "The thing about Genevieve is that she got her Ph.D. at age twenty-six, and she got her degree through us. She was born in Ghana and came to the States at age five, and she is a dynamo. But she had been in a 'dissertation funk' before she joined SisterMentors. It had been six months since she had relocated from California to living in Maryland, and she felt stuck. Now she is doing a post-doc. She's the youngest Ph.D. we have helped.

"We have a woman who is sixty-seven years old; she's a grandmother, and she's getting her Ph.D. with us! And it's wonderful to see her working. Her Ph.D. work is in social work on black women's mental health.

"One of the most exciting things is that we are helping women and girls from eleven years old to as old as sixty-seven, from teens to twenties and every stage of life, all through the generations, all along the generation scale.

It's wonderful to see that, to have women and girls of all those ages in one room helping each other. A lot of experience in that room."

An underlying reason for SisterMentors is the feminization of poverty, which has been a serious, growing concern on Capitol Hill and in think tanks for at least two decades. As mentioned previously in this book, the statistics are alarming. In short, women live longer than men, and on average, women are paid seventy-seven cents for every dollar a man makes. For women of color, the gap is worse. According to the National Organization for Women, African American women earn seventy-one cents for every dollar a man makes; Latinas only make fifty-eight cents on the dollar. Women often take time off to have a child or to be a caregiver for a parent or a child. Therefore, overall, women have fewer earned resources, live longer after caring for others, and are far more vulnerable to poverty. One way to stem the tide of this trend is education.

SisterMentors is part of that effort. As Shireen pointed out, "To be taken seriously as a woman, a woman needs her education. I've seen a whole lot of backlash against women in general. And it's very hard to be taken seriously as a woman of color. And then it's very hard to be taken seriously as a woman of color who is an immigrant. I see all those levels."

And Shireen believes there is more to it than simply getting your own education set. She said, "You want to help others along the way. The whole thing is about giving back. One of the things that happens with the women in SisterMentors is the giving back."

Before a woman joins SisterMentors, she meets with Shireen and that is merely to get on the waiting list! Explaining the process, she said, "I talk with them one-on-one. Why are you getting a Ph.D.? There's more to this than teaching or doing whatever. It really means a responsibility to give back to your community. I talk about it at every meeting and every celebration. The fundamental thing is that everyone says, 'Go to college and get a good job.' What about saying: 'Go to college and learn more about who you are and the world around you?' I think for the first time these women begin to think about the larger meaning, the larger context of getting a Ph.D. Besides getting a job and having a Ph.D. behind your name, what is the larger meaning for society?

"We have a session at least once a year called the 'Oprah Session,'" Shireen said with excitement. "And what we do is we set up a stage, and someone is designated as 'Oprah.' And then we have a panel of experts: three women and two girls. And the rest of us sit back as the audience. The whole discussion is, 'Why is school important and why is it relevant to our lives? How is it important to my future?' A lot of the girls have never really thought about it. 'Why does it have meaning for me in my life?' For the women, they are asked, 'How long have you been in school?' So they think for a bit and say about twenty years. To the girls, they say seven or eight years. Then one session—after hearing 'twenty years of school'—a girl's eyes went really big and said, 'Don't you get tired of homework?' And we all laughed. These women have never thought about the length of time they've been in school. And what I say is that you have had all these years of education, and what you should really think about is, 'How has this improved my life?' Or, 'How can I use this education to improve my life and the life of others?' It's poignant. It shifts the focus from getting a degree or a job to more of a focus on contributing to the community."

Shireen has a specific vision with SisterMentors, which is far more than a mentoring program. This woman is on a mission—a mission for community-minded women who will have an impact on young girls and other women and the nation. She explained, "One of the things I talk to women interested in SisterMentors about is that we're looking for two things. One is women who are serious and committed about getting the doctorate. And second, women who are willing to give back by mentoring girls. If either one of those things is not there, then this is not the group for you. And we have a waiting list constantly."

Shireen could speak all day about how proud she is each of the women in SisterMentors, past and present. As she has written, "Most of us are the first generation in our families to get an advanced degree or a doctorate." She has made lasting friendships with women who are already making a difference. One example is Losang Rabgey, a Tibetan who is earning her Ph.D. through SisterMentors. Shireen said, "From what we know, she may be the first Tibetan in the West—meaning outside of Asia—to receive her Ph.D. Her parents have built the *first* school in her father's village in Tibet. She and her sister put in a requirement in the village school that 50 percent of the students must be girls. Traditionally, it's only boys who were schooled through the monastery, and girls traditionally stayed at home. At the school, they have the same kind of energy our teachers had in Trinidad, and those kids are taking off—passing all kinds of exams and are going to do well!"

Everyone has a background that forms his or her perspective. Shireen brings to the table an awareness and point of view that form her daily life. First, she sees herself as an immigrant. She moved to the United States when she was in her early twenties and became a citizen in the intervening years. But she feels in her heart that she is an immigrant, explaining that it is harder on an immigrant the older you are. Secondly, she considers herself a woman. And third, she sees herself as a woman of color.

Some people achieve a great deal, never pausing to take stock of how they achieved so much and never reaching back to help others along the way. Through SisterMentors, Shireen has taken time to do both. Ultimately, Shireen believes that "education is a catalyst for social change and economic advancement in communities of color." Much like her hero, Prime Minister Eric Williams, Dr. Shireen Lewis is a change agent, a social entrepreneur in our midst. Imagine all the fine achievements her program's "graduates" will conquer and inspire others to strive for. And imagine how much better the young girls of color will do as they face challenges in the coming years. They will already have their North Star guiding them from within.

UPDATE ABOUT SISTERMENTORS

IN THE SUMMER of 2007, SisterMentors celebrated its tenth anniversary. As of 2008, SisterMentors had helped thirty women of color receive their doctorates, and two of the "doctorate graduates" in the past year were the first in their family to earn a college degree as well. One of the recent participants earned her Ph.D. in applied mathematics and is currently teaching at West Point.

In 2007, SisterMentors took a group of twenty-two girls, ages eleven to seventeen, on a four-day college tour in the Northeast. In the fall of 2007, five twelfth graders, who had been with SisterMentors since eighth grade, graduated from high school and began college. Their schools include Duke University and Virginia Commonwealth University. SisterMentors has now expanded its program to include elementary school girls.

Tisha Lewis, daughter of Tom Lewis (the founder of The Fishing School), joined SisterMentors in the fall of 2006. Tisha credits SisterMentors with helping her make significant progress on her dissertation. She is slated to receive her doctorate in May 2009.

Contact information for SisterMentors & EduSeed:

Shireen Lewis, Ph.D.
Founder SisterMentors
Executive Director of EduSeed
1666 K Street, NW, Suite 300
Washington, D.C. 20006
Phone: 202-778-6424
Web site: www.sistermentors.org

If you like SisterMentors, you might be interested in these organizations:

1) Academy of Hope
   Washington, D.C.
   Web site: www.aohdc.org
   Phone: 202-269-6623

2) Teach For America
   National headquarters in New York, New York
   Web site: www.teachforamerica.org
   Phone: 212-279-2080

3) Women's Opportunity & Resource Development, Inc.
   Missoula, Montana
   Web site: www.wordinc.org
   Phone: 406-543-3550

THE SEED FOUNDATION

M ANY FORCES CAN push a life in one direction or another. Without a guiding force, where would many of us be? Whether a grandfather who sacrificed everything for his children's education or a former student who showed courage and then triumphed against all odds, some are blessed by the inspiration of another's life. Such were the influences for Rajiv Vinnakota and Eric Adler, respectively. Believing that a fine education should be more accessible, Rajiv and Eric together created the SEED Foundation and its first SEED School, an urban public boarding school for inner-city children in Washington, D.C.

In some ways, it would have been easy *not* to select the SEED Foundation for this book. Their budget is huge compared to some of the other nonprofits chronicled here. The founders have already been honored widely. And their school in D.C. is a public charter school, which is not a "slam dunk" in some political circles.

But here is the bottom line for me. The SEED Foundation created a school that gets results. I've seen the inner city of Washington. I've worked there and seen the hopes and disappointments in the faces of children and mothers and fathers there. D.C.'s inner city encompasses a wide swath in addition to the Anacostia neighborhood, but Anacostia (which is also known as East of the River or Southeast) is where I focused my energies when I taught my program to inner-city teens. The one thing I believed before working in Anacostia and certainly knew *after* working in Anacostia is that the children simply needed a chance to shine. Given that chance, the vast majority of the kids would hit the ball out of the park, and that is what happened for the teens in my program.

The SEED Foundation resides in its own stratosphere of success, and The SEED School is ripe for replication. It is self-evident that the visionaries behind the SEED Foundation, Rajiv Vinnakota and Eric Adler, have achieved where others have failed. Their SEED Foundation epitomizes what it means to help inner-city children realize their potential. All the children attending The SEED School are urban children from D.C. When Rajiv, Eric, and I first spoke in 2005, the school had a 100 percent record of sending all their graduates to college. *100 percent!* Whatever they are doing, it is remarkable. To top it off, when it was launched in 1998, the SEED Foundation's SEED School was the *first* urban public boarding school in the nation.

Rajiv and Eric each had a vision for a better way to educate inner-city children, shared their ideas with each other and then together made it happen.

Like the former business consultants they are, Eric and Rajiv run their nonprofit like a well-oiled machine. To create a successful organization, they thought about everything from a corporate perspective, which included planning strategically, mastering the art of fundraising, making connections where there were none, building a strong board of directors, and hiring the best teachers they could find. And then they opened their doors.

As of 2005, thirty-five kids had graduated from The SEED School in D.C. and they have all gone to college. There were 320 kids at The SEED School at that time, and those kids were on target to graduate and go to college.

The SEED Foundation makes The SEED Public Charter School (or SEED School) possible. The SEED School's official mission is "a public college preparatory boarding school whose primary mission is to provide an outstanding, intensive educational program that prepares children, both academically and socially, for success in college."

The SEED School has a four-building campus in Anacostia. In addition to two dormitories, one building has classrooms, science laboratories, administrative offices, the student affairs office, the mental health center, special education services, the technology center, and the main library. Each dormitory houses up to 165 students and eighteen boarding faculty members, and each dorm has private living accommodations, study areas, and kitchen facilities. The welcome center, admissions office, parent resource center, dining hall, gymnasium, school store, and student meeting rooms are in the fourth building known as the Student Center. With a staff of fifteen, the SEED Foundation is focused on fundraising, financing, government relations, alumni support, program support, and logistics, as well as laying the groundwork for a SEED school in Maryland, in Oakland, in Los Angeles, and elsewhere. All those teachers, staff, and buildings cost money. The SEED Foundation's 2005 annual budget was $1.5 million, and The SEED School's 2005 budget was $9 million, which included the school's buildings and maintenance, boarding the students, teachers, administrators, nurses on duty around the clock, books, supplies, athletics, an art department, and after-school programs for choir, drama, and debate.

From the word go, every day the students at The SEED School are focused on their academics and every single day, the students are talking about college. The school is high energy. One SEED graduate named Monique said, "SEED helped me live my dream, which was to be the first of my family to go to college."

If there is one downside to The SEED School, it is that there are always many more students who want to go there than the school can handle. So that is why Rajiv and Eric are working diligently on a second campus for The SEED School in Washington. In the meantime, they have a lottery system. There is no testing. There is no official or unofficial system of knowing the right person to get your kid in there. Rather, each child's name goes in the proverbial hat and then they see if their name is drawn. Pure, simple, and fair. The chance of being chosen to attend The SEED School varies year to year, but currently, the kids have anywhere from a one in two chance to a one in five chance of getting picked to attend. Half the students are male and half are female.

At SEED, a great deal is expected. First, unlike most schools, it's a boarding school. SEED students wear uniforms, and they are held to a rigorous academic standard. The students are literally and totally immersed in The SEED School's philosophy and intense workload, and the students' pride in the school is palpable. The fact is that the kids want to be there. It's not only the parents who are trying to get their kids in there. The environment is friendly and accepting for the students, all of whom arrive in the seventh grade. Contrary to other schools, a student can only join The SEED School in the seventh grade. In addition to academics and sports, The SEED School works with each student as an individual on his or her own strengths and areas to improve, including any learning or emotional issues.

Before school even begins, SEED also wants to ensure that everyone is on the same page and is comfortable when he or she starts in the fall. So the school has a summer introduction program, which has proven to help bond the students to the school and to each other, thereby setting the stage for lasting friendships and a sense of community on campus.

It all started with a couple of young fellows, Eric and Rajiv, who believed that there had to be a better way to reach kids in the inner city, that education was the key to a life of choices, and that each child deserved an equal fighting chance. They were committed in their own lives to making it happen. The fact that they met each other, got along and joined forces to create this phenomenal program is miraculous.

In the Foundation's offices in downtown Washington, photos of The SEED School's kids line the walls. Eric and Rajiv share an office, which is really big enough for one person. In their office, two old, wooden desks form an old-fashioned double desk. Eric said he and Rajiv had worked at a double desk since the beginning, and they weren't going to change that now that they had a larger budget.

When I first met them for their photo shoot, Rajiv joked, "He's Tweedle Dee and I'm Tweedle Dum." Eric immediately replied, "No, no. He's Tweedle Dum and I'm Tweedle Dumber." For some reason, it was funny. Standing there in their sharp suits, they laughed easily and enjoyed the photo shoot—teasing each other as guys can do. In contrast, their work could not be more serious. Still, they are enjoying the journey and their enthusiasm is contagious, pulling in others all the time. Their goals are an extension of their values, and their goals have been straightforward from the beginning: Help the kids get an excellent education so they have a fighting chance.

Even as a teenager, Eric Adler knew he was blessed. His gratitude and desire to be involved in making things better have led him to this day. His experiences as a student and a teacher fuel his drive.

"I taught high school physics for eight years. That's where the kernel of the idea came from—for me," Eric, age forty-one, began. Then upon reflection, he added that the "kernel of the idea" actually took root years earlier.

"My parents pulled me out of Montgomery County public schools even though it was a great education and I was enjoying school," Eric recalled. "They put me in Sidwell Friends School, a private school in Northwest D.C.

"I knew from people at other public schools that their education was good, but I knew I was getting an extraordinary opportunity beyond the basically terrific opportunity I was already having in Montgomery County. So as I grew up, I knew there were haves and have-nots.

"I knew almost immediately that I was being given an extraordinary opportunity at Sidwell Friends. It got ingrained in me in ninth grade that the quality of one's education could make or break a life. I knew it at fourteen years old.

"That fact coupled with being raised in a Quaker school with its strong emphasis on service really made me think a bit about the world around me, about the opportunities that I had and that I knew that other kids didn't have. I went to Swarthmore College, which is also a Quaker school, and again, I spent a lot of time thinking about service. I knew I was going to teach as a first career, not as a permanent career, because I wanted to help create the terrific opportunities I had when I went to Sidwell. I got degrees in engineering and economics. Never took a course in education but just knew my first job was going to be teaching, and my first job was teaching at St. Paul's in Baltimore.

"St. Paul's was a mostly white prep school in Baltimore. It was an Episcopal school. I had a wonderful time there. One of the things I saw there was that we did have some kids who came in on scholarship from South Baltimore. They came in usually in ninth grade and were cherry-picked from their public school. My first day at St. Paul's, the first thing I did was have homeroom. I had fourteen kids. Never met them before because it was the first day of school.

"There was this one kid in my homeroom who was African American. I figured he was an upper-middle class, African American kid. I was wrong. He was one of these kids from South Baltimore, and it was his first day of school at this dramatically different place than he had been before. And I didn't know that. I also didn't know his father was not in the picture and that his mother was an alcoholic. I didn't know that he had a long commute on three different buses to get to school. I didn't know that he didn't want to be in our dress code, which was a shirt and tie. In his neighborhood, that presented a problem for him. I didn't know that there were nights where he was having to take care of his mother rather than his mother taking care of him. And so it was very difficult for him to do homework. And yet there we were. We're in the business of holding a kid accountable for doing their homework. And we got a kid who is not doing his homework. In school, not doing your homework is not good. And the other thing is that I saw something happen to other kids. We had kids come in from South Baltimore and they would ask themselves, 'What do I think these rich, white kids are going to be carrying their stuff around in?' And they would show the first day carrying a briefcase. And that is needlessly torturing a child."

Of course, the white kids carried their stuff in a backpack and didn't think twice about it. The child from South Baltimore wanted to fit in and inadvertently drew attention to himself. Kids tend to tease each other about anything they can find. It must have been torturous.

"I thought there were things we could do to better prepare these kids for us and prepare ourselves to serve their needs," Eric continued. "There is no reason we couldn't have brought these kids in in May before school started to see how kids are going about doing things. Stuff we could have done to help them. But we didn't. We didn't know at the time. Similarly, that the school would assign me a child from South Baltimore with an alcoholic mom and no dad, then one would think I, as a twenty-two-year-old teacher, would need to be prepared by the school.

"I figured it's great that we're making this high quality, college-prep experience available to these kids, but the truth I came to realize is that we weren't making it all that available. You had to be a 'super-human kid' to do this: to show up with your briefcase; to handle the social pressures of switching schools; to withstand the academic pressure when you're a couple of years behind at a school that is going to have high academic expectations for you; to deal with your multi-bus commute; to help your drunk mom; and then do your homework and show up at school the next day. That's not the average kid who can do that. So only the 'super-human kids' could have achieved that. What's the rest of the kids supposed to do? If we want this kind of college prep to be accessible to more ordinary kids, we are going to have to figure out a way to deliver it so the more ordinary kids can go, too.

"I left St. Paul's because I had an entrepreneurial bug. So I went to Wharton [for an M.B.A.] because I wanted to build some kind of business. I went to work at a consulting firm, but after a while, I wanted to build something. That's when I started to talk about building a public boarding school for urban kids. And someone mentioned I should meet with this fellow named Rajiv Vinnakota, who was looking into the same kind of program. Rajiv and I met for dinner one night and discussed our ideas.

"I remember going home to my wife and saying to her, 'I could work with this guy, and I know we could do it.' And we met again about a month later. He had taken time off as a consultant, and he was traveling around the country talking with experts all over the country—academics, etc. What worked and what didn't. He compiled all these interview notes and arranged a weekend-long meeting with people from around the country. And he invited me to attend. The group spent the weekend in meetings hashing out the ideas and discussing things. At the end of that second meeting, it was Sunday night, and everyone, except Raj and I, flew home. So there the two of us sat with this big whiteboard full of notes. It was going to be a lot of work to launch this.

"It was February of 1997, and we'd want to open the school in fall of '98. We wondered, 'Can we do this?' Yeah, it would take somebody full-time. Then we said, 'Nah, it would take two people full-time.' And we were the only two people in the room!" he said laughing. "Then I turned to Rajiv and asked, 'You in?' And he said, 'Yeah.' At that moment, we agreed to go in and quit our jobs the next day. We gave notice and started working full-time for SEED in March 1997."

Rajiv did a ton of legwork interviewing people and compiling all those notes. I wondered if he felt it was proprietary. Eric said immediately, "Raj has been unbelievably generous from the start. He had done all that work and was willing to share."

Like leaders or partners at any company or nonprofit, they do have their disagreements, Eric admitted. But as he emphasized, "It's always about the idea, never personal. In eight years, we've never had a blow-up. We're very lucky. Now we're the closest of friends, and our wives and children are all friendly. You find this common driving goal as a bond. We had the same idea in what we wanted to do, and we work well together."

In another conversation, Rajiv agreed with Eric's telling of their story and added, "The most serendipitous thing is that I met someone who felt as I did."

Two guys who leave lucrative positions with big consulting firms are not ordinary. But like roots of an old oak, both had their values formed at a young age.

"My mom was a second grade teacher in the Milwaukee school system, and my dad is a professor at Marquette in Milwaukee," Rajiv said. "Education was the first, second and third priority in our family. It is impossible for that not to become part of what you think and believe.

"I went into business consulting after college. In the end, I wanted to go into education. I had come up with this idea with my friends from Princeton while at an alumni event. In fact, one of my friends asked, 'Why aren't there boarding schools for inner-city kids?' I spent a lot of time talking with people about what's been tried before."

Rajiv explained his motivation by saying, "The single most influential person in my life was my grandfather who I never met. My grandfather died a few months before I was born. He was a farmer in southern India in a tiny village of perhaps a few hundred people. My grandfather spent twenty-four of the thirty rupees he earned every month on his six children's education. That was the value my grandfather put on education. Today, all six of those children have gone on to receive degrees from college.

"My father, for example, is a professor of engineering at Marquette University. That is my background as well. Education was everything; it was the biggest priority in my family. So I found myself growing up in Switzerland, then Ithaca, and then moving to Milwaukee by the time I was in third grade. I studied molecular biology and international relations at Princeton. It was at a Princeton reunion while talking with friends, some of whom had become teachers, that I got the idea for the SEED Foundation. I began wondering why there are no boarding schools for urban kids. And that got my mind working. And for the next three years or so, I thought about it and read about it.

"I thought, 'I've been thinking about it for three years. If I don't take some kind of action, then in twenty years, I'll still be thinking about it.' So I took a leave of absence from work to do that investigating and compiling. And you know the rest."

Strategic in their management style of SEED, Rajiv and Eric think corporate, a trademark which is critical for any nonprofit to thrive in the future. Rajiv agreed, "We tend to think that way. We are very deliberate about the things we decide; we think about exactly what the consequences are, about the best way to think through decisions from a financial, philosophical, and practical perspective."

"For me, there was no 'Aha' moment," Rajiv philosophized in late 2005. "There was a realization. Even though consulting was a great life, it wasn't the social footprint I wanted to leave. Both my parents are educators; education permeates my very being—the leverage it can provide for everyone. Now at thirty-four, I've been running SEED with Eric for almost nine years. I want to do things that will help others for the rest of my life."

Among many options on the table for SEED, Rajiv and Eric are working hard on creating a second campus for The SEED School in Washington. There is certainly the need; the word has gotten out about their successful track record. Rajiv said, "We need to find a second space and the money. The chances are quite good."

One project is the launch of a SEED School in Maryland, perhaps in Baltimore or in Prince George's County. The idea of replication is in the works but still on the drawing board. Rajiv elaborated, "We're working on the legislation in Annapolis [where the Maryland state legislature meets]. We're building bipartisan support for the school, which will be a publicly-funded, state-overseen, privately-incorporated entity. We're hopeful it will happen.

"The big picture is to be able to demonstrate that there is a cost-benefit to this boarding school concept. There is a need that is served, that a boarding-school concept should be part of every urban school system," Rajiv believes.

The kids at The SEED School are between the ages of twelve and nineteen, grades seventh through twelfth, all of whom live at the school five days a week, ten months a year.

The SEED School has a reason that the kids can only enter in the seventh grade. "The number allowed in a seventh grade class depends on how many seniors graduate, how many beds they have, and other variables," Rajiv explained. "What we have is a waiting list for the seventh grade class that is three to four times the size of the seventh grade class, which depending upon the year is fifty to one hundred kids. We want our students for six years. We want them to get into the culture. It all takes time." Most of all, it takes time to catch them up and build them up academically. Ultimately, SEED has high expectations for the students, and the students thrive on it.

There are rules at The SEED School. It's part of SEED's success story. "Of course you're going to have kids being kids," Rajiv said regarding any problem behavior, drugs or alcohol. "We have absolute rules—certain rules so that a kid knows that if you place yourself and others in the community at risk, there is a zero tolerance." In other words, actions have consequences. Being part of SEED is a privilege—a privilege that a student can lose. SEED will try to work with a child but the kids know the rules coming in. As one might expect, some kids simply don't make it.

Rajiv added, "Children end up leaving the SEED School for three reasons: families who move out of the District and cannot be served by this D.C. public charter school; or the child would rather go to a full-service school with football programs, other athletics, vocational education; or some students get asked to leave when they are violating the rules of the school."

Of the 320 kids at the SEED School in 2005, more than 90 percent are expected to graduate from their high school program, and that is in sharp contrast with the D.C. school district, where the graduation rate is between 49 and 65 percent, depending upon which statistics you follow.

At The SEED School, any medical needs are handled. The school has a full-time nurse during the day and a full-time nurse during the night. Other than that, if they need a doctor or if they break an arm, for example, they go to the hospital.

"We do look for strategic partnerships with other nonprofits where it makes sense," Rajiv mentioned. "There's no sense in reinventing the wheel. We spend time with programs like Hoop Dreams. [The Hoop Dreams Scholarship Fund is a successful nonprofit in D.C. that mentors and sends high school students to college.] Their founder, Susie Kay, is working with kids once they're in high school. So she's getting them from a different pool, but we're in touch with her, certainly. We work with others such as Heads Up to learn from their programs." (Heads Up is a D.C.-based nonprofit that helps at-risk children and youth focus on academic skills; college students and others serve as tutors and mentors.)

Working with the kids directly is a part of Rajiv and Eric's makeup. Rajiv said with excitement, "I teach all the kids! The first year, I taught public speaking, which was required back then; now it's an elective. Currently, I'm involved teaching the junior and senior college prep program. I do tours with them. I know about their life, their families. It's very personal. That's how you keep yourself grounded. If you're too far out from the school, you forget why you started this work in the first place." Eric often goes on college tours as well and at times teaches SAT prep.

The mission of many high schools is to have students graduate from high school. The overall mission of The SEED School is to provide a support system so that they all graduate from *college*. High school graduation is a given at The SEED School. The school has a full-time director of alumni support, and like any other boarding school in the nation, The SEED School has programs where it asks alumni to come back.

"We've had a family with four kids at one time!" Eric added proudly.

While the offices for the SEED Foundation are located in downtown Washington, The SEED School is located in Anacostia. Rajiv and Eric see the separation as a part of running the school. They're in touch all the time with the administrators and teachers, but as Rajiv put it, "Letting the people who know how to run the school run the school is important. They're doing a great job. We need to focus on building new schools, construction development, lobbying, and fundraising—running the Foundation."

Rajiv feels that the work they do at The SEED School is personal. When asked to select an anecdote about one of the kids, he paused and said hesitantly, "It's hard to select. Everyone is special." Eric had the same response. And they meant it.

Sitting with Eric and Rajiv can at times feel like a friendly ping-pong match where one helps the other through a story and the repartee is fast.

Though it was hard to single out a story about one child, they felt a story about a child they decided to call Fred, which is not the child's real name, exemplified the purpose and success of The SEED School and Foundation. (It should be noted that describing Fred's young life is difficult. Eric, Rajiv, and I absolutely want to protect Fred's feelings. Nothing here is a judgment, for we believe the vast majority of all kids simply need a chance to shine. Telling Fred's story pays tribute to his courageous journey and will hopefully inspire others.)

Eric began about Fred, "A nice, gentle kid—a good soul."

"In 1999, I did a home visit to Fred's home in his apartment complex," Rajiv said. "We do home visits with all the kids."

Fred's home was in a dilapidated apartment complex in Southeast. It is in a rough neighborhood with few options for rising above. The high school dropout rate around there is high and the crime rate is higher. The conditions can be grim and harsh, especially for the children. Typical for many inner-city kids in D.C., it was all Fred had known.

Rajiv continued, "Fred was having trouble in school. I spent half an hour with him at his home, getting to know him. While he was in SEED, his brother died. It was a violent death. Fred had questions whether he should go back home to support his mother." Rajiv paused and then added, "She had her own issues."

"Any other siblings?" I asked.

"A sister who had a child and dropped out of high school," Rajiv recalled. "So we had to work with Fred for a number of years, and we supported him in all kinds of ways. We made sure we took him to the doctor at the hospital to get any shots."

"We got him glasses—a nice, sweet kid," Eric said. "The kids are with us [boarding at SEED] five days a week and go home during the weekends. We often made sure that he had a place to go—a family to stay with— during the weekends if he couldn't go home."

"Talk about probabilities against him," Rajiv felt.

"The odds were *stacked* against him. He's now a freshman at Tuskegee University," Eric said beaming as if Fred had been his own son. "We worked with him on financial aid. When it came time to start school, his mother couldn't go with him, so we had a staff member fly down with him."

"He's now an engineering major," Rajiv said to Eric, and they both chuckled. Engineering had been one of Eric's college majors as well. Talk about having an influence on others.

UPDATE ABOUT THE SEED FOUNDATION

THE SEED SCHOOL, which opened in 1998, celebrated its tenth anniversary in 2008. It currently serves 325 students in grades seven through twelve. In 2008, the SEED Foundation opened its second SEED School in Baltimore, Maryland, and it will serve up to four hundred students in grades six through twelve. This school is the nation's second urban public boarding school—the first one being The SEED School in Washington. The SEED Foundation is not aware of any other school that meets the same description.

Approximately 75 percent of SEED's entering ninth graders graduate from high school. Of those who graduate from The SEED School, 98 percent have been accepted to four-year colleges or universities, and 90 percent have immediately enrolled in college.

Including the class of 2008, eighty-eight students have now graduated from The SEED School.

Contact information for The SEED Foundation & The SEED School:

Eric Adler & Rajiv Vinnakota
Co-Founders & Managing Directors
The SEED Foundation, Inc.
1776 Massachusetts Avenue, NW, Suite 600
Washington, D.C. 20036
Phone: 202-785-4123
Web site: www.seedfoundation.com
mailto:eric@seedfoundation.com

If you like The SEED Foundation, you might be interested in these organizations:

1) The Children's Storefront
   New York, New York
   Web site: www.thechildrensstorefront.org
   Phone: 212-427-7900

2) City at Peace
   Washington, D.C.
   Web site: www.cityatpeacedc.org
   Phone: 202-319-2200

3) The Hoop Dreams Scholarship Fund
   Washington, D.C.
   Web site: www.hoopdreams.org
   Phone: 202-414-4774

4) Oregon Native American Business and Entrepreneurial Network
   (ONABEN)
   Tigard, Oregon
   Web site: www.onaben.org
   Phone: 503-968-1500

5) The Suzuki-Orff School of Music
   Chicago, Illinois
   Web site: www.suzukiorff.org
   Phone: 312-738-2646

D.C. Central Kitchen

WHO WOULD HAVE guessed that a young bartender/nightclub manager would come up with an idea that would change lives in a major metropolitan area? That is exactly what Robert Egger did when he came up with a way to help homeless men and women, some of the most vulnerable in the Washington area. That was 1988, and at first glance, young Robert Egger might have seemed like the last fellow to start and manage a winning nonprofit program, but he had passion and he's always had a big heart. This is a story about someone who listened to his heart.

Robert wasn't even interested in getting involved, and he admits that he was a reluctant champion of the cause at first. You could say that his leap into the nonprofit sector happened to him.

Robert didn't go to college. In the late 1980s, for three years, he had been a bartender and manager of bands at a well-known Dupont Circle establishment in the heart of Washington, D.C. He was in his mid-twenties and engaged to the woman who would become his wife. They lived in Georgetown, a ritzy and historical part of Washington that also has its share of homeless on the streets. Robert recalled, "We were looking for a church to get married. There was this church in Georgetown that had 'The Grate Patrol,' and they went out at night delivering meals out on the street. I didn't want to go; I looked for every opportunity to avoid going. I was a recovering hypocrite!"

It's not that he didn't feel for others. Robert not only jammed to the music of the '60s and '70s; he also felt inspired by that era of music and the themes of peace, love, and understanding. But like many, he confessed, "I wasn't really willing to go out of my comfort zone. I had no interest. I had interest but I was afraid, maybe skeptical. The church's program forced me to deal with it. I got *dragged* one night out in this truck. I was struck almost immediately by that sense, 'This can't be all you're doing. You can't just be satisfied.'"

He also noticed that a ton of food was getting thrown out late at night by the restaurants and hotels—all while the homeless and hungry were on the streets begging and barely making it to the next day. Robert asked around if anything could be done about the waste of perfectly good food, but no one had an answer. Someone even mentioned something about the liability associated with discarded food.

Robert didn't take that answer. He saw a better way and decided to try "recovering" the food. So he went around and arranged to pick it up late at night. The next day, he figured out how to "redistribute" it. It was a win-win situation. The restaurants and hotels felt great about doing the right thing and being associated with Robert's idea, and the hungry ate. Robert soon created a nonprofit called the D.C. Central Kitchen.

The D.C. Central Kitchen has always had a simple mission. Yet, it was so simple that no one had thought of it until Robert Egger came along. Today, the Kitchen, as it is known, is so vital in the region and they do their job so well that D.C. wouldn't be the same without it.

The D.C. Central Kitchen "uses food as a tool to strengthen bodies, empower minds, and build communities." The nonprofit recovers *two to three tons of prepared food every day*. They have a slew of volunteers who help prepare the food into 4,000 meals every day for distribution to area agencies that serve the hungry and homeless. And here is the kicker: A significant part of the D.C. Central Kitchen's mission is that it also trains unemployed men and women for jobs in the food service field. As their motto captures, the Kitchen is "feeding the soul of the city."

The D.C. Central Kitchen is located in a part of downtown D.C. that includes Capitol Hill, Georgetown Law School, and numerous hotels. The Kitchen is right in the midst of it all, and yet, the nonprofit exists in another world. Within its vast building that fills desperate need, the D.C. Central Kitchen is adjacent to a large homeless shelter as well as an extensive free health clinic. The parking lot behind the building looks like a war zone hit it, and cars are parked there in a "creative" pattern.

After I figured out how to "park" my car in their lot, I walked through major potholes to get to the door for the D.C. Central Kitchen. A group of men and a few women were loading carts of food into a truck. A few were taking a break. Everyone was friendly. A hallway filled with donated furniture led to a large kitchen inside. Looking for Robert, I stumbled into a class that was preparing to take the GED exam. The teacher pointed me in the right direction.

With his cropped, gray hair, quick smile, and engaging personality, Robert has qualities that make you want to bottle him up. He is total energy and talks fast! Like most of the visionaries in this book, Robert is a fellow on the move all the time and focused on new possibilities. The fascinating thing about Robert is that he is not one to rest on his laurels.

Sitting with him in his tiny, square, windowless, beige, cinder-block office in 2004, I could hardly get him to tell me about his successful, entrepreneurial nonprofit operation. All Robert wished to discuss was his vision for a better system for the nonprofit sector as a whole. He is focused both on his nonprofit as well as how it fits into the big picture, about the possibility of creating systemic change. The wheels were turning so fast; his words spewed out in bursts of conversation. So this essay is written in a fast, "Egger-like" way to reflect Robert's sense of urgency.

Years earlier, at a small charity event I had organized for the Kitchen, Robert had spoken passionately to the crowd about the cause and how proud he was of their graduates. He conveyed the same urgency that day in his office.

The whole time he and I chatted, there was a constant buzz of activity outside the doorway. People were doing their jobs of getting food, preparing food, and shipping food. The hustle in the air was real. Being there was like getting a B12 vitamin shot. Robert now has a staff of sixty and thousands of volunteers helping the cause. Together, they are making things happen. But it wasn't always that way. Back in 1989, Robert took his idea and generated support from friends and the community. The Kitchen grew steadily through the years.

"In the beginning, I met with a group of Jewish men and women, and I learned about *tzedakah* [meaning justice or charitable giving]. They explained that *tzedakah* is about justice and creating balance. In addition to hunger, how can we pretend there's not larger work to do? What evolved is that people became enamored with the idea that we were simultaneously addressing hunger and the cause. Once your eyes are opened, are you allowed to close them again? Is there a larger obligation besides feeding someone on the street?" Robert said and then added, "Everyone has value at the Kitchen."

Support, large and small, started to come from around the region. Every dollar has had impact. In Robert's office on the wall, there's an enlarged copy of a $10,000 check from Mr. and Mrs. Bruce Springsteen, THE Boss himself! When Springsteen has played a concert in the region, he has sent a major check to the Kitchen and insisted that the concert managers have collection sites for non-perishables wherever he plays. As a lifelong fan of Bruce Springsteen, I was thrilled for Robert's nonprofit and somehow in the same instant, I wasn't surprised by Springsteen's consistent support of the Kitchen and other hunger programs. Springsteen has never forgotten what it was like to struggle. A poet of everyone's pain and hopes, Springsteen often writes songs full of images and people who remember their youth and first love, who long for a better day, who work hard, and who miss the way it was in their one-company town.

President Clinton visited the Kitchen twice during his presidency and rolled up his sleeves and cooked during the holidays. At the time, Mr. Clinton said, "This place offers a recipe for opportunity. It's an empowerment classroom...I hope that where this message goes out...they'll look at the D.C. Central Kitchen model and they'll go to work."

Robert remembered Clinton's visits well, saying, "Here's the president working side by side with men and women in the program, with someone who is homeless. And here are people who are homeless who are holding knives and showing him how to make lasagna or stuff peppers, which are the two things he made while he was here. And First Lady Hillary Clinton sent a $5,000 check; the money came from proceeds from her book, *It Takes A Village*."

So how does the D.C. Central Kitchen manage to feed 4,000 people a day? As their materials state, "The Kitchen safely recycles more than thirty-five tons of food each month. Every day, the Kitchen safely retrieves surplus food from restaurants and food service businesses around the city. This donated food is brought back to the Kitchen where it is recombined, re-prepared, and then sent to serve over 4,000 each day." The D.C. Central Kitchen feeds hungry children and adults at social service agencies throughout the region. The Kitchen "converts donated foods into balanced meals while at the same time training unemployed individuals in basic culinary skills." In 2004 alone, volunteers contributed over 48,000 hours to the Kitchen.

Far more than a "feed the hungry" program, the Kitchen's stated mission is "to combat hunger and create opportunity." Michael Curtin, the Kitchen's Chief Operating Officer, has the same high energy and commitment as Robert, and said, "All the people we serve have been homeless; many have been in jail, but they all deserve and get a chance at a fresh start."

The Kitchen has the following programs: Food Recovery/Meal Distribution Program; Job Training Program; First Helpings Street Outreach Program; the Campus Kitchens Project (opening similar programs at university halls throughout the country); and two revenue-generating projects that employ graduates, called Fresh Start Catering and New Beginnings Contract Foods. Its Job Training Program has an impressive record with a high job placement rate; most graduates have jobs on graduation day and typically earn well above minimum wage. Most have kept their jobs after six months. The Kitchen's Fresh Start Catering is a professional catering company that employs only graduates of the Kitchen's Job Training Program. The catering business further prepares their graduates for jobs in the food service industry. And finally, they have their First Helpings Program, which "uses food as a tool to guide people off the streets and...toward resources needed to overcome problems of substance abuse and mental illness," as their materials state. The Kitchen did all that with an annual budget of $6 million. Of that total, $3.8 million came in in-kind donations, which means that the organization operated with $2.2 million.

One part of the Kitchen's Job Training Program is to have professional chefs come once a week and teach in the classes. Robert explained, "The volunteer chefs [program] was designed to help men and women in the program, who have stereotypes about what a chef looks like, realize that a chef can be black, white, yellow, brown, man, woman, big, tall, gay, straight, doesn't matter. If you ask them in the beginning what a chef looks like, they'll say, 'A white guy with a French accent.'

"We'll ask a chef, we'll say, 'This week, we want you to teach de-boning, but we're also talking about a life skills class. How do deal with it when a chef yells at you? Can you talk about your history and how you've dealt with chefs who yell.' So it's great. It really personalizes it. And normally after every guest chef thing, the chef will say to us, 'Hey, man, I really want to do this again. Can I send my sous-chef? These students were really great. Let me know when the class is up. I'll come speak at graduation.'

"It breaks down every possible barrier. That's the class in a nutshell. It's twelve weeks long. Between fifty and sixty graduate every year. And they're all over town, all over the city," Robert boasted. "We have a graduate on our board of directors, which I think is very important."

Of the sixty on staff, he said, "That includes our program called Campus

Kitchens, which are all across the country. We have six different Campus Kitchens at universities and we're launching efforts in high schools as well."

A significant part of the team effort at the Kitchen, volunteers are all ages, from teenagers to middle-aged to retired persons. Robert estimated, "About 7,000 a year come through. And that's extremely purposeful. That's how we fight hunger. We want our volunteers to love the experience here, to feel appreciated, and to be inspired to act and see that everyone has a role."

Numerous individuals and groups help with food preparation and kitchen work or job training in the mornings. They also have an opportunity to help with food outreach at night. One nonprofit called Brainfood, which is based in Columbia Heights, brought a team of teens to work in the Kitchen during their December break. The Kitchen believes in partnering with other nonprofits as much as possible. The list of strategic partnerships with other nonprofits is long.

Robert is the kind of person who reminds you how you might have felt when young. He lays it all out on the table. His beliefs and vision were set long ago when he was a boy. Staying grounded with those beliefs feeds his soul and continues to motivate him when things get difficult.

I knew about things getting difficult. A few days after Christmas in 2005, I had not yet secured any major funding to underwrite this book. Still, I was determined to complete it. I didn't even have an agent or a publisher yet! Nothing. Yet, something within me just told me to keep at it. By late December of 2005, I had written drafts of many of the essays but the essay on Robert continued to elude me, partially because we had taped our conversation—something that seemed like a fine idea at the time in mid-2004. I dreaded the tapes and kept going forward with the other essays. Though proud of how much I had accomplished on the book, I was embarrassed about where I was with his essay. Something about Robert's reaction put me at ease—maybe the way he wasn't judgmental, the way he understood how hard it was to write a book. Whatever it was, that's when I knew why he does what he does. Within a few days, I finished this essay.

When we spoke in late December, the joys of the holidays and family filled the air. Robert talked about how glorious it was to have so much family in town over Christmas. Of course, at a typical family dinner, he chuckled to himself about being outnumbered by the women in his family—his wife, daughter, and sisters. I understood. My father and uncle had the same lot with their wives and many daughters, and they always told each other right before any medical procedure, "Don't you leave me with all these women." Though my father and uncle died earlier in the decade,

Robert asked me about their lives. We chatted about our fathers, how our families like to laugh a lot, and how we treasured the original film version of *The Producers*.

"I always laugh at my father," Robert quipped. "He asks if I have money in the bank. Or he'll say, 'Are they paying you when you go speak somewhere?' I tell him or tease him, 'You sent me to Catholic school all my life. You ruined me for profit, old man.' It's hard for me to charge. I always tease them [my parents] about that. As a kid, it was always about what you do for others. At dinner every night with six kids, my mother would pass around the Bible. Every night, one kid would read one chapter of the Bible. It was a kid's Bible. It had history, morality stories, and lessons. So you knew the Bible."

At forty-seven, Robert thought back to the turbulent times of the '60s. Growing up in Los Angeles, his family enjoyed the beauty of Balboa Park and Joshua Tree, not to mention the beaches of Southern California. But then his father went to Vietnam as a pilot for three different tours during the '60s and '70s. Robert was at home with his mom and sisters. The nation was gripped by protests in the streets and on college campuses.

"There were two or three underpinnings. 1968 was important to me," he said instantly about that pivotal year when he would have been about ten years of age. "The year of the double assassinations of Dr. King and Bobby Kennedy. We lived in L.A. when Kennedy was shot. And I saw all the adults crying. That affected me.

"I remember getting out of school the day that King was shot. Some kids and I were walking home, and there was a lot of construction going on. A bunch of construction guys were around there. And these construction guys asked us why we were out of school. When we told them it was because of King getting shot, one yelled back, 'They let you out of school because they shot that *nigger*?' I remember that," he said, pausing. "I had never heard someone talk that way before. All the nuns were weeping, all the adults I knew. And he said that."

Participating in church was another underpinning. "I was eight or nine, and I was waiting in line to get to school. Someone asked me if I wanted to be an altar boy," he said. "I wasn't sure at first, but this fellow said he would signal me when I needed to ring the bells. So I tried it and realized that it was like being a part of theater. I was ringing the bells on cue. Thereafter, I got there in time for the 6:00 A.M. mass, wearing vestments, and I lit the candles. There was an audience there. Within a month, I was telling the Father, 'We're going to do it this way today.' And the Father was probably thinking, 'Who is this kid?' But I loved it. It was morality and the theater:

making the Bible into some kind of theater.

"When we moved to D.C., I was twelve, and I was not happy," he emphasized. "I grew up on the beach—me and my five blond sisters. I came here and I was really bummed. My mom sat with me and we watched *Casablanca*, which I've seen many times now. But I remember that everyone is there at Rick's because everyone else is there. It's the place to go. Underneath all the gambling and fun is that it's an escape hatch. It's about freedom. In that scene as they pan the place, there are all these people talking about getting free. There are two guys whispering in Chinese! It's theater as a disguise for liberation—the idea of freedom. The D.C. Central Kitchen is my version of Rick's. It's joyful to be here. It's the coolest place to volunteer, to work. Underlying all the work we do here, it's about freedom. There is energy. It's a portal to freedom. Everything I do is a show to get people to lower their guard and be a part of it. All kinds of freedom, including spiritual freedom. Freedom fascinates me.

"Here in my office, I have pictures of those who fascinate me. I have a picture of Harriet Tubman. I'm fascinated by people who help others find their freedom: liberators. Look at people like Gandhi and Chavez. I'm much more interested in people who were the tacticians. Like Gandhi's simple metaphor of salt. King took the same idea with the bus and it only cost a dime. Chavez did the same thing with the grapes boycott."

Similarly, it is not hard to see that the D.C. Central Kitchen liberates men and women from hopelessness and helps them help themselves. Also in his office is a picture of Frederick Douglass, the abolitionist who bravely spoke out against slavery.

Robert doesn't usually talk about his own health, but he had scoliosis as a teen and had a body cast for a year at age sixteen. He said, "One minute I was getting a quick physical to play on the soccer team, and the next minute I was at Walter Reed Hospital having surgery on my spine. A lot of amputees from Vietnam were there. I had a body cast that I was going to have to wear for a year! I remember whimpering in the car on the way home from Walter Reed, and my mom pulled the car over and said, 'There are two ways to deal with this. You can either feel sorry for yourself and that's not going to go too far in this family. Or you can deal with it.' And that was it." That experience provided a stronger back and steel core.

In the past decade, Robert hiked the Himalayas and traveled to India to learn more about Gandhi. Robert explained the basic story about Gandhi and salt: "Gandhi was saying to the Indians that if you don't spend your pennies on salt, the machine will stop. The Indians were divided—divided by caste, race, religion, and gender. Gandhi wanted to unite the Indians. So he organized a march to the port city of Dandi, where he scooped up a handful of salt. The making of and selling of salt was prohibited even though it was naturally produced in India. The Indians were *forced* to buy salt through the British. The British never had more than 3,000 officers in India and yet they were able to control all those millions of Indians. It was simple. As long as you can keep people divided, the rest is simple. Gandhi was saying that if we don't buy it, even though it only costs rupees [or pennies], it will have an impact. We need to be united.

"Gandhi was saying that the oppressed and the oppressors are equally afflicted. He said that the Indians had to reach out to the salt miners in Liverpool as well, those who inadvertently were part of the problem. By telling them what their salt was doing to the Indians, Gandhi was reaching out to the miners and saying, 'How can you participate in this? Do you want to help us?'"

Now you might be sitting there thinking, What the heck do Gandhi and his salt protest have to do with visionaries and the nonprofit sector in America today? I believe nothing happens in a vacuum. Robert Egger is a visionary because of those who struggled before he came along. He is paying tribute to those who came before, recognizing that he stands on the shoulders of these brave souls. Robert thinks about the possibility of a better way, about how an individual standing with other individuals can make a difference.

Pennies for salt. Dimes for buses. Saying no to grapes. It's all connected to standing together for one another.

And it leads to his belief that the nonprofit sector could be far more effective if different nonprofits joined forces. His newest idea is known as the Nonprofit Congress. "I'm the co-convener of the Nonprofit Congress, which will be launched in January 2006," he announced. "There's a declaration that says the nonprofits need to join forces. It says that slaves can't liberate slaves, that people we serve will stay in their situations unless something changes. A *united* nonprofit sector would be a vibrant force for change in America. One of our goals is to be influential in the next presidential debate in 2008. We hope to host presidential debates. There are eighty million boomers and the greatest transfer of wealth is going to happen. The candidates need to be asked, 'What's your vision? How can you use the richness and generosity of our people?'

"I was always intrigued but skeptical about unions because of what happened with Jimmy Hoffa and the corruption. But I was also aware of why they came to be. I'm a populist at heart, and I wondered, 'How do you get working people aware?'

"The future of philanthropy is not how much you give away at the end of the year. It's how you spend your money every day. That's what King, Chavez and Gandhi said. If you don't ride the bus, if you don't buy the grapes, and if you don't buy the salt, the machine stops. It's amazing. Gandhi went up against the British Empire. We're much stronger than we think. One-tenth of our economy is in the nonprofit sector. That's larger than most countries. We'd be the fifth biggest country in the world if we were a nation, if we were organized!

"Here are the main points of the Nonprofit Congress. First, we need a greater sense of identity. We need to replace the name, nonprofit. It has a negative imagery, which keeps us from seeing the amazing positive side. As a sector, we need regular, consistent coverage on the business pages of the papers.

"Second, we need a full-time advocacy organization on the nonprofits' behalf. I want a 501(c)4 to represent the nonprofits, but especially the small ones. Most of the nonprofits are less than $1 million or even $500,000. Third, we have to focus on the political process. We have to politicize the volunteers. We can't 'charity' our way out or 'volunteer' our way out of the problems we're working on. We have to have this conversation as a nation.

"Eighty million baby boomers are beginning to retire. What are they going to do with themselves? On top of that, a smaller workforce is going to replace them. Are we going to drag the boomers into philanthropy? As cool as the Kitchen is, someone who was an executive is not going to chop vegetables for hours in the Kitchen. That's not utilizing what they have to offer. We need to create a whole different way for people to volunteer and have impact and to measure impact. The end goal is to be aware of how you spend your money every day."

King and dimes. Gandhi and salt. Chavez and grapes. Robert wants people to see that they can have an unprecedented impact by rethinking their spending, their giving, and our nation's nonprofit sector. He's saying that if nonprofits join forces and organize, then they'll have greater impact and efficiency. It's ultimately about long-term change or systemic change, not merely feeding a family for a day or a week. How can we help them not become hungry in the first place?

"In India, salt was the metaphor," Robert summed up. "Gandhi was saying that salt is the basis of life. We all need salt. We are all Indian, not divided by caste or race or religion or sex. We're all in this together—just like the nonprofit sector. And that's what the Nonprofit Congress is all about."

Robert's views on the nonprofit sector and philanthropy are laid out in his book, *Begging for Change*, which describes his vision of how things work and how things could work better in the sector. His perspective is based not only from his years as the executive director of the D.C. Central Kitchen, but also from when he was asked to help resurrect the United Way of the National Capital Region after a ruinous scandal.

"One of my frustrations is that when you divide yourself into categories of the causes *du jour*, like breast cancer, AIDS, starving children, when you create this caste system, it's intellectual laziness. Then you're giving to the lowest fruit. When you get into a cycle of which disease [or cause] is popular this year, then you create a cynicism within the sector. The awkward dance for most of the nonprofits is that they can't say we need money to pay for the phone bill. But that's critical, too. But no one wants to fund that," he said candidly.

Sometimes a founder or executive director of a successful nonprofit can lose sight of the mission. A nonprofit can inadvertently become a cult of the originator, and it takes a big person to see that and stay focused on the mission. As Robert observed, "There's a weird trap founders or executive directors can get into. But the Kitchen is not about me. It's about a larger conversation about whether there is a smarter way to do this, to feed people. It's not about me and building up a large capital campaign. It's about the good of the organization. It's about how many meals can you serve and what's the cost per meal. Our cost per meal is $1.67, and that's hard cost. But instead of building up the Kitchen, we're interested in creating Kitchens all across the country. That's why there's a bill before Congress called The FEED Act, which would fund Kitchens elsewhere."

The FEED Act stands for Food, Employment, Empowerment, and Development and would coordinate programs. It would be a coalition of nonprofits such as Meals on Wheels, the AIDS Nutrition Network, and state colleges working together in existing kitchens. The mission is to engage schoolchildren in healthy eating and in feeding the hungry from their own school's kitchen. So it's engaging young people in the mission, it's nutritious foods, and it's a job-training program. Plus, they don't have to build new kitchens when the schools already have facilities. As Robert put it, "The idea is to teach the children from a young age that their day-to-day lives have impact on others."

Robert is philosophical about philanthropy in America today. As he has said in speeches around the country, "De Tocqueville said about Americans that we as a people are willing to lend a hand to a neighbor. We are a generous country." But Robert also wondered, "In this country, people give their surplus money and surplus things. What then happens to these nonprofits when the surplus money is tapped out? About 80 percent of donations come from people who make between $25,000 and $50,000, and they're getting squeezed." Thus, while Robert Egger continues to run the D.C. Central Kitchen, he is also committed to the Nonprofit Congress, so all the nonprofits can be a force together and then the nation will benefit from that cooperation.

"Hunger is always wrong. All hunger is wrong. We have enough food to solve this," Robert pointed out. "The climate has too many organizations saying whatever they think the public wants to hear, rather than creating a *movement for real change*. Our house is divided. What if the public loses faith with the nonprofit sector as they have with organized religion and politics? People long to believe. They want to see that world. I believe that is possible. But we need to show the results; we need to say, 'Here is how we are decreasing future need.'"

One inspiring image that continues to guide Robert's compass is the idea of the prodigal child. When he speaks about the prodigal child, his heart is laid bare.

While the D.C. Central Kitchen has moved over a million pounds of food, it's a place about the people in the Kitchen and for the Kitchen. After all, they've placed over fifty people a year in jobs since 1991. Many return to the Kitchen for all kinds of reasons, and the door is always open.

"A lot of them come back and volunteer," Robert said proudly.

"A woman showed up today," he recalled in 2005. (Please note that for this story, I changed this woman's name to protect her privacy.) "Charlene was an employee here and went back out [to the streets]. It was sad. It happens all the time, but that's one of the great joys," he said, pausing to explain. "It's Friday. It's been a tough week. All weeks are rough. If you work hard, you're really tired by Friday. I'm sitting here and there's a little knock on the door. I look up and there's Charlene! I haven't seen her in ages and she says, 'Well, you know, I went to prison but I got myself really straightened out again and I've been clean now.'

"In other words, she's back. It's like the prodigal child, and it's so joyful. This happens all the time. And I think the lesson is that not everyone is going to succeed the first time out. And the joy of this is that sometime people need to fall five, six, twenty times. It's not my call. But by finishing the program, oftentimes it's the first thing people [have] finished. 'Let me see if I can do it again.' It's that sense of belief. 'I did it!' It's like people who quit smoking for two weeks. You can do it again. It might take you eight times, but you can do it if you keep trying. And I think that's our bag at the Kitchen. We always will welcome people back.

"Again, it's that prodigal children thing. I love the idea of the prodigal child. There's a great painting by Thomas Hart Benton that was done during the Depression. It's about a prodigal child returning home. I think it's called, 'Return of the Prodigal Son.' It's a picture, and they flipped it. The idea is that here's a strapping, young, return-from-college, educated child who returns to the family farm, and the family farm is deserted.

"I was fascinated by the idea. Historically, you see the prodigal child is the errant son who comes back. What kind of table are we setting for returning prisoners, for young men and women aging out of foster care, for people who have done everything we've asked them to do? Are we ready as a society for the return of the prodigal child? I don't think we are. I like setting a big table." To Robert, that big table is always set and ready.

"So when Charlene came back—" I began.

"Well, she's going to work with Fresh Start."

"So you gave her a job?"

"I always give somebody a job," Robert said without hesitation. "They always say, 'Are you a faith-based program?' Yeah, we have faith in people."

As of 2006, Charlene was still doing well. She worked with the Kitchen's Fresh Start catering program, and through that program, she found some work in a kitchen at a private school in the Washington area. Eventually, they hired her to run their cafeteria! So she's not only working there; she is managing others. Robert was thrilled by the turnaround and added, "A lot of our people end up guiding others. It's a long road to change. And guiding others is a way to stay healthy and to give back."

It's all connected. It's that "ripple of hope" that Robert Kennedy spoke about in 1966. Robert Egger's Kitchen sets forth a ripple of hope with each person who passes through his doors and comes out with new job skills and a second chance. Many, in turn, are then able and inspired to guide others.

Chavez said that workers deserve a fair price for their grapes. Gandhi said that we are all Indians. King said that we are all entitled to any seat on the bus. Maybe Robert Egger is saying that we are all Charlene, that we all benefit when someone gets back on their feet, that we all deserve another chance. We are all the prodigal child.

Update about the D.C. Central Kitchen

Since inception in 1989, the D.C. Central Kitchen has distributed 21 million meals and helped 730 women and men gain full-time employment. In 2008 alone, the Kitchen had 11,000 volunteers and distributed 4,500 meals each day. In January 2009, the Kitchen graduated their 73rd Culinary Job Training Class. Also in early 2009, the D.C. Central Kitchen opened its twentieth Campus Kitchen in the country.

In 2006, Robert served as the founder and co-convener of the Nonprofit Congress, which brought hundreds of nonprofit leaders to Washington to discuss their common goals and the nonprofit sector.

In 2007, the FEED Act was referred to the Senate Committee on Agriculture, Nutrition, and Forestry, which did not take any action. Therefore, it was never brought to the Senate floor and voted on.

In addition to being president of the Kitchen, Robert continues to see a critical need for a unified voice for the nonprofit sector. In early 2009, he launched the V3 Campaign. As Robert described his vision, "V3 is about speaking with one voice as a nonprofit community. When we speak with one voice, we speak about our value, what we bring to the table economically in every city in America. We're major employers and economic stimulators throughout the country. With fourteen million employees, eighty million volunteers and 10 percent of the Gross National Product, if nonprofits started to think and act collectively based upon our shared interest, then we could be a tremendous political and economic force not only in America, but around the world. Our goal is to be involved in every political election and push each candidate to articulate how they would partner with the nonprofit sector and strengthen it to achieve their vision for that city, state, and this country."

Contact information for the D.C. Central Kitchen:

Mr. Robert Egger
Founder/President
D.C. Central Kitchen
425 Second Street, NW
Washington, D.C. 20001-2003
Phone: 202-234-0707
Web site: www.dccentralkitchen.org

If you like the D.C. Central Kitchen, you might be interested in these organizations:

1) ASHOKA
   Arlington, Virginia
   Web site: www.ashoka.org
   Phone: 703-527-8300

2) Bean's Café
   Anchorage, Alaska
   Web site: www.beanscafe.org
   Phone: 907-274-9595

3) Boca Helping Hands
   Boca Raton, Florida
   Web site: www.bocahelpinghands.org
   Phone: 561-417-0913

4) City Harvest
   New York, New York
   Web site: www.cityharvest.org
   Phone: 917-351-8700

5) Computer C.O.R.E.
   Alexandria, Virginia
   Web site: www.computercore.org
   Phone: 703-931-7346

6) The Delancey Street Foundation
   San Francisco, California (national headquarters)
   Web site: www.delanceystreetfoundation.org
   Phone: 415-957-9800

7) Feeding America
   Chicago, Illinois
   Web site: www.feedingamerica.org
   Phone: 800-771-2303

8) Greyston Foundation
   Yonkers, New York
   Web site: www.greyston.org
   Phone: 914-376-3900

9) Manchester Craftsmen's Guild
   Pittsburgh, Pennsylvania
   Web site: www.manchesterguild.org
   Phone: 412-322-1773

10) Miriam's Kitchen
    Washington, D.C.
    Web site: www.miriamskitchen.org
    Phone: 202-452-8926

11) Project H.O.M.E.
    Philadelphia, Pennsylvania
    Web site: www.projecthome.org
    Phone: 215-232-7272

12) Sisters of the Road
    Portland, Oregon
    Web site: www.sistersoftheroad.org
    Phone: 503-222-5694

13) The Stewpot (of First Presbyterian Church)
    Dallas, Texas
    Web site: www.thestewpot.org
    Phone: 214-746-2785

14) St. Patrick Center
    St. Louis, Missouri
    Web site: www.stpatrickcenter.org
    Phone: 314-802-0700

15) Target Hunger
    Houston, Texas
    Web site: www.targethunger.org
    Phone: 713-226-4953

HORTON'S KIDS

ONCE IN A while, driving through a neighborhood can be life altering. Life is like that. You miss a train and then while waiting for the next one, you meet someone who inspires your life. It's the little, unplanned moments that seem fleeting at first, but looking back, those are the moments that stand out for their impact and make us grateful. But first, we must be open to that moment in time.

Such was the case for Karin Walser when one day, as she recalled, "I was commuting from Baltimore to D.C., and I stopped to get gas at a really cheap gas station. It was eighty-nine cents a gallon! That was a while ago!" she joked.

"And I met some children who were trying to pump gas for money. I was interested in what could compel a child to cross four or six lanes of traffic at 10:30 at night. The children said they lived at the Capital City Inn, which was the city's largest homeless shelter. It's been torn down since then. So that's how I first met them."

She wasn't scared but she admitted, "Looking back on it, I should have been. But I wasn't. I said to the kids, 'What's it like living there?' And they said, 'It's boring.' So I asked them if they wanted to go to the zoo. And they said, 'Yes!' So days later, I went back and picked them up to go to the zoo. Of course, when I went there, there were thousands of them swarming all over my car, begging to be able to go. I stuffed as many as I could into my car and ever since then, I've been trying to get my friends and other people to go with me so that we don't leave anybody behind."

As chronicled here in other chapters, Washington is a tale of two cities, but in Washington, the shift in reality from one part to the other can be jolting to the unsuspecting soul. Other parts of the nation have the same issues of grave poverty and hopelessness. It's just that in Washington the land feels compressed, so you may drive from the gleaming white dome of Capitol Hill with its powerful halls of Congress and go to the depths of poverty in five minutes!

Certainly, Washington, D.C., is not alone in its socio-economic divide. The divisions of a community or a nation have always existed; it's just less pronounced in some communities—perhaps divided by a railroad, a river or even a road. Even in the smallest of towns, there is a divide. Years ago while driving across the country, I stopped along the way and saw wealth and poverty divided by some old, imaginary line. Nowhere was it more startling than the magnificent community around Asheville, North Carolina. There within the shadow of the great estates of the stunning Great Smoky Mountains were impoverished neighborhoods inhabited by Native Americans and others. The difference was like night and day. Washington is no different.

So Karin stopped for cheap gas on her way to Capitol Hill. A twenty-something campaign staffer at the time, she had taken a turn to get gas and within a few minutes found herself in another world, and knew instantly where she was, a place she had heard about but didn't know. I had had a similar experience before I worked in Anacostia. All the stories run through your mind as you try to traverse the unknown streets and ensure your doors are locked.

Driving through Anacostia in the late 1980s and early 1990s would have given most people pause. It was the height of the crack wars. Drugs and violence were rampant there. It boasted the highest poverty and unemployment rates in the District. Test scores and high school graduation rates were among the lowest. Yet, D.C.'s political leadership was incapable or unwilling to tackle the needs there.

Karin Walser wasn't just driving through; she *stopped* for gas. Some would have put the pump in the gas tank and gone back to sit inside their car. But Karin chatted with the children and continued to think about them and their words. The children simply wanted to have something to do. Karin returned and started something small and glorious. That was 1989 and she unofficially established her program, Horton's Kids, all while working on the Hill. But starting Horton's Kids was not really the plan Karin had in mind. One thing led to another.

"In the beginning, I generally did cheap things with them," Karin recalled in mid-2007. "If I needed to do something, I just dipped into my pocket. Then people started giving me money to do things with the kids. They'd say, 'This is for the kids.'

"I thought that maybe I should open a separate bank account. I never set out to start a nonprofit. I just wanted to help some kids. But to open a bank account, you have to incorporate. So in December 1991, we incorporated. Today, in 2007, our budget is $900,000, including approximately $100,000 in in-kind donations," she estimated. "Three out of the seven full-time staff people, including me, started out as volunteers. I'm a little biased toward people who have paid their dues in the neighborhood."

With about 500 volunteers per year and the seven on staff, including Karin, Horton's Kids worked consistently with 163 children from Anacostia in 2007. About fifty other children were involved with Horton's Kids intermittently. The kids' ages ranged from four to nineteen.

When I called Karin about this essay and the book, she exclaimed with her signature exuberance, "NO WAY! I'm so honored." She paused and added, "But there are so many others who are the real saints. When I go to meetings or conferences, I am so awed by these other leaders. There are people who pay for things like staff salaries out of their own pockets." But Karin in her own way is a saint, too. She simply loves the children. It's really not more complicated than that.

"They call me Kern or Miss Kern," she chuckled. "It's a southern version of my name." (Karin is pronounced as if it starts with the word, 'car.')

Horton's Kids has a significant impact for a variety of reasons. First, Karin believes in Horton's Kids' holistic approach. "We let the whole family in: the mom, the other kids, the dad if he's around," she said. "What I've seen is their [the child's] confidence grows, and they relax a little bit more. And their academic skills improve. If you don't know your 'times' tables, you're never going to learn algebra. If you're reading comprehension skills are low, then you're not going to get very far. So we work with them on their math and reading skills so they can do better in school. They're grades behind in their schoolwork."

"And they're not learning it at school?" I asked.

"Not if you're in DCPS," she said, frustrated with the D.C. Public School system. (The D.C. Public School system finally began a proposed makeover in 2008.) "Our children go further in school, and they don't get into trouble when they're youngsters. If they get into trouble, they get into trouble later, and it's not as serious as some of their neighbors. It is basically noticing what they need and trying to get it for them, paying attention to them. It comes down to tutoring and PBJ sandwiches."

According to their written materials, "Horton's Kids provides wrap-around services to Anacostia's children designed to improve the quality of their daily lives and nurture each child's desire and ability to succeed."

For the children's sake, the programs are constantly running and include Monday night tutoring with supper; Tuesday night tutoring with supper; Wednesday night tutoring with supper; Sunday afternoon mentoring field trips with lunch; medical care; dental care; enrichment activities; Thanksgiving dinners; Halloween costumes; Easter baskets; Christmas presents and Christmas trees; advocacy; and learning disabilities testing and specialized, additional tutoring.

Karin added, "We have a van and we take them to gymnastics, ice hockey, tennis, golf, and tae kwon do. And we have Saturday afternoon enrichment programs. We also have a dental program with Howard University, and we put on a summer camp. We take them to the pool every day."

The thing about Karin is that she gives it to you straight. "They live in Southeast, the most dangerous part of Washington. They live in Ward 8 in Section 8 housing, which means their rent is subsidized. They live with the highest crime rate in the city. They go to the worst schools in the city. There's neglect and abuse. All combined makes it extremely hard to succeed," she said.

It is not that Karin is an angry person, but when she summarizes the kids' situations, you can tell she is speaking out on behalf of the children. She is angry *for* the children. She yearns for a day when things wouldn't have to be this way and lives by the motto Robert Kennedy often said when he quoted George Bernard Shaw, "Some people see things and say, 'Why?' But I dream things that never were, and say, 'Why not?'"

A press secretary for different members of Congress for thirteen years on the Hill, Karin's longest stint on Capitol Hill was working as a press secretary and speechwriter for Congressman Joe Moakley of Boston. Thus, public service was a part of her life before she stumbled upon the children of Anacostia. Actually, a sense of mission took root long ago.

"My parents are good people," she credited immediately. "I went to a really good school while growing up in Baltimore. I went to Bryn Mawr, a K-through-twelve private school. I was brought up with 'To whom much is given, much is expected.' I got a sense of responsibility to the world. I definitely got that from my parents and my school. My husband and I can barely afford to send our children to preschool, but it's all relative. See, I always thought I was very lucky."

A graduate of the University of Virginia, Karin earned her degree in foreign affairs before starting work on the Hill. With Horton's Kids established, she started work on a master's in social work at Catholic University but would have had to stop Horton's Kids in order to finish the degree and she didn't want to do that.

"One little boy, we gave him a new book," Karin remembered. "His mother said he took it home that night and took it to bed with him, and he didn't want to take it to school because the other children would *mess* it up. So we went and bought one for every child in the class."

As far as donations are concerned, Karin is grateful for any and all donations and said, "We always love new books. Money is easier so we can buy the books. When we receive books, we try to give everything away as fast as possible so we don't have to store it.

"We have a lot of parents who are very sweet to us and write us thank-you notes. One mother wrote to us and referred to us as an 'army of angels'. She said she didn't know where she and her girls would be without us. I save those, by the way. The families tell me all the time how much Horton's Kids means to them."

Horton's Kids likes to involve the parents. "We hire some of the parents, primarily mothers," Karin explained. "We started this out selfishly, because we thought the mothers would contribute to the programming and we were right. What we do is hire them to work for us and they get on-the-job training, and then we send them to other classes like CPR, First Aid, and a course called Advancing Youth Development. They become more valuable to the organization, and their confidence improves visibly. One parent serves on our board. A bunch of parents and one of the kids of Horton's Kids, who is now grown, are on our staff. They get the kids to cooperate really well. And they tell us what is going on in the neighborhood and they tell us things that need to get done. Like a child needs their hair done or a dental appointment, and we get it done."

With regard to replication, Karin is certainly open to that but really has her hands full with Horton's Kids. She added, "YES, there is interest. After the NBC piece aired, some people asked me about starting a Horton's Kids program in other states. I certainly I want to do all I can to help. Horton's Kids is what it is because of the perfect storm of Washington, D.C., with all of its need and all of its plenty and Capitol Hill and my pushy personality."

Except for her pushy personality, the perfect storm exists all over the country. Karin agreed and advised, "A comprehensive program, a neighborhood-based, holistic program is a good idea for other communities. The urban neglect isn't unique to Washington. There are children all over the country with academic needs, health needs, and nutritional needs."

Above all else, Karin has a wish. She said, "I wish my children and their families would find peace and succeed and be happy."

For all the kids who have come through Horton's Kids and done well, there are those who haven't made it. Karin hesitated and then said, "A bunch of them have been killed on the streets of D.C. You never really know why. I have no idea. We lost a teeny-tiny baby once. A lot of our children have lost their mothers, I think because of bad health care.

"Sometimes, the kids stay in touch. They say, 'Hey Ms. Kern, I have a job, and I'm doing well, and I miss you.' Some come back and volunteer."

It's hard work, the work of Horton's Kids. Despite Karin's wit, fast-talking exuberance and positive outlook, sometimes the stress tucked away in her voice comes through if you really listen. At some point, in any program for at-risk youth, there is a realization that some kids are not going to make it. Karin and her team stay focused on doing what they can. There is no magic; it's just hard work and you fight to keep your high hopes in check.

As Karin spoke passionately about the kids, it struck a deep chord for me. The dire situation in Anacostia and other parts of D.C. cannot be emphasized enough. And yet there is an Anacostia in every major metropolitan area in America. It is all over: the inner city of our nation, the dilapidated school, the rough streets, the unemployment and under-employment, the lack of a living wage. And the children are born into the chaos.

While working in Anacostia in the mid-1990s, like Karin, I became tied to the well-being of the youth in my nonprofit program. It's impossible not to feel attached. Part of the glory of teaching is mentoring the children, helping them achieve in school and in life. Similar to Karin, I had high expectations for all of the kids and felt protective of them. I was thrilled when a kid did well and then quietly devastated or worried when a kid failed to show up or when a kid dropped out or disappeared. The incessant threat of violence hung in the air like a live wire knocked down and swinging from a street pole. That's what the streets of Anacostia felt like, and yet, the land was lush and the people were friendly and devoted to the kids. But the statistics were real, and even school was dangerous.

Rayvon, one of the teens in my program, watched the news one night about a teenager who was shot in the back and killed after a fight at another D.C. high school. That teen was Rayvon's friend, but Rayvon didn't want to dwell on it. He had lost many friends and felt that any day he could be next. In the shadow of the nation's capital, I often wondered why a safe neighborhood could not be ensured for the children of Anacostia and the Anacostias across the nation?

Given the hurdles of Anacostia, my over-arching goal was for my kids to have the tools to tap into their dreams and believe anything is possible. Like Karin, I wanted them to realize their potential. I believed that each of them was special and that they were going places. And I told them so each day. I also knew their hope was fragile, so I got them to articulate their long-term goals and focus on the everyday tasks to achieve those goals. Finally, I told them about the four things that I believe are critical for life. I asked them to imagine if everything was suddenly gone tomorrow and you had to start over. In such a situation, always remember there are four things that no one can ever take away from you. First and foremost, your education. Education is the fastest way to create options for your life. If you lose everything, no one can take your education away from you. Second, your values. Live your values. Don't just talk about it on Sunday. Third, your integrity. Know that your integrity is impenetrable. Surround yourself with a core group of people who share your values and integrity. And fourth, your dreams. No one can take your dreams from you. Hold them dear and launch them.

I thought about all of this as Karin spoke about the remarkable and often fragile youngsters in Horton's Kids. I can recall being so worried about the kids in my program and the short film we were making that I began to have headaches. A board member told me that if only one of the kids stayed with the program, then that would be everything. The quality of the film didn't matter, she said. What mattered was if I reached even one kid. In the end, I was proud and relieved that seven out of eight went to college. Survival was not a given for these kids, and they had all survived their high school years and were on their way.

Karin and her team at Horton's Kids have known that level of pride and relief each year since 1989. The program name of Horton's Kids is based on the well-known Dr. Seuss book, *Horton Hears A Who*. As Karin kindly reminded me, "A 'who' is a little tiny person who lives on a dust ball."

"A dust ball?" I questioned, wondering where this was going.

"Don't you remember the book?"

I hesitated and blurted out with laughter, "It's been a while!"

"Well, Horton says, 'There are people out there who you can't see but they still need us to take care of them.' Horton realized there was suffering. He never actually saw Whos, but he took responsibility for alleviating their suffering." Thus, Horton's Kids was launched, committed to the children behind the invisible veil.

At age forty-one, Karin chuckled at how it all started back in 1989 when she was only twenty-two.

"It is hard to believe. In those days, I would walk through the shelter, stepping through the crack deals. They'd be in the middle of handing money back and forth and drugs, and I would say, 'Hi!' I cannot believe nobody killed me. It was crazy. I think someone was watching over me," she philosophized, and paused. "I think somebody is pushing us along to do this work, those of us in this field. I feel somebody is pushing me along," she added quietly.

Sometimes we are too busy to stop for life, so life stops for us and forces us to pause and see things more clearly. Karin Walser did not have to stop and care about the children of Ward 8. She could have chatted with them at that gas station, driven off, and never returned. But she returned. She could have returned and taken a car full of kids to the zoo and then felt that she had done her part. But she returned again. She could have taken them to the zoo and not created a nonprofit with weekly educational and recreational programs. But she returned—this time with an army of those who also cared. That was Karin's choice. She chose to stop for life, for their young lives.

Robert Kennedy often said that one person can make a difference. Karin decided to do what she could in her own backyard.

UPDATE ABOUT HORTON'S KIDS

WRITING ABOUT THE children's summer activities during the summer of 2007, Karin reported, "Our free, all-day summer camp ran from June 25 to August 3. The children swam, dissected frogs, danced the Charleston, and learned about Monet." I would guess that Karin personally taught the Charleston to the children. She is that kind of person. Each day, she and her team are giving that love of life to all of the Horton's Kids.

In 2008, the Catalogue for Philanthropy selected Horton's Kids as one of the best small charities in the Washington, D.C., region. This is the second time that Horton's Kids has been selected for that honor.

As of early 2009, Horton's Kids was serving 145 children in Anacostia.

Contact information for Horton's Kids:

Karin Walser
Founder/Executive Director
Horton's Kids, Inc.
110 Maryland Avenue, NE, Suite 207
Washington, D.C. 20002
Phone: 202-256-7194
Web site: www.hortonskids.org

If you like Horton's Kids, you might be interested in these organizations:

1) Harlem Children's Zone
   New York, New York
   Web site: www.hcz.org
   Phone: 212-534-0700

2) Latin American Youth Center
   Washington, D.C.
   Web site: www.layc-dc.org
   Phone: 202-319-2225

3) Save the Children
   (Particularly their work in New Orleans, Louisiana, and the Gulf states after Hurricane Katrina)
   Westport, Connecticut
   Web site: www.savethechildren.org
   Phone: 203-221-4000

4) Self Enhancement, Inc.
   Portland, Oregon
   Web site: www.selfenhancement.org
   Phone: 503-249-1721

IN CLOSING

PRIVILEGED TO KNOW LOVE

I would like to leave this legacy to the coming
generations. To know that the power of love
is the strongest, and no monument has been
built to people like Hitler and hate. But
when you think of it, the little Diary of Anne
Frank, which was found among the debris,
and was swept out of the pitiful attic, where
she said she still believes despite everything,
I believe this must inspire us. I heard
somewhere the saying that pain must not be
wasted, and I believe in that, and I do believe
that love must be elevated. It is the strongest
emotion that can heal most pain. And I was
privileged to know love.

— Gerda Weissmann Klein
Author & Holocaust Survivor
Excerpt from an interview on
ABC News' *Nightline*, 2000

GERDA WEISSMANN KLEIN knows about coping with loss. Ms. Klein's
pithy memoir, *All But My Life*, tells the story of her family and
community and how the Nazis killed everyone and everything she
knew. That is, all but her own young life.

In her account, there was chaos and terror when the Nazis took over
her hometown of Bielitz, Poland, in September 1939. Within a short time,
the Nazis rounded up several Jews and burned them alive in the Temple.
By late October, the town's boys and men from age sixteen to fifty were
ordered to register with the Nazis. As required, Ms. Klein's beloved, older
brother, Arthur, who was nineteen, reported to the train station, never to be

seen again. Almost three years after the invasion, though it was hot in the middle of June, her ailing father insisted that his eighteen-year-old daughter wear her ski boots the next day, a decision that Ms. Klein wrote years later "played a vital part in saving my life." The next day, her father and other Jewish men were put on trains. Ms. Klein never saw her father again.

The following morning, Ms. Klein and her mother and many other Jews did as the Nazis had requested and walked to a nearby field. They had been ordered to go there for a transport to a work camp. They waited for hours in the rain with their suitcases until the SS officers arrived. First, the SS men set up a table and checked names on a list. Some people were pushed onto trucks and driven away. Ms. Klein wrote of their crying and screaming. The SS men had the remaining crowd march for hours through the streets of the town. Though growing exhausted, Ms. Klein and her mother did as they were told. Forced back to the field, the crowd continued to march around, and suddenly the Nazis created two sections, tearing Ms. Klein from her mother's side. There was no chance for goodbye. Little did Ms. Klein know that that would be the last time she and her mother would see each other.

Ms. Klein was thrown onto a truck, already packed full of traumatized people. Despite the din and panic, she cried out for her mother. Somehow, her mother heard her and shouted over the crowd and turmoil the last words Ms. Klein would ever hear from her: "Be strong." And that sustained her and sustains her.

Skin and bones at the end of the war, Ms. Klein, who was liberated the day before her twenty-first birthday, barely survived the concentration camps and was the only member of her family to survive, except for one relative in Turkey. The young American soldier who drove up in a Jeep to assess the situation at the concentration camp holding Ms. Klein was the man she would eventually marry.

When she says "in spite of everything," she is not only quoting Anne Frank; she is speaking from her own unspeakable experience about everything she lost, suffered, and witnessed. She says she was privileged to know love. Her quote speaks to how grateful she is for the love she knew with her parents and her brother and about feeling eternally blessed to have met the love of her life, her young American soldier, Lieutenant Kurt Klein. They married in 1946.

In 1998, they founded the Gerda and Kurt Klein Foundation, which is committed to promoting education, teaching tolerance, lessening prejudice and discrimination, and encouraging community service. At age eighty-one, Mr. Klein died in 2002. Today in 2009, Ms. Klein is a mother, grandmother, and great-grandmother. She is the author of several books and speaks to young people about what she witnessed and about living a caring, giving life.

At its core, the stories of courage and vision in this book have been about being strong, being loved, and ultimately being grateful and giving love. That, in turn, creates a community's soul, enriches your soul and the souls of others.

A life of indifference is not the answer. It leads to a hollow existence. A life of active engagement and caring leads to an enriched existence, and builds bridges of understanding and acceptance of others. In an era of hatred and violence and suffering, being engaged is a connection that can transcend all boundaries. Each of us can build a bridge of understanding. Each of us can do something and reach out to another. It only takes a listening heart. It doesn't have to be a complicated effort. You don't have to change your whole life. But doing something will change your life. You will know you have set forth a ripple. Live a life with an immense dash.

Memories of our lives, of our works
and our deeds will continue in others.

— Rosa Parks

POSTSCRIPT

D URING THE WRITING of this book, which began in mid-2004, I
suspended my monthly, schmoozing Film Biz Happy Hour and
had its last gathering in the fall of 2004. Film Biz had begun
in the early summer of 1996. By the end, Film Biz had given more than
$50,000 to local nonprofits in the Washington region. A number of those
nonprofits and their leaders became the basis of this book. Because of Film
Biz, I learned their stories.

Film Biz was simple. All the proceeds from the door went to a carefully
selected nonprofit of the month. In the process, Film Biz raised awareness
about more than one hundred local nonprofits. People went to schmooze
with each other and ended up getting to know the nonprofits beyond the
donation. Some attendees arranged to donate an unused computer, fax
machine, or printer. Some became volunteers for the nonprofits while

a few joined the board of the nonprofit of the month. Almost all of the Film Biz nonprofits are still thriving, a few are struggling, and all of them are making a difference, creating their own ripples of hope. Film Biz was a happy hour with a twist. While people went to socialize and make business contacts, they also gained a deeper understanding of a world not that far away, perhaps a few blocks at most. Awareness leads to action, which creates change.

Telling the stories of these eighteen visionaries and their programs is a tale about a much broader set of problems throughout our nation. Aspects of these stories warn of the potential of a tale of two cities.

Such a tale seems un-American. The Founding Fathers envisioned a nation in which everyone would have an equal chance at the pursuit of happiness. The courageous in this book have done their part for others. Now it is critical to identify and invest in nonprofit programs that work. Public investment and corporate support for these programs will make a difference and thereby pay for themselves. These pages are filled with visionaries who believe it is in everyone's best interest to ensure that the playing field is even and that every one of us has a chance and sometimes a second chance to realize his or her potential. As *Time* magazine announced boldly in a cover story in August 2007, the time for a new wave of national service has arrived. With passage of the Edward M. Kennedy Serve America Act in 2009, President Obama has ushered in a new era of public service.

The stories of this book salute not only the vision, but also the courage and grit to get something done. If you find the visionaries in your midst, thank them, give them some time, and ask how you can be of help to them. Become a voice and visionary with them as they gather support from community leaders, elected officials, and the private sector.

GUIDELINES FOR
SELECTING NONPROFITS

Selecting nonprofits is meaningful and unquestionably fun; however, there are some guidelines that I follow when evaluating where and how to give. Giving funds to a nonprofit requires some measure of care. I call it giving intelligently. You are investing in a nonprofit. Having greater impact means selecting nonprofits carefully, earmarking funds in partnership with a nonprofit, and creating an ongoing relationship with a nonprofit. Before giving, there are numbers to crunch, a mission statement, a track record, and other public information. If possible, a site visit can be enlightening. Then there is old-fashioned judgment, the unexplainable ability to size up an entity and its leadership.

Having started and managed Lights, Camera, Action!, a Washington nonprofit, I learned how rewarding and at times difficult it can be as an executive director of a nonprofit. I have a deep appreciation for the nonprofit sector and its leaders. As I have given to nonprofits over the past decade, nonprofit leaders have boasted about results while at other times confided about shortfalls in the sector. The nonprofit leaders and staff I have known work extremely hard and accomplish an enormous amount with few resources. They are far more efficient than many outside the sector realize. The nonprofit sector generally attracts do-gooders whose hearts are in the right place. But no industry is perfect. When there is a rare bad apple in the bunch, it becomes abundantly clear, and typically that person does not last long.

Many nonprofit leaders have expressed their concerns and, at times, frustrations, which I remember from my days as an executive director. The main frustration among the leadership is that fundraising is never-ending and the job can be stressful. Burnout is a threat, even for successful nonprofit leaders. One award-winning leader admitted out of sheer exhaustion, "You know what it's like. It's twenty-four/seven. It never ends." She says that and then runs a major fundraising event for her cherished nonprofit and gets her energy back. In short, there is an art to managing a nonprofit and an art to giving effectively.

For both large and small donors, here are a few online resources that I have found to be helpful. Checking out a nonprofit requires seeing the nonprofit's official 990 statements submitted to the Internal Revenue Service. Documents can be viewed easily through GuideStar (www.guidestar.org), which offers a rich source of information about nonprofits. The Foundation Center (www.foundationcenter.org) is a valuable resource for information about the nonprofit sector and philanthropy in the nation. The Catalogue for Philanthropy (www.catalogueforphilanthropy.org) and Network for Good (www.networkforgood.org) offer insights about well-managed nonprofits and ways to get involved. Idealist (www.idealist.org) provides lists of paid and volunteer positions in the nonprofit sector and foundation world. The Chronicle of Philanthropy (www.philanthropy.com) provides a world of information about nonprofit organizations, foundations, and opportunities. Local organizations, such as the Center for Nonprofit Advancement in Washington (www.nonprofitadvancement.org), can be a helpful resource if you are starting a nonprofit, if you are managing a nonprofit and would like to learn more about best practices, or if you are looking to get involved in the nonprofit sector.

When selecting a nonprofit, I prefer to call the organization out of the blue and have a conversation with at least one staff member, and preferably the executive director, founder, and/or director of development. If there is another staff person or a receptionist who answers the phone, I will have a conversation with that person. It is not good enough to see a nonprofit's financial statement alone; I prefer to hear it from the staff and discuss the meaning behind the numbers. Finally, if possible, I ask around the community and get a sense of a nonprofit's reputation, specifically its management and history. Similar to assessing the value of a corporation, selecting a nonprofit involves more than agreeing with its mission or assessing its numbers. It's the quality of the nonprofit's management, the integrity of its work and staff, and the direct impact on the community.

The following is a set of criteria for selecting nonprofits:

- Mission
- Shared passion
- Types of direct services offered
- Specific programs that make a difference
- Track record
- Measurable impact on the community
- Resource allocation
  - Effective use of funds, budgeting, strategizing

I may also inquire about the following:

- Management team
- Financial statements
- Business plan of organization: capacity building
- Long-term investing, budgeting, and strategizing
- Public-private partnerships
- Returns on investments
- Data-driven decisions
- Top technology for fundraising and communication

QUESTIONS FOR READERS AND BOOK CLUB DISCUSSIONS

- Which stories and which visionaries in the book touched you the most? Why do you think that is?

- How did you feel about urban and suburban poverty *before* reading *Visionaries In Our Midst*? How is that different from your perspective *now*?

- Did you know much about suburban poverty before reading *Visionaries In Our Midst*? Do you think the media cover urban and suburban poverty and innovative solutions enough?

- Describe some of the problems in your community that you have noticed. What nonprofit programs already exist in your community to help the most vulnerable?

- Do you know any visionaries in your midst? How would you describe them and their work in the community?

- What unmet social needs in the community need more attention?

- If you could do anything in your community and make a difference, what would you do? Is someone already doing something like that? Could you join their efforts? Can you think of a few friends who might want to join you?

- Do you think our national priorities need to be more involved with issues of poverty? Do you think it is worth it to invest in programs that make a difference?

- Do you think that awareness of the most vulnerable and thinking about solutions is something that we want our nation's children to ponder and participate in as a form of community service? Do philanthropy and volunteerism begin at a young age? Does it teach a sense of community and gratitude? Does it instill a sense of social responsibility? Would you support a year-long national service program for all high school graduates?

- In terms of giving of time or resources, do you think you might want to get involved more or involved less with challenges in your community? Going forward, do you think you will be more aware of poverty in your midst? Is that awareness enough? Is it possible to be part of the solution? What legacy do you want to leave?

- Do you think it takes courage to get involved? What would you gain from being involved as a volunteer, connecting with your community's needs, or working within the nonprofit sector?

- Do you know a visionary's story to share with Allison Silberberg for possible inclusion in future writings? E-mail her at the listing below.

To learn more about Allison Silberberg's work, please visit her Web site, www.allisonsilberberg.com.

To join Allison Silberberg's e-mail list for announcements of her upcoming readings, to ask her to participate in your book club's gathering, to send her feedback, or to ask questions, please feel free to contact her at allison@allisonsilberberg.com. Please know that the e-mail list will not be shared with anyone. At any time, should you want to be taken off the e-mail list, simply e-mail your request.

ACKNOWLEDGMENTS

I wish to express my gratitude to those who helped make this book possible. There are many individuals, far too many to list, whose efforts made a significant difference during the writing process. I would especially like to thank my mother, Barbara Silberberg, for her advice, friendship, and humor during every phase of the writing. Her editor's eye is unmatched. Though my father, Al Silberberg, is no longer alive, his years of teaching me about fairness will always be my moral compass. I would like to express my deep gratitude to my grandparents, especially my grandmothers, Betty Schwartz and Adele Lorie Silberberg, as well as my great-grandmother, Grandma Epstein, who all carved a path of service, which my mother has shared with me. My gratitude to Trudell Williams, whose compassion and conscience are with me. My thanks to my sisters, Susan Silberberg and Dana Bartholomew, and Dana's husband, Richard Bartholomew, for their support. I would like to thank Alan Kraut for his insightful guidance. I am also indebted to Rabbi Gerald J. Klein of Temple Emanu-El in Dallas, whose lifelong friendship will always be present.

I am deeply grateful to nine readers—Michelle Ganeles, Dana Gerard, Deborah Kalb, Caryn Kboudi, Judy Martens, Maria Moreno, Cynthia Muller, Susan Roth, and Liz Trice—who provided thoughtful, detailed feedback. I would like to thank Lisa Brachman, Peggy Brown, Jeff Campbell, Carla and David Cohen, Inge Goettler, Andrew Lotwin, Helen Thomas, Joe Uehlein, and Don Wortman for their encouragement and help. For assistance with deciphering current statistics, I would like to thank

Colleen Pawling, Marian Barton Peele, and Adam Tenner for their careful guidance. I am incredibly grateful to the gifted Karen Elliott Greisdorf for her photograph of me for the book's cover. I would like to thank another talented photographer, Richard Latoff, who was instrumental in helping me select and digitize my photographs for the book's cover and Web site. I would also like to thank Aviva Kempner and The Ciesla Foundation for administrative support with the grants.

Special thanks go to Jack Taylor's Alexandria Toyota and NCB Capital Impact for their generosity in providing grants to help underwrite the research and writing of this book.

Many thanks to my enthusiastic agent, Diane Nine, for believing in the book's vision, for her hard work and friendship. For the book's design, I would like to thank Ilana and Scott Gordon, as well as Andrew LaGow, of Word Wizards. I would also like to thank my editor, Brooke Bascietto, and all those who helped put this book together at the publisher, University Press of America, an imprint of Rowman & Littlefield. For legal advice, I would like to thank Janice Lawrence of Folger Levin & Kahn in San Francisco, and Amy Shelf, formerly of the same firm.

Finally, my heartfelt thanks to my remarkable circle of family and friends for their everlasting bond. I am blessed.

ABOUT THE AUTHOR

ALLISON SILBERBERG is a writer, advocate, and photographer who has extensive grantmaking experience. She is the author of *And Life Will Be a Beautiful Dream*, a memoir she was commissioned to write about the meaningful life of a philanthropic family. Her writing has appeared on PBS.org in conjunction with Ken Burns' and Lynn Novick's documentary series, *The War*, as well as in conjunction with David Grubin's documentary series, *The Jewish Americans*. Her columns and articles have appeared in *The Washington Post* and *The Dallas Morning News*. In 1989, she wrote an episode for the television series *Mama's Family*.

In the early 1990s, Ms. Silberberg worked on Capitol Hill for Senator Lloyd M. Bentsen of Texas. It was the height of the crack wars in D.C.'s most troubled neighborhoods, and Ms. Silberberg, who had also been teaching a screenwriting course at American University, founded and managed Lights, Camera, Action! (or LCA!), a nonprofit committed to helping inner-city teens realize their potential through film. Seven of the eight LCA! participants went to college, and *Poppy*, an award-winning, short film they made together, aired on local PBS stations. After a return to writing and consulting, Ms. Silberberg created monthly charitable gatherings, which she organized for nearly a decade and where all proceeds from those events went to a different local nonprofit each month. In 2005, The World Bank asked her to serve a three-year term on its Community Outreach Grants Committee, which disbursed major funding to nonprofits in Washington. She has received two awards for her community work.

Ms. Silberberg's photography, which specializes in portraiture, has appeared in major newspapers and magazines in the States and abroad. Her photograph of Coretta Scott King has garnered national attention.

Ms. Silberberg has a B.A. in international relations and history from American University and an M.F.A. in playwriting from the University of California, Los Angeles' School of Theater, Film and Television. Originally from Dallas, Texas, Ms. Silberberg resides in Alexandria, Virginia.